NO SECRET SO CLOSE

For Rupert, Tana and Georgina

"There is no secret so close as that between a rider and his horse."

Surtees: *Mr Sponge's Sporting Tour*

NO SECRET SO CLOSE

The Biography of Bruce Hobbs MC

by

Tim Fitzgeorge-Parker

Pelham Books, London

First published in Great Britain by
Pelham Books Ltd
44 Bedford Square
London WC1B 3DP
1984

ISBN 0 7207 1552 1

Typeset by Alacrity Phototypesetters,
Banwell Castle, Weston-super-Mare.
Printed by Hollen Street Press, Slough
and bound by Dorstel Press, Harlow

Illustrations

1 Bruce aged 4
2 Three generations of the Hobbs family
3 Bruce on Fisherman
4 Bruce on Lady Marvel
5 Reg, Battleship and Bruce at Lambourn
6 Jumping Becher's
7 Bruce being led into the winner's enclosure after winning the National
8 The triumphant return to Lambourn
9 Presentation after winning the Cedarhurst Grand National
10 Trooper Hobbs
11 Four Grand National winners
12 Bruce on Agility
13 Bruce, Neville Crump and Hector Gordon
14 Outside Buckingham Palace, 1945
15 Bruce's last ride as a professional
16 John and Eileen Rogerson
17 Betty and Hobblette
18 War Risk with Bob Turnell up
19 Bruce's string on the sand
20 H.M. The Queen at Newmarket
21 Henry Cecil, Arthur Boyd-Rochfort, David Cecil and Hobblette
22 Meld
23 Absolved
24 Jacinth
25 Betty Hobbs and Stilvi
26 Bruce with the Cambanis family
27 Mrs Fyfe-Jamieson and Tony Villar
28 Tromos

29 Tyrnavos winning the Irish Sweeps Derby
30 Tyrnavos from Henrietta Micklem's painting
31 Bruce and the late Tom Blackwell
32 Tom Pettifer, Bruce and Bill Payne
33 Jocelyn Hambro
34 Royal Ascot 1984
35 Charles and Hobblette with their family
36 Bruce and Betty Hobbs

Photo credits

The author and publisher are grateful to the following for permission to use copyright illustrations: Associated Press no. 5; Central Press no. 19; Colorlabs International no. 31; Daily Express no. 20; David Hastings no. 28; Jack Knight no. 34; Brian Love no. 36; Henrietta Micklem and Michael Smith no. 30; Desmond O'Neill no. 16; W. W. Rouch no. 25; Sport and General nos. 7 and 15; Peter Sweetman no. 27; The Field no. 11. Every effort has been made to trace copyright owners but in a few cases this has not been possible.

Contents

Acknowledgements	viii
Foreword by Peter O'Sullevan	ix
Chapter 1	1
Chapter 2	5
Chapter 3	14
Chapter 4	29
Chapter 5	46
Chapter 6	56
Chapter 7	64
Chapter 8	78
Chapter 9	104
Chapter 10	112
Chapter 11	125
Chapter 12	136
Chapter 13	146
Chapter 14	155
Index	173

Acknowledgements

My heartfelt thanks to Bruce and Betty Hobbs for their enthusiastic, time-absorbing co-operation in the production of this book. I would also like to thank Peter O'Sullevan for his Foreword and Harry Carr, Douglas Gray, Jocelyn Hambro, Simon Lycett-Green, Dick Micklem, Bill Payne, Monica Sheriffe, Jeffrey Simmons, Maynard Tomson, Fulke Walwyn and Tony Wingfield for their help.

Foreword

by Peter O'Sullevan

Tim Fitzgeorge-Parker's succinctly titled story of Bruce Hobbs, the boy wonder of his time, not only reflects the finer aspects of the sport of horseracing, and jumping in particular; it illumines an era in the process.

This is a racing scenario with a difference, far removed from the saga of uninterrupted success which a generation primed with the knowledge of his teenage attainment, and familiar with the handsome image of him as boss of Palace House Stables, Newmarket, might expect.

In fact, the achievement of Reg Hobbs's teenage son in becoming the youngest rider to win the Grand National when Battleship beat Royal Danieli by a head in 1938 obscured as much as it highlighted his talent.

The very magnitude of the performance of the young man, who characteristically acknowledges the debt he owes to Fred Rimell for redeeming his post-Bechers error, inevitably left him with a public tag similar to that endured by Dick Francis.

Just as few who are aware of the disastrous circumstances under which Dick failed to win the National in the Royal colours appreciate his status as champion jockey; so fewer still may know that at sixteen the Lester Piggott of the jumping firmament was a close third in the National Hunt jockeys' table.

There is in fact an unmistakable degree of affinity between Bruce and Lester for each of whom, maybe, there is "No secret so close as that between a rider and his horse".

Each has accepted the spotlight of publicity with more resignation than pleasure and it was no surprise to learn that while Bruce was a £10-a-week assistant to Sir Cecil Boyd-Rochfort and the great but ailing filly Meld, for whom he cared so deeply, was running in the St Leger, he felt unable either to attend the Classic or watch it on TV.

Instead he drove to Boy's Grave (the melancholy landmark where a gypsy shepherd is buried who was so distraught over losing one of his sheep that he hanged himself) and sat there with a book until the race was run.

It was no surprise either to learn that while working for Gibson's, the Newmarket saddlers, he reacted with disfavour to the order of a potential show-jumping client.

The firm he represented had a good line in leather shin-boots with tin-tacks sticking out to stop horses chewing their bandages — a habit usually confined to yearlings and two-year-olds.

When a famous show jumping star showed interest in purchasing a quantity, Bruce's curiosity was aroused. "I'll turn them inside out with the tin-tacks sticking into their shins", the man told Bruce "When they hit a pole with those and feel those nails in their shins, that'll larn 'em, they won't knock one again. They'll jump over the moon rather than that happen!"

Bruce Hobbs's reaction was predictably forthright. "I told him exactly what I thought of him," he relates, "refused to sell him any, left the yard and have not seen him since."

I have had the pleasure of knowing both Bruce and his infinitely charming father Reg. While it is true that this happily related chronicle will have greatest appeal to a pre-war generation, it is a marvellous story for young readers too, and turf literature would have been a great deal poorer without it.

Chapter One

Bruce Hobbs lay flat on his back in the hospital bed. He had been there for nearly three months, unable to walk, unable even to raise his head. He was paralysed all down his left side. He did not know whether he would ever walk again. He was just eighteen years old.

It was morning. Such a fine crisp winter morning that the patients' beds had been wheeled out onto the verandah of their private wards in Oxford's Wingfield Morris Hospital.

"They were fresh-air fiends in those days," says Bruce. "Every morning, winter or summer, as long as it wasn't raining, we were shoved straight outside. Now, as I looked at the sunny, frosty scene in the garden, I thought of that splendid chap in Surtees, looking out on just such a morning at the start of another hunting season. Do you remember?

"'Hoorah! Blister my kidneys! It is a frost – the dahlias are dead!'

"I laughed about it to my mother. But it was a bitter-sweet laugh. I don't think either of us really believed I would ever hunt again."

As usual, Bruce's mother had arrived at daylight to take up her daily vigil by his bedside. He would never have made it through those months of despair if she had not been there.

"As soon as she heard of my accident, she moved down from Melton, found herself digs in Oxford and spent every single hour of every single day by my bedside."

Marge Hobbs, five feet eight inches tall with a good figure and a wonderful smile, idolised her only child. If she had had her way, Bruce would not have been there because he would never have become a professional jockey. Now, sensing his mood, she met his eyes and guided them to the next bed, saying for the umpteenth time in her quiet voice, "You'll be all right, my darling. But *he* won't. He'll never walk again, poor chap."

There was genuine despair behind the large pale blue eyes and the brave smile in the handsome face of Edward Courage, all that was showing above the iron lung. At the age of thirty-two polio had stricken this fine sportsman with paralysis from which not even the wealth of his famous brewing family could save him.

Later, from his wheelchair, he was to do so much for National Hunt racing. Now, unconsciously, he was to save one of the best products of that sport, giving young Hobbs the will to live.

Bruce recalls: "About the second week I was there I looked across and saw this fellow in an iron lung. I had been told that I would probably be all right and I knew very well that he wouldn't. That was the best thing that could have happened to me. I was feeling pretty low at the time but he made me feel that, with the grace of God and a following wind, I should recover but he, poor chap, would never move. He had been out shooting and, that night, felt sick. He got into bed, felt sick again, could not get out of bed and never moved again."

Bruce was no ordinary eighteen-year-old. Ever since the crash, letters and get-well cards had flooded in, many of them from people he had never met. Nurses had stolen in to ask for his autograph. It took him three minutes to write the ten letters of his name with a trembling right hand while able to see the paper and the expectant smiling faces only in the mirror above his head. He was living in a Through-The-Looking-Glass world. Everything and everyone was upside down. The whole world was upside down.

It had been such a stupid accident, in a little selling hurdle at Cheltenham; the hurdle in front of the stands. The crowd must have enjoyed it. Despite his youth and his height – he already stood six feet one and a half inches in his stockinged feet – Bruce was lying third in the Jockeys' Championship, equal with Fred Rimell in that year of 1938. He was already a star, riding winners all over the country, but this was the first autumn meeting at Cheltenham, his unlucky course.

"Although I was to train my first winner at Cheltenham, I rode there a lot but never managed to win a race. I fell at that hurdle in front of the stands, a normal fall, part of a day's work, but Billy Parvin's horse landed on my back. I wasn't unconscious but I was in terrible pain. I got up, crawled away and went to the ambulance room, where the doctor examined me and said, 'I think you have broken a couple of ribs. You should be all right. Come and see me before you ride tomorrow.' As the afternoon wore on I found myself in more and more pain and, although she couldn't drive, I was grateful to have the company of my stepmother's sweet younger sister, Freda.

"I was in such a bad way that I stopped off in Swindon for a quick check-up with the masseur Dickie Dowson, who looked after the Swindon football team. I can see it now so vividly. When I went into his room he stripped me off, laid me down on his table and ran his fingers down my spine, stopping momentarily before going on. Then he said simply, 'Are you on your own? I said, 'No'. 'Have you got a driver?' 'No.'

"He thought for a moment, then said 'Go carefully.' So I went carefully back through Shrivenham, past the famous White Horse. It was sheer agony changing down to get up that hill in Ashbury."

Thank God for Dickie Dowson. As Bruce turned into the driveway of his home, Ronehurst in Upper Lambourn, he found an ambulance, a doctor and a nurse waiting for him. He had broken his spine.

Bruce's father, the famous trainer Reg Hobbs, was most upset. Of course he had to find other jockeys to replace his son on his runners at Cheltenham the following day. Bruce said, "Will you telephone Mummy and let her know?"

"Yes, I'll do that. You'll be all right, my boy. Now I must get on the telephone and chase those jockeys."

The ambulance men were more obviously concerned for their precious burden. They drove slowly and carefully through the bends of Lambourn, up Faringdon Road and down the other side to Wantage, Abingdon and then to the Acland Nursing Home in Oxford.

But Bruce's troubles were only just starting. "They tried manipulation – to manipulate the thing out. Not only did it not work but it paralysed me completely down the left side. I was still in agony, terrified to find myself unable to move my left arm or leg. Then they took me to the Wingfield Morris Hospital where, thank Heaven, they handed me over to the great orthopaedic surgeon Professor Girdlestone, with whom I was soon to become very friendly. He did a spine graft on me, taking a piece of bone out of my left shin and putting it on either side of my spine before encasing me in plaster."

For ten weeks he lay in that plaster casing. The plaster went from head to foot. "Fortunately I was not worried about growing a beard," says Bruce today, smiling. "I was very slow maturing."

Only time would tell whether the graft had taken. Only time would tell how great the damage had been.

Sister Masters came over for a quick comforting word. About the same height as Bruce's mother, in her early fifties, she was a lovely, buxom, inspiring woman with a wonderful smile. "She was never strict and was loved by everybody, even the nurses," says Bruce. "a tremendous help in my recovery."

As his mother left his bedside, she stretched out her hand to his. "Do you remember the last time, darling – the last time you were in bed sick?"

He did indeed. Although he broke his collar bones seven times, Bruce was only once confined to bed. This was at the age of seven after his first hunting pony, Tom Thumb, had put his foot in a rabbit hole and turned over. "I was unconscious for five days," says Bruce. "Then, when I came to, I found myself upstairs in a room that was pitch dark. I was very frightened to begin with, but that was the treatment for concussion in those days. They kept me in that black room for a fortnight. Since then I have had headaches on and off all my life. My mother was by my bed then. Yes, I could certainly remember the last time."

Chapter Two

Sitting on the crest of Brixworth Hill in the late afternoon of a November day, Captain Tom Hobbs was reliving the past as he gloried in the present. He had always loved Brixworth, not so much for its parish church, reputed to be the oldest or second oldest in England, nor for the elegant spire that for centuries had served as a landmark to so many travellers, but because, since 1825, the little town had been the headquarters of the famous Pytchley Foxhounds, with whom he had enjoyed the best years of his life.

From a wonderful position on its hilltop, that church, in the thirties, looked down upon mile after mile of the most beautiful grass in the shires and on a landscape dotted with numerous coverts and spinnies, in any of which, from Creaton to Haselbech on the distant hill, you could find as good and strong a marauding fox as anywhere in England.

Only that morning, as the church clock chimed eleven Tom had stood to watch the cavalcade move off from the meet, to shake hands with Master and huntsman, anxious to wish his many friends good luck. A huge man, six feet two inches and broad-shouldered, he was still upright, although his handsome face was lined and his big moustache was grey beneath the curly-brimmed bowler hat. The dark overcoat was impeccably cut, the narrow trousers beautifully pressed, the black brogues glistened and the kid gloves proclaimed the great showman.

Captain Tom and no other had been fated to holloa the first fox away on that memorable day.

At the top of the hill there was an old seat by the wayside; not a thing of beauty or of grace, but a welcome resting-place no doubt for the homecoming housewife, who had carried her shopping basket up the steep ascent from the railway station below.

There, as the sun started to sink below the ridge of Creaton, sat Tom Hobbs, remembering all the days when he had led the Pytchley field over those fences and obstacles. He was waiting.

From his point of vantage he was able, thanks to a pair of field-glasses, to see something of the final phases of the hunt. Earlier the cry of the hounds in the vale had brought back his youth for a few precious moments. The final issue was hidden from his eyes, but he would forget his chest trouble, braving chills, rheumatism, and all the penalties that the climate of cold Northamptonshire could inflict, rather than go back before he had waylaid the homecoming pack and learnt whether the hounds had killed their fox.

He was soon to know. The sound of horses' feet, the jingle of bits and the whipper-in's voice told him that they were coming and, as he rose to meet them (not without an effort, alas !) a velvet cap appeared above the shoulder of the hill.

The question which his lips had framed was answered without his actually needing to ask and instead he offered hearty congratulations. For in front of the muddy tan shapes which clustered round their huntsman's horse trotted the leader of the pack, peerless Pytchley Statesman, head up and stern erect. Grasped between his jaws with a gesture that proclaimed to the world his triumph, he carried the mask of the gallant fox from "Old Poors Gorse".

When Tom arrived home at Nitsdale, his large, comfortable house on the Northampton road out of Market Harborough, he saw a familiar car outside and went in to find his son, Reg, and fifteen-year-old grandson Bruce, who had called in on their way back to Lambourn from Leicester races.

Before Grandfather could tell them about the famous Pytchley gallop, Reg, tucking into the whisky, told him proudly: "Bruce rode a double today. Yes, two winners over those big black Oadby fences."

When they had gone, it was a very happy old man who coughed his way to bed. His chest trouble killed him in 1938.

Yet, only ten years earlier, the three of them, Tom, Reg and Bruce, had been out together one day with the Quorn.

Bruce says: "Those were the days of the big dealers. My grandfather had a large dealing-yard at Great Bowden, which was then his house outside Market Harborough. He was a wonderful man across country – as famous with the Pytchley as my father was in Leicestershire."

Dick Fanshawe, later to be so well-known as Master of Hounds, then a cavalry subaltern, says: "Tom Hobbs was most impressive. A brilliant horseman and a formidable figure with enormous personality. We were all terrified of him!"

Small wonder that he was Britain's top showman, leading the

parade in the twenties on his champions at the Mecca of the show ring, the International Horse Show at Olympia.

Great indeed was his pride in 1928 and 1929, when he was followed in that parade of champions by his grandson, Bruce, on the unbeaten white pony Lady Marvel.

Captain Tom and his charming, lovable wife had three sons, Tom, who farmed in Lincolnshire, Cecil, the delicate one, who had to leave the horse scene because of asthma and lived outside Liverpool, and Reginald Clonsilla Edward who, as his name suggests, was born during a period when his family were living in Ireland.

During his childhood Reg, or Reggie as he was later to be known to his many girlfriends, had the undivided attention of his famous father, just as his son Bruce was to have in the next generation. He was never spared. He had to learn every single branch of the horse trade. Buying, selling, wheeling, dealing, riding, driving, making, breaking, hacking hunting, showing, point-to-pointing. Captain Tom loved his son and took tremendous pride in his development as a horseman and horse-master.

Reg grew up in the palmy days, the golden days of the shires, whose galloping grassland provided the finest fox-hunting in the world, when Leicestershire was described by Whyte Melville as "Where the business of life is to hunt everyday and the nights may take care of themselves as they may!"

Captain Tom Hobbs's livery and dealing yard at Great Bowden just outside Market Harborough was rivalled only by that of Harry Beeby at Melton Mowbray. The two were great friends for many years.

It was not unusual for Captain Tom Hobbs to buy as many as a dozen hunters in the Saturday sale at the Leicester Horse Repository. All the horses that he bought carried a warranty. So on Monday morning Reg, accompanied by the grooms and tack, would go from Great Bowden to Leicester, saddle up the horses and ride them off to the meet of the Quorn. By lunchtime, when the field was changing over to their second horses, Captain Tom, his son and their grooms would have decided which animals they wished to keep, to sell on at a substantial profit. Those that were unsound or just bad hunters would go straight back to Warner, Sheppard and Wade's Repository and the Saturday sale would be annulled.

Reg said that he acquired the "racing bug" while fox-hunting as a boy. Off the Newark-Nottingham road in the South Notts country, then known as Lord Harrington's Hunt, was Cropwell Court, a hunting lodge that was shared by George Williamson and Danny Maher. George Williamson was the steeplechase jockey who won the 1899 Grand National on wonderful Manifesto, with the joint record burden of twelve stone seven pounds, and every other major steeplechase in Europe. Perhaps an even greater childhood hero was the good-looking, dapper, intelligent little American stylist Danny Maher who won three Derbys in four years, on Rock Sand, Cicero and Spearmint and, more than fifty years later, was to be described by Atty Persse, trainer of The Tetrarch, as "the greatest jockey of all time".

With his tiny hands, the hands of a lovely girl, Maher could hold any horse alive. He loved his fox-hunting and was a wonderful landowner. His carefully planned covert, planted entirely of privet, always held a fox. Imagine having two such men as Williamson and Maher in one ordinary country house for the whole hunting season, although, of course, George Williamson would be away race-riding a good deal. Then, in the spring, when hunting ended and he too was needed on the racecourse, Danny Maher would leave his house and the stud of hunters in the hands of top-class servants.

Whether it was the example of his heroes or the point-to-points which he rode on his father's horses that inspired him most, Reg's love of racing was instilled at an early age.

In 1906 Lord Annaly had engaged Frank Freeman, described by Henry Chaplin and many others as "the best huntsman in the world" as huntsman to Captain Tom Hobbs's own particular pack, the Pytchley. This then was the heady atmosphere in which Tom Hobbs raised his son Reginald who, even then, in his teens, was establishing himself as one of the finest horsemen in the world. I can truthfully say that, in a lifetime spent with horses, I have never seen his superior.

Around the turn of the century hunting in Leicestershire and British steeplechasing were becoming extremely popular with the rich fox-hunting American sportsmen, who usually lived either on Long Island or in the southern states. This popularity and their enthusiasm was increased when American-bred Rubio won the 1908 Grand National. It was hardly surprising because Rubio's story is one of the most romantic of all those associated with the National. Bred in California, he came to this country as a yearling. Although his dam was a half-sister to the mighty Sceptre, he fetched only fifteen guineas at the Newmarket sales. Resold for ninety-five guineas to Major F. Douglas-Pennant as a hunter, he proved such a success that he was sent into training and, in 1903, as a five-year-old, won three chases. He then broke down and, once sound again, was sent to The Prospect Arms at Towcester to pull the hotel bus. This drastic treatment was entirely successful and by the end of 1906 he was back in training – this time with Fred Withington. The following season he won four races including the Grand National at the magnificent odds of 66 to 1!

Among those to whom this performance gave extra inspiration was Ambrose Clark, who, together with his brothers, Stephen and Robert Sterling (owner of the 1954 Derby winner Never Say Die), shared a thirty-million-dollar fortune derived from the Clark Thread Company and Singer Sewing Machines.

The Clarks were men who not only loved sport but also knew their own minds. In 1946 Robert Sterling Clark decided not to run any more horses in America since the New York Jockey Club refused to register for racing the produce of certain Arab mares that he owned. Thinking back to Rubio, Mr Clark observed that " a cab horse can be raced in England."

One spring day in 1913, five years after Rubio's National triumph, young Reg rode one of his father's horses, an all-quality brown lightweight six-year-old, ten miles to a point-to-point meeting, won his race and hacked all the way back home. The following morning he was summoned to his father's study to meet a shortish man with a hump on his back and a very deep American voice, who spoke down his nose all the time and was introduced as Mr Ambrose Clark. Captain Tom Hobbs was smiling in a way that Reg knew betokened a highly successful deal. "Mr Clark has bought your little horse, Reg," he said. "He wants you to take the horse over to America and to stay with him over there, helping with his stud."

So "Brose" Clark, graduate of Columbia University, dedicated hunting man and point-to-point rider, world-wide exporter of sewing machines, imported to his Long Island home young Reg Hobbs as Master of the Horse.

In the next thirty years both "Brose" and Reg were to achieve their life's ambition by winning a Grand National each.

After many vicissitudes American fox-hunting, not only in the states of Virginia and Maryland but also in New England and Long Island, was settling down. In 1907 the Master of Foxhounds Association of America was formed with Major Austin Wadsworth as its president. It was this descendant of an old English north-country family who had finally revolutionised fox-hunting in the States by getting a proper pack under proper control. From 1880 he had been importing very good English hounds and by 1900 he had what Mr Higginson, another of the most famous American enthusiasts, later to be Master of the Cattistock, called the best pack in America. It was wholly private. The field were his guests. The country was sporting and the foxes plentiful. Sadly, before the Second World War, bricks and mortar were to swallow up that Meadow Brook country in Long Island, but it is fascinating to see that in those days soon after the turn of the century Major Wadsworth, who had had trouble with ill-disciplined thrusters in the hunting field, which in turn had caused him trouble with the farmers, had drawn up a celebrated set of rules which was widely printed and read. It was a splendid document, stern without hectoring and witty without loss of seriousness. Essentially the rules were that farmers must be shown consideration, since the hunt depended on their hospitality and goodwill; that the Master of Hounds was absolute master – he must not be spoken to nor interfered with, though at any time he might be offered a drink!; and that horsemen must keep well clear of hounds and never head a fox. This document, known as the Genesee Valley "Bible" was warmly approved by all English fox-hunting men when it was printed over here in *The Field*. The sporting philosophy of Major Wadsworth and the other dedicated American fox-hunters of those days is demonstrated by his dictum: "I would rather see a farmer's boy on a mule at a meet than the most elaborate creation of a London tailor."

From the start, Reg's supreme skill overcame all problems, particularly those associated with colour, because all the stable work was done by negroes. However, they soon recognised that their white English boss was a true horsemaster in every sense of the word.

Starting at first light every morning in the hot summers, to get the best out of the early part of the day, Reg and his nagsmen worked throughout the morning, making and breaking hunters, show-horses and particularly polo ponies. Then after a light luncheon and siesta, the horses would be worked again in the long evenings. Reg was producing good horses and perfectly trained polo ponies. He played a lot of polo himself. Also in the family were those magnificent horsemen Pete and Brother Bostwick and the Stoddards. They were a great hunting family and Louis Stoddard had horses in training in England with Aubrey Hastings and later with Ivor Anthony. Pete Bostwick, of course, was not only one of the finest amateur riders in the world, but also a superb international polo player.

"Brose" Clark kept many of his polo ponies standing at Belmont Park Racecourse, where he could hire extra boxes and stalls. This was the racecourse which the late, great Atty Persse – then leading amateur rider in five countries, including America – was asked to build. He told me that he imported from his native Ireland an expert who designed the course as a facsimile of Baldoyle.

In earning immortality for himself as the fastest racehorse of all time, The Tetrarch, or the "Spotted Wonder", as he was called, performed the same service for his trainer, who was widely quoted for a very brief conversation he had in America at this time.

After Atty had ridden the winner of a top steeplechase, he was guest of honour at a celebration dinner. The successful owner asked his jockey, "Now, Mr Persse, just what do you consider to be the first and primary asset of a racehorse?"

He was slightly put out to receive the answer in one word – "Speed."

"Yes, yes," he said rather tartly. "And after that?"

"More speed."

"Yes, yes," said the American sportsman again. "But after that?"

"Still more speed!"

Atty was as popular outside his own stables as he was feared within them. In an old book called *Over the Open* by H. S. Page, an American who was for many years secretary of the Meadow Brook Hounds, I read: "H. S. Persse, the 'Atty' of Stockbridge and of The Tetrarch and Aunt May fame, hunted with us in the nineties and always went at the top. What a good fellow he was, singing a song or holding more than his own against our steeplechase jockeys, amateur or pro."

Aunt May was the mare on whom Persse finished third to Ascetic's Silver, ridden by Aubrey Hastings in the Grand National of 1906, having been brought down at the Canal Turn.

Ambrose Clark was already spending the latter half of each hunting season at Warwick Lodge in Melton Mowbray and in the spring of the year he would come back to Long Island, bringing with him a string of tip-top Irish ponies bought at peak prices. This was where Reg got to work. He was catering for people who knew what they wanted. They had no time for ill-behaved or fractious horses. He already knew that nearly every horse could be sorted out by long hours of expert, sympathetic schooling and by judicious feeding. At no time of his life did he undertake such extended hours of schooling as during his thirteen years with "Brose" Clark in Long Island.

By 1915 guns were blasting holes in a generation of sportsmen across the Atlantic and critics of the war effort in England were indignant that racing could continue on the slogan "Business as Usual". Others considered the sport to be as important to morale as theatres and music halls. Those in uniform lucky enough to be on leave on Grand National day, 1915, splashed patches of khaki and navy blue in the Aintree crowd as Ally Sloper won to make Lady Nelson the first woman to own the winner.

It was a perilous ride for Jack Anthony, who was later to play such a big part in the life of Bruce Hobbs. He was nearly down at the second, saved only by his brother Ivor, who was alongside on Ilston. Ivor reached out, grabbed him by the seat of the pants and dragged him back into the saddle. Twenty-three years later history was to repeat itself for Reg Hobbs's as yet unborn son.

At the end of 1915 Aintree was taken over by the War Office and closed to racing. The National was transferred to Gatwick and called "The Racecourse Association Steeplechase" with the prize reduced to

£500. In 1917 the name was changed to "The War National Steeplechase". It was won by Ballymacad trained by Aubrey Hastings, although Limerock must have won if, like the Queen Mother's Devon Loch nearly forty years later, he had not collapsed a few yards from the winning post.

The last substitute National in 1918 was the best of them. It was won by Poethlyn, a magnificent Aintree type of horse and the finest chaser of his time who had, however, had a humble start. He was sold for seven pounds to a hotelier in Shrewsbury and then bought for fifty guineas by Major Hugh Peel who gave him to his wife. His jockey was Lester Piggott's grandfather, that fearless cavalier Ernie.

By now Reg Hobbs was old enough to enlist. He travelled back to England and joined the Army, lending his priceless skill to the Remount Service until he was demobilised soon after the Armistice in November 1918.

A new hunting season had just started. The war was over, "Victory" had not yet become a sour joke and "a land fit for heroes" was still the politicians' promise. Men celebrated their release from trench, destroyer and merchant ship by rushing to Aintree in the spring for a race that seemed to stand for England in a shattered world. Crowds were larger than ever before; the mood was one of desperate gaiety. It was a day when the favourite had to win and Poethlyn, a hot favourite at 11 to 4 after his success at Gatwick, duly obliged.

Meanwhile Reg Hobbs, quickly released from the Army, had gone back to Great Bowden to hunt with the Pytchley and to collect some more horses for Ambrose Clark before returning to Long Island.

He was not as tall as his father, only five feet ten and a half inches. But he was dark, good-looking and possessed tremendous personality and charm – a charm that few women could resist. And Reg, like most horsemen, loved women.

He was slim with a good leg for a boot and invariably immaculate; and fussy to the point that the garter strap of his boots, like those of a good cavalry officer, always had to be positioned between the second and third button of the breeches. It was his sophisticated charm that captivated one of the most attractive girls in Northamptonshire. Margery (Marge) Robertson was the daughter of the Superintendent of Police at Market Harborough. Five feet eight inches tall, fair-haired, with a good figure, softly spoken, tremendously kind and well-liked, with a keen sense of humour, Marge came from a marvellous family. Her father was a fabulously kind man whose name was a legend in the district. Nobody ever came to the police station, however down and out they might be, without going away comforted in some way. He was very well loved and respected in the local community and in the force which he served for more than thirty years. He used to call Bruce

Tixie. Margery's mother Florence was a perfect complement to her husband, immensely kind and supremely popular.

After a short courtship Reg and Marge were married in 1919 and sailed across the Atlantic to Long Island, where on 27 December, 1920 their son Bruce was born.

Chapter Three

Bruce first saw the light of day at Mineola, Long Island. All he can remember is that he had a black nanny called Pearl whom he adored and he remembers a photograph of her, neat and slim in her white hat and white apron, not at all typical of the fat Momma-type of black so beloved by the film producers.

"The only other thing that I can remember," he says, "is that my favourite food in those days at the age of two was corn cobs and water melons. I still love corn on the cob."

When Bruce was two years old Ambrose Clark, the multi-millionaire who lived for sport and was now known as the Lord Lonsdale of the U.S.A., decided to set up a hunting establishment at Melton Mowbray. Reg Hobbs was to be his Master of the Horse.

Despite all her entreaties Pearl was not allowed to accompany little Bruce to England. On the quayside she bade Reg, Margery and baby Bruce a tearful farewell as they sailed from New York in the *Majestic*, crack liner of the White Star Fleet. Bruce enlivened the voyage. "Apparently I use to hurtle round the deck in my little kiddie-car to the amusement of all the passengers," he says. He was met by a new nanny and promptly fell in love with her – a dark, attractive, fun-loving girl called Peggy Pepper with whom he kept in touch until her death only a few years ago. "I use to pull her leg a lot," he says, "and she took it very well indeed."

The little family was now introduced to an incredible world of fantasy, a dream world that had never been seen before and can hardly even be imagined today. Each season people who lived in palaces, castles and mansions competed to occupy little houses in and around Melton. From early days Melton Mowbray had been the Mecca of fox-hunting pilgrims, chiefly because it is built on a site where the countries hunted by the Quorn, Cottesmore and Belvoir meet. In

1638, according to Gabriel Plattes, "the vale of Belvoir was the best corn land in Europe," and Leicestershire as a whole was under plough. Hence the high ridge and furrow (produced by the ox ploughs of the period) for the purpose of drainage and of presenting as large a surface of the land to the sun as was possible. If you think about it, you will realise that there was method in their madness!

In 1784 Marshall described Leicestershire as "not long ago an animal country, now it is a continuous sheet of green sward." Such it was in 1920, although perhaps rather a bumpy sheet owing to the ridge and furrow still remaining. As Nimrod said, "both nature and art have contributed to make Leicestershire the county for fox-hunting." Nature had supplied a soil which held scent. Agriculture had supplied well-drained land and negotiable fences while art had placed fox coverts at nice distances apart. Last, but not least, unlike most of the provincial counties, there was no game shooting.

Leicestershire life in the period between the wars, during which Bruce and I were growing up, was unique. Before 1914 the wealth of the fox-hunting fraternity, who were in the main the upper classes, whether it stemmed from industry or from genuine land-owning aristocracy, was solid. But now after four years of bitter conflict which had brought the deaths of many true fox-hunting men, against a background of industrial unrest, the General Strike and the Depression, the ice began to wear thin; there were visible cracks and in many cases the wealth, although still there on the surface, was in danger of disappearing. Imagining that they could still recapture "the golden age", the dancers skated on even more furiously than before with a forced gaiety, but in the knowledge that it would not last.

However, those who played out the charade would never forget it. Whatever else might die, their memories of that glorious time in Leicestershire would live forever.

A remarkable fact about Leicestershire in those days is that it was responsible for one of Britain's two annual "migrations". The upper classes migrated to Scotland for the twelth of August and the advent of each hunting season brought a steady influx of hunting visitors, not only from England, but from America and the Continent. The Midland Hunts, unlike those which were practically self-supporting, depended largely on these visitors. The local hunting population was comparatively small. There was nothing new in this. Leicestershire had always attracted fox-hunters from outside and it was said that the whole of a Melton field changed entirely in the course of every ten years.

There was a hard core of completely dedicated fox-hunting people, by no means confined to Leicestershire. One dedicated hunting man was Earl Fortescue, who, with his wife Daisy, a superb horsewoman side-saddle, and their family used to travel from their Castle Hill in Devon up to Melton Mowbray at the end of October every year in their own special train, containing their complete retinue of servants, horses, children, dogs, etc. They would stay in Melton, hunting six days a week until the end of the season, when they would return to their glorious Devonshire home where their daughter Lady Margaret Fortescue now lives. But even she says, "When I can no longer hunt with the Quorn on Fridays and the Belvoir on Saturdays, I'll give up. It is the only true fox-hunting left in England today."

Whyte Melville wrote "fox-hunting is a wild sport, the wilder the better."

Nevertheless the pick of our fox-hunting countries is a county famed not only for agriculture but for manufacture. Leicestershire, in fact, is full of towns, railways, canals and roads, not to mention ironworks and coalfields, while Melton Mowbray itself, the reputed metropolis of fox-hunting, has been better known locally over the years for its manufacture of such items as stockings, lace goods and pork pies! Indeed, even in the palmy pre-war days, unless you happened to see a string of hunters passing through the streets, there was no town which looked less like a sporting centre than Melton.

Warwick Lodge is still there today, at the top, right at the apex of Ankle Hill on one side and the Dalby road on the other, with the hospital below. Now it serves as council offices. Bruce says, "Then, it was an enormous house with a wonderful stable yard, something akin to Stanley House at Newmarket and completely self-contained. Like Stanley House it was painted black and white with highly-polished brass knockers on the doors." When the lovely Countess of Warwick left Warwick Lodge, it was taken first by Lord Hamilton of Dalziel with his splendid, hard-riding, immensely popular wife, and then, in 1922, by Ambrose Clark.

His Master of the Horse and family moved into a compact five-bedroom house on Burton Road, almost opposite, just above the famous Craven Lodge, scene of so much nocturnal revelry. Major General Vaughan, a retired officer, had already turned Craven Lodge into a hunting guest-house with stabling for guests' horses. They took either a room or a suite for the season and it was here that in 1923 the Prince of Wales, later King Edward VIII, installed himself. From the Royal suite he gave dinner parties and dinner dances, to which invitations were much coveted. Even more socialites flocked to Melton each season after the heir to the throne started hunting in Leicestershire. The slender Prince of Wales had not the skill across country of the Earl of Lonsdale ("the Yellow Earl") but at least he had the courage. In his magnificent book *Fields Elysian*, Simon Blow writes, "Inevitably Melton Mowbray had all the making of a snobs' paradise.

By the middle Twenties it not only had a galaxy of titles but three capital Royal Princes hunting. Prince Henry and Prince George were also to be regulars, sharing the Royal suite. Practical jokes became a fashion, one of which was to ask those women known to be in pursuit of the Prince of Wales to an imaginary dinner party. The girl would desperately search for a flattering partner and then turn up on the steps of Craven Lodge to be told that the Prince was in London!"

He adds: "A few men with foreign names decided it would help to add a title after a season and Mr Jack de Pret suddenly returned as Count de Pret!"

Monica Sheriffe, a magnificent horsewoman who hunted six days a week and attended nearly all the Craven Lodge parties, frequently in fancy dress, told me, "I only dined at home one day a week!"

Of all the Melton establishments Warwick Lodge was the biggest. Every box had to be occupied throughout the season. There were fifty boxes and fifty glorious thoroughbreds at all times. Bruce says, "At the end of every season before Ambrose Clark went back to America, he and father with six nagsmen would go to Ireland where they would buy a bunch of horses. They would try them thoroughly and only buy them if they were good enough. They were all thoroughbreds good enough to be novice chasers or top event-horses today. Throughout the summer father and his nagsmen would school them until they were absolutely foolproof and perfectly trained by the time the Clarks came over. When old Ambrose Clark and his wife got on their horses, they rode with the buckle of the reins in their hands. The horses had to go straight and there was no question of pulling them up or anything like that.

"Apart from all the servants in the big house, butler, footmen, maids, etc., there were two separate lots of staff in the yard, those that used to groom the horses and those who were the nagsmen and second horsemen."

Monica Sheriffe says, "On a fashionable day there would be as many as four hundred out and two hundred second horsemen."

Bruce remembers twelve second horsemen, all dressed in livery, top hats with cockades, silver buttons, etc., pulling out from Warwick Lodge, each riding one beautiful thoroughbred and leading another.

"The second horsemen never groomed the horses. When they came back from hunting at night, they would take the tack off and hand the horses over to the strappers. The tack was their responsibility. They had to keep it perfect in every respect, clean and polished. They would go into the wheelroom to look at the order book and see which horses they had to equip to go out the following morning. I don't know why it was called the wheelroom. It was what, in racing circles, might be called the best tack-room. There all the tack was hung up, behind glass, obviously, because all the bits were burnished steel. Then, in the morning the second horsemen would come down. They would never muck the horses out. All they had to do was to wipe them over, put on the tack and away they would go. They wore black coats with white breeches and mahogany top boots. My father's second horseman, Leonard Gregory, had his own buff-coloured breeches and black boots. In those days there was a hunt servant, the huntsman's second horseman in charge of all the second horsemen. He too was in livery, wearing a distinctive leather sash over his shoulder, and when hounds moved off, he would lead them trotting round the roads. He would know where the draw was and where they were likely to go. All the other second horsemen followed him and they never went faster than a trot."

This then was the atmosphere in which Bruce was brought up. Six days a week, horses, horses, hunting, hunting.

Small wonder that one of his happiest memories of those early days is associated with his mother's parents, grandfather and grandmother Robertson of Market Harborough. "My grandmother was undoubtedly one of the kindest people I have ever met in my life and my grandfather was wonderful with me as a child. My mother would take me over from Melton on a Sunday and grandfather would take us out for a drive in his bull-nosed Morris Oxford. I shall never forget those Sunday afternoons when grandfather in his open car with his grandson beside him used to race the trains!"

Bruce's first school was a little kindergarten near his home on Burton Road. There he made lasting friendships with two little girls who were to become famous in the years to come. His first girlfriend was Diana Carlos-Clarke, whose good-looking father Charlie, despite his Etonian nick-name of "Shit" Clarke, was popular in hunting circles as an amusing raconteur and rhymester. He acted as agent to the Marquess of Blandford at Lowesby and lived with his wife and two children, Sandy and Diana, in a fairly large house with lawns and paddocks that swept down to a stream at the Dalby road. His little girl grew into the most beautiful woman that anybody in racing can remember and married Fulke Walwyn. There was also Prim Rollo, who was to be universally loved and who married David Niven. Both were to die early, mourned by all.

"We were up to all sorts of mischief," says Bruce, "and I, being the smallest, used to get most of the stick, but I enjoyed every minute of it."

He learnt to ride when he was four years old and on his fifth birthday was given a little black Shetland pony called Bombo. The groundwork was well laid for his introduction to a decent active pony called Tom Thumb on whom he started hunting when he was six. He was not a very good show-pony because his hocks stood too far away from him, but he was quite a good hunter.

In retrospect one of the landmarks in Bruce's life came when he was seven years old and was given a very good pony called Lady Marvel, "Kiss Me" as she was known in the stables. "She had belonged to Doreen Hearth whose Leicester family, in the boot and shoe trade, were great friends of ours. They had bought this grey pony from a fishmonger's cart in Leicester. Now she was white, a superb show-pony and a magnificent hunter. Doreen had grown out of her and they gave her to me. I hunted her for three seasons and showed her everywhere and, without boasting, I can state unequivocally that we were only ever defeated twice in riding or pony classes, and that was when she was in season. We won the championship at Olympia in 1928 and 1929." Bruce had been ready for such a pony for a long time.

The games at the kindergarten with Di Carlos-Clarke, Prim Rollo and the others had not been like those of other children with dolls, bears, kiddie-cars and scooters. They had always been with imaginary ponies. "We would practise jumping. Prim and I would hold a little stick while Di would run in and jump. Sometimes she would pretend to refuse and another child would come behind her, urging her on, pretending to smack her, then we would change over and the girls would hold the pole while I jumped. One day I hurt myself quite badly when staging a fall!

"We would enjoy gymkhana games, pretending to be the ponies, bending between little poles, playing musical chairs and so on. One day I got into trouble for teaching the girls how to win apple-bobbing competitions. The rules are simple. The contestants line up, then gallop to one end of the arena where they find a stable-bucket full of water with an apple floating on the surface. They must dismount from their ponies, pick the apple up in their teeth and then, still holding it like that, gallop back to the finishing line. It's easier said than done, because, of course, as you try to get your teeth into the apple, it bobs up again and it usually takes quite a long time to complete the exercise. But, as with everything else connected with horses, my father had the vital trick up his sleeve and I heard him chuckling about it to my mother several times. The secret is to throw yourself off the pony onto your knees in front of the pail, take a deep breath, open your mouth over the apple, plunge it under your head to the bottom of the bucket, hold it there hard and bite into it. No messing about with bobbing apples. Just a racing certainty. Of course, the only trouble is that you are apt to get your head and also your clothes soaked with water. I was not at all popular with the headmistress when we arrived after break, soaking wet, particularly the girls with their long hair!"

It was all right for the other children. Riding was fun for them and was to remain so. But for Bruce, it was to become his life.

"Keep your elbows in, Bruce. Sit up, boy. Sit up!"

Before he was six playtime was over for him. "My father was a fanatic," he says. "Once he got me going, he was not going to allow me to stop until I was champion young rider. He drove me very hard and, in fact, he and mother used to argue like hell because she resented his treatment of me. I could hear them while I was in bed at night. At one stage he frightened me to such an extent that for three months I wouldn't go near a pony.

"We'd be in the yard at seven a.m. and I had to ride for three hours every day. All the time he seemed to be over-facing me. He asked me to negotiate obstacles that terrified me. He would send me off on a nappy pony and tell me to school it in a field for an hour all on my own. I couldn't do it. I used to stand in the gateway and blub my eyes out. I couldn't move the stupid pony and there was nobody there to help me. Then, when father came back again, he would say 'What have you done?' and I would say 'I can't move', knowing very well that he would be furious.

"My father loved his job and was very good at it, brilliant at schooling, with a first-class team of nagsmen. He applied the same rules to me as he did to his horses, perfection, perfection and still more perfection. He was so ambitious for me that I had to be a success. His strict firmness upset my mother. After all, I was her only child and, when he was extra firm – he used to bloody well frighten me – I would turn to Mummy."

The routine at Warwick Lodge was simple. At the end of the hunting season the Americans went back to Long Island and Reg was in sole charge. He loved point-to-pointing, trained the likely ones to run and rode some of them himself with considerable success. He had already acquired the racing bug. The others were turned out to grass where they were joined later by the point-to-pointers. Now the new entries from Ireland were being nagged. Once again there was only one standard – perfection. Bruce says, "They were taught what is now called dressage to a very high standard. In those days it was just normal training, horse P.T. Anyone of those horses would have gone to the top in the eventing world today. It may be hard for the modern generation to believe, but they were all as good as anything that you see at Badminton; all of them.

"Any with flaws were turned out. All had to be ridden in double bridles. Apart from anything else, it was considered undressed in Leicestershire in those days to hunt in any other bit. There were never any martingales or other forms of adornment."

After the horses had been at grass, they came in and had to pass a test to ensure that they were still up to standard. Those that did not pass or were too old were sold at Leicester Repository.

"Father did no showing. He had a very good woman called Kay Newcombe, absolutely brilliant side-saddle, who used to ride Mrs Clark's horses in the show ring. In 1925 she had the champion Popham."

Reg was the most brilliant man at teaching a horse to jump I have ever known. Bruce says, "Yes, he was brilliant all right. We had a little school at Warwick Lodge which he had copied when he went to Lambourn, and later Fred Rimell copied the same pattern with considerable success. Boarded round the outside, oblong, with a cinder track, it had a fence and some poles on one side and on the other there was an open ditch and a pole. Let a horse in there loose, with just a headcollar on, and he couldn't go fast because there was not enough room. Reg would stand with a whip in a little dip in the middle and he would begin by getting the horse to go round; he would just give him a crack round the hocks to give him a lift before he took off and was away. The horses got to love it and by the time they had finished in there, with the poles gradually going up so that they jumped three feet six, they were near perfect. If they hit those jumps they went straight onto their noses, and they never did that twice. But there was no one hanging on to their mouths and so they really revelled in it. When you put a saddle on them and took them out to jump fences, there was never any question of them turning their heads. On occasion father would make me get up on one of those horses in the school, which was very unpleasant, quite unnecessary and slightly dangerous because of the confined space.

"From the loose school the horses graduated to the natural fences in the fields over which the local farmers used to let us jump. We had *carte blanche* over the Wilson Newcombe land and that of many others and, whenever we damaged any of the fences, our men used to repair them. Below Burton Lazars there used to be a gated road up to Croxton Park where there were two polo grounds, jumping fields and fences.

"Even if he was asking an awful lot of me as a six- and seven-year-old, my father certainly inspired his nagsmen. 'Come on, follow me,' he would shout, taking us over the trickiest little places. His number-one nagsman was a magnificent chap called Leonard Gregory, who came to us straight from school at the age of fourteen, looked after my ponies, graduated to nagsman and then to father's second horseman. Later he came to Lambourn as our head man."

I well remember Leonard Gregory at Lambourn as the smartest man in the place. Tall, handsome with an outstanding figure and leg for a boot, he was a different class of horseman from any other in the village – a true Reg Hobbs Leicestershire product.

Like the young hounds with the Quorn, Belvoir and Meynell, the Warwick Lodge horses were ready for their introduction to the hunting field with cub-hunting in the late summer. Remember there was no standing corn to worry about in those days in Leicestershire. Monica Sheriffe says, "If you ever saw a ploughed field you would stop and say 'good God, there's a ploughed field!'"

Reg was almost as dedicated as the late Duke of Beaufort who told me: "Once, about that time, when I was hunting hounds, I had nine days in one week cub-hunting. Six mornings and three evenings!"

This was the drill for Bruce at the age of six and seven, first with his pony Tom Thumb. He believes that he was one of the founder members of the Pony Club because his badge was in single figures. The very first children's meet ever held was at Baggrave Hall, the home of Major Algie Burnaby, the renowned master of the Quorn whose fame dated back to the 1890s when he had won the Moonlight Steeplechase. On the spur of the moment, it was decided that all the jockeys should ride with nightshirts over their hunting clothes but Algie Burnaby had forgotten his nightshirt and won the race in a pink ribboned nightdress lent by Lady Augusta Fane. The major was, by all accounts, no stranger to ladies' nightwear! Bruce says, "I can see it all now. Before we moved off from that first children's meet, Major Burnaby stood on the steps of his house and called us round to give us a briefing on what to do and what not to do. Apparently, after the talk, I went up to him and asked whether I could help him with the children. I had had a fair amount of practice."

Monica says, "Bruce was always impeccably dressed, marvellously turned out. He looked like a miniature huntsman with his black coat, white hunting-tie and velvet cap. I shall never forget his wonderful manners and the way that, no matter how awkward a gate was, Bruce was always there to open it."

When the hunting season proper started in November, Reg had the Warwick Lodge horses to himself for at least six weeks until Ambrose Clark and his "family" arrived. Bruce says, "My father hunted six days a week all through the season. There was no such thing as boxing horses onto the meet. We would hack twelve or thirteen miles to a meet and I would go trailing after them. Then perhaps fifteen or sixteen miles home in the afternoon and evening, with no lights or anything about your person to indicate your presence in the dark."

As a boy he never saw much of the Clarks, although he did receive some nice Christmas presents, such as leather-bound volumes of Rudyard Kipling from Ambrose Clark. "As I was born only two days after Christmas, I was rather apt to be 'the little boy that Santa Claus forgot!' because I would be told 'That will do for Christmas or that will do for birthday.' As far as presents were concerned, I had to have all my riding kit before anything else. A saddle, a bridle, breeches, jodphurs, boots, etc., etc. I was never allowed a bicycle. As for books, even those that Mr Clark gave me, I never read anything until I joined the Army – except the form book! Now I never stop reading.

"There were no wirelesses in those days, so sometimes after lunch on a Sunday we would crank the old gramophone up and my job was to play it to father and mother. I used to get terrible stick if I didn't change the needle often enough, put on the wrong side of the record or hadn't wound the machine up sufficiently.

"Mother and father played bridge. Mother was very keen on the game and would do a twelve-hour session at a time but father's real game was poker."

The only other relaxation during the year was a short holiday in the summer at Skegness, where Reg used to play golf with the Whittons. "We had a house along by Seacroft golf course there and the Whitton boys, who were my chums, were very keen golfers. I wasn't very keen. By now all I wanted to do was ride, despite the discipline and the falls."

When he was eight years old Bruce went to Neville Holt near Rockingham Castle, Medbourne, Market Harborough, which was a preparatory school for Uppingham.

He says, "I don't know whether the discipline was good or not but I loved it. I loved the atmosphere and everything about that school, where I made some very good friends. One of my best chums there was Billy Griggs, the son of Walter Griggs who used to train at Newmarket. He and Michael Marsh and I became firm friends. My parents were great friends of Michael's mother and father, a very respected solicitor from Melton.

"Michael became a judge and recently met an untimely end when he and his wife were burnt to death in their own house. His sister, who lives at Burton Lazars, is married to Britain's top showman of today, Vin Toulson.

"Another of my great chums was John Warrender, son of Sir Victor Warrender, later Lord Bruntisfield, who had a lovely place at Croxton Park. I was to meet John some years later when he was in the Royal Scots Greys."

Unlike his own father, Reg was no Vin Toulson. His heart was in the hunting field and more particularly in racing, fired with enthusiasm by Pete Bostwick, who, while still hunting with Ambrose Clark from Warwick Lodge, rode in races and indeed took the Imperial Cup on Flaming; he was an outstanding jockey and a brilliant international polo player. Not surprisingly, some of the Warwick Lodge hunters, given a chance to race under rules, became useful chasers, including

Gogglegoose, Garadice and of course that stout-hearted, consistent bay son of Jackdaw, Kellsboro' Jack, whom Reg bought as a yearling in 1927. Six years later, trained by Ivor Anthony, Kellsboro' Jack won the Grand National for Ambrose Clark and his wife Florence.

Incidentally, unlike Dorothy Paget and many other greedy owners, Mrs Clark refused to allow her young champion to risk the hazards of the National again, but he continued to race for five more seasons, winning his share every year and running third to Golden Miller three times in succession in the Cheltenham Gold Cup before being retired to the United States. He was buried there along with the Clarks' Welsh National winner Sorley Boy, on the summit of one of the foothills of the Adirondacks.

Nevertheless Reg was determined that his young son would become well-known throughout the country as a horseman and he thought that the best method available at the time, after the arrival of the pony Lady Marvel, was through the medium of the show-ring.

Bruce says, "Funnily enough I adored the showing. The training wasn't so funny because father used all his tremendous skill to bring Lady Marvel and me to perfection. Though I say it myself, he succeeded. Father loved the glory of it and every time we won, there he was in the forefront when the photographs were being taken for the press. Then he would meet us at the station and see that the rosettes were stuck on properly before we walked home through the streets of Melton. Leonard would unload us, put the rosettes right and on we would go in glory through the streets. We would have gone to the show by car but the ponies went everywhere by rail because there was a station every five miles.

"When we went to the International Horse Show, the ponies were led through the streets of London from Kings Cross to Olympia. We used to exercise in Hyde Park's Rotten Row.

"As I said earlier, in three seasons of showing, we were beaten only twice – and that was when Lady Marvel was in season. Being a showman, my father had several tricks up his sleeve, several secrets, one of which was the band. He would always show where there was a band, knowing that Lady Marvel liked to dance to the music and would really stick her toe out.

"Also, when I was called on by the judge to give my show, cantering and then galloping round the ring, it was essential to get off on the proper leg and father had always drummed into me that I must never look down under any circumstances. He told me I must not take off and break into a canter until I got into the corner, when I must lean over and do it properly. So at big shows he would position himself on the turn somewhere in the stands and I would look up for his signal – either yes or no. Whatever happened I mustn't look down and

I was never to take off until I got his signal on that corner. As a result I was always right, and then how we galloped. They used to say that my grandfather won his championships by the speed and power of his gallops. I was made to do the same.

"I think the happiest day of my childhood was when my grandfather led the final parade on the champion heavyweight and I, champion in my division, was placed second to him with Lady Marvel.

"That little white pony was not just a show pony. She won innumerable jumping competitions, and one of my toughest rivals was Lord Belper's daughter, Lavinia Strutt, later to be Duchess of Norfolk, a most attractive girl and always an outstanding rider."

No pony ever gave greater service than Lady Marvel. In the hunting field she is described by Monica Sheriffe as "Bruce's wonderful white pony".

Monica adds, "On a fashionable day with the Quorn or Belvoir with whom Reg was hunting, accompanied by his little son, you needed two horses out. There would be as many as four hundred people and about two hundred second horsemen. It was like a cavalry charge, a full-time job struggling through that crowd. If you weren't in the first twenty through a gateway, you had had it.

"And Reg was always in the lead. In all my hunting days I am convinced that Reg Hobbs was the finest man across country I have ever seen."

Bruce says, "Whether I wanted to or not – and often I didn't – I had to follow father. He was always at point. The master of hounds used to send him off to the point of the covert, with the result that he got a bit of a start. He had a top-class thoroughbred horse whereas I had a fourteen-two-hand pony. 'Come on,' he would shout and off he'd go. Quite incredible. I was doing my best and I had to jump every obstacle, following him. If I fell off he never waited for me, just gave me a bloody good rousting when I caught up again. Father was a very very hard taskmaster and he never spared me."

Bruce smiled as he thought back to his childhood. "My first pair of boots were given to me by Di Carlos-Clarke. I know they were because they had pointed toes! My word, she grew into a lovely woman."

Although not perhaps brought up "in the lap of luxury", Bruce's lifestyle throughout the first eleven years of his childhood, as the son of a multi-millionaire's Master of the Horse, was comfortable indeed.

"I certainly never had to get a pony ready or do it up when I came in. Nor did I ever have to clean or press my clothes. We had servants and grooms to look after everything.

"The whole period seems like a dream now, but I suppose I was a very lucky, privileged little boy. I was blooded when I was six and was only eight years old when I was given my hunt buttons with the

Quorn. That was quite a distinction in those days. Those were the days when, in riding classes for children under the age of fifteen, with father standing in the corner making sure I started cantering on the right leg, I was sweeping the board although I was only eight. I suppose there was a bit of rivalry among the older competitors but I didn't know about it because I was young and innocent and getting on with the job as a professional.

"At home I had an enormous great playroom in the garden and at the back of the playroom there was a fence and between the fence and the playroom there were sticks and piles of wood. I had tremendous hunts there on my own. I would get the terriers in and I'd get the horn out and I'd be blowing them away. I was always hunting. I knew Leicestershire backwards by the time I was nine and, although I couldn't read the signposts properly, I knew how to get home. I must admit that I once got lost in a fog! I found a track and followed it and it just happened to be going in the right direction.

"My father used to play polo in those days and I tried my hand at that on Lady Marvel. I was occasionally allowed to take a stick to the ball. My father was a four-goal man, which was fairly good, and used to play at Roehampton and Hurlingham. George Beeby used to play with him locally on the grounds at Croxton Park.

"In August father would go up to Scotland to shoot grouse, and one year he and mother brought back a fox cub which I called Charlie and proceeded to tame. It used to go for walks with mother and me, around the shops in Melton on a lead. Naturally as Charlie grew older he got wilder and eventually the day came when he had to be reintroduced to the wild. So he was put in a box and taken off by father and one of the earthstoppers at the dead of night. Before turning him loose we clipped his ear and tagged him so that we would know him again. Right next door to the stables at Craven Lodge the river runs down to the railway and the first time hounds drew, they got away on Charlie. He went a wide detour, swam the river and came back to his box where luckily the door was open and he was able to pop in over the top. Hounds were called off and we took our black-faced Scottish fox into the wild again. As far as I know they never caught him.

"Father had a terrible fall which prevented him from riding Chaddsford in the Grand National for the second time. He was taken to Melton Hospital, where he was in traction with heavy weights on his leg. One afternoon when mother and I were visiting him, the whole lot snapped and the twenty-one-pound weight fell with a crash."

By the time he was ten years old, Bruce was riding any number of other ponies for different people. "When I outgrew Lady Marvel, father tried to breed from her but I think she must have been too old.

So he gave her to Mrs Aubrey Hastings for Peter Hastings and his sisters to ride and she finished her days with them. About that time Pete Bostwick gave me a good hunter called Fisherman. I won a number of hunter trials and pairs-jumping all over the country on this fifteen-two-hand horse. I was very small for one of that size but he had a perfect mouth and manners and could really gallop and jump. Although I was still not quite nine, we were competing in an under-sixteen pairs class just below Craven Lodge and the last fence was an in-and-out over a pair of railway gates. We won all right!"

These ponies and others were Bruce's childhood. On them, at least two days a week, school or no, throughout the hunting season, he would follow his father, who went as straight as a gun-barrel over the glorious Leicestershire grassland. They must have been wonderful ponies to have stuck the pace behind such hounds as the Belvoir bitches, even though Bruce would often go home when the field changed to their second horses. "There were a lot of people then who went out to hunt just to gallop across country," he says. "Once you got going, there was nothing greater. You would look round and there were hundreds of people behind you. It was all grass, not a bit of wire. Even a grown-up had to have a good horse if he was going to be up there, let alone a child."

Among the owners for whom Bruce now trains is Sir Thomas (Tommy) Pilkington. This association reminds him of those days, because Tommy's grandfather was famous Major Jack Harrison of Melton with his eight lovely daughters who "went like hell". For Bruce is one of the only people still in his prime today who really took part during the twenties in that fabulous hunting scene. "I remember George Barker who hunted the Quorn, and George Tongue with the Belvoir. They were both rather short, and George Tongue was quite plump, but they were marvellous men. I think that their greatest asset was their ability at one time to work hounds and to leave them alone. You had to be so alert. It was no good standing by the covert coffee-housing. You had to listen or else you were left behind. All of a sudden there would be a holloa the other side of the covert and the hounds were gone.

"If anyone made a noise or got in front of the Fieldmaster they were sent home at once. I have seen it happen time and time again. One day someone lost control and rode into hounds. He was expelled from the country."

Despite many disagreements at home owing to his father's amorous escapades and his domineering treatment both of Bruce and Margery, the future looked secure. Bruce firmly believed that he would go on from Neville Holt to Uppingham and then become a veterinary surgeon. "I had set my heart on being a vet," he says.

It was not to be. All his boyhood hopes and dreams were shattered after a day's hunting towards the end of the season in 1930. Ambrose Clark in his scarlet cutaway coat, drinking his whisky and soda, told Reg that he had decided to give up the English hunting scene after one more season at Warwick Lodge and then go back to the States. "I know you want to go racing," he said. "So you find the place and I'll support you right to the end."

It was Reg's old friend Harry Cottrill who found them the right place. Harry, a buoyant, debonair character, always looked on the bright side and derived a great deal of fun from racing. A native of Cheshire who had hunted a lot before 1914 and ridden in point-to-points, financing these pleasures by making and dealing in hunters, he had eventually established a small stable of jumpers at Tarporley, but was now a highly successful flat trainer at the famous Seven Barrows, just outside Lambourn. It was in Upper Lambourn that Harry found the place for Reg – Ronehurst, a little old house with a small, cosy, enclosed yard, nestling at the foot of the downs.

For horsemaster Reg, who had ridden in the Grand National and nearly crippled himself in a steeplechasing fall, it was the beginning of a dream.

For horselover Bruce, who also loved school and longed to be a vet, it was the premature end of a childhood that seemed like a horse-obsessed dream.

For horseless Margery, who now disliked her domineering, philandering husband as much as she adored her only child, it was the beginning of the end of her married life.

Chapter Four

Bruce, like Sir Noel Murless, has never shared Sir Gordon Richards's love of the downland country. "Once a downsman, always a downsman," says the immortal Gordon. But Bruce has always disliked Lambourn as much as Noel disliked "cold, damp Beckhampton".

The reason is not far to seek. As the Hobbs family drove through Wantage, with its Bear Hotel and statue of King Alfred, out on the road towards Lambourn, ten-year-old Bruce, who had been feeling sick for most of the way from Melton, realised once and for all that his childhood was over. Leicestershire was gone, along with his beloved Neville Holt prep. school, the hunting and his burning ambition to be a vet.

As they started to climb the long hill up towards the ridgeway, Reg pointed. "You're in God's own country now, my boy," he said. "That's Letcombe Regis over there, where old Jack trains the greatest horse in the world."

There was no need to ask the name because Bruce had heard of nothing but Easter Hero for the last three years since the little, all-quality chestnut had won his first Cheltenham Gold Cup, and only the previous year Jack Anthony had brought off the great Cheltenham double, winning a second Gold Cup with Easter Hero and the Champion Hurdle with Brown Tony. Now forty-one years old, the rider of three Grand National winners and a former champion jockey before he took out a training licence in 1927, Jack had visited them often at Melton. It was ironic that this small, dark, humorous Welshman, the youngest of the three Anthony brothers, so fearless a rider who had survived so many circuits of Aintree unscathed, should permanently have lamed himself stepping off a hack while on holiday in America. He was at once a hero and the loyalest of friends, and was to play a vital part in the life of young Hobbs.

As for Easter Hero, he too provides a link to this story by introducing one of the most important characters in Bruce's life, Bill Payne. In the summer of 1927 the Irish-bred horse, a son of My Prince, had been bought by Frank Barbour, a rich, eccentric, extremely shrewd linen-thread manufacturer, who had owned and trained the previous year's Gold Cup winner Koko. Easter Hero won eight chases during the 1927/28 season, including the Molyneux and Becher Chases over the Grand National fences at Liverpool, but it was not until the last of these eight victories, in the prestigious three-and-a-half-mile Coventry Chase at Kempton, which he won with twelve stone seven pounds, that the pundits really sat up and took notice. Hitherto their admiration had been qualified. It was an age when the top steeplechasers were big, burly powerhouses with enormous quarters, and although today we have become used to all-quality stars like Mandarin and Arkle, one contemporary scribe thought Easter Hero "full of quality but rather lacking in substance" and another wondered "where he finds all his powers of jumping and endurance".

However, by winning the Coventry Chase, proving that he could stay the distance in top class company, the chestnut had become a star overnight and was to preserve the status for the rest of his brilliant, sensation-strewn career.

Briefly, he won twelve more chases including two Cheltenham Gold Cups and was an extremely gallant second in the 1929 Grand National under twelve stone seven pounds, despite being handicapped by a grotesquely twisted plate over the last mile.

He could well have run up a sequence of Gold Cup victories, like Golden Miller and Arkle, but before the Cheltenham Festival of 1928, he was bought for £7,000 with an extra £3,000 contingency should he win the Grand National, for which race his new owner wanted him to be trained to the exclusion of the Gold Cup.

The man who paid what was then this astronomical price for a steeplechaser was well known to the hunting Hobbs family. It was eventually announced after a great deal of speculation that the buyer was the Belgian millionaire financier, Captain Lowenstein, called "Low" by his Melton friends, who kept a yard of magnificent horses in the near-by village of Thorpe Satchville and gave investment advice on the hunting field!

In the Grand National Easter Hero led a then record field of forty-two runners. He sailed over those huge upright fences with supreme contempt until he reached the Canal Turn, which was then an open ditch. Here he took off outside the wings, crashed on top of the fence and straddled it, apparently stuck, baulking those behind and putting more than twenty horses out of the race. Not until Popham Down came a cropper in 1967, in Foinavon's year, was there to be another mêlée like it. Two fences from home in 1928, there were only three left in the race. Going by far the best was Great Span, ridden by seventeen-year-old Bill Payne for his father, a former champion jockey who now trained near Epsom. But the saddle slipped, dumping young Payne and frustrating his achievement of an age-record which he would have shared ten years later with the man who became his greatest friend.

After the other survivor, Billy Barton, had fallen at the last, Tipperary Tim, who had come to Aintree with the reputation of being a "thoroughly bad horse" won the great chase at 100 to 1. Billy Barton was remounted to become the only other finisher.

Easter Hero then went to Paris for the Grand Steeplechase, the nearest French equivalent to the Grand National, but his jockey Dick Rees, the British champion, who was always a *bon viveur*, had wined and dined rather too well in Paris before racing and, although renowned and respected as one of the all-time greats, now allowed his mount to refuse at the famous water jump in front of the stands, the Tribune de la Rivière, and was himself shot off. Nothing daunted, Dick got up, shook himself and, facing the packed stands, gave a rude sign to the crowd and had a much needed pee in full view of the delighted Gallic spectators who shouted "Vive l'Anglais!"

Easter Hero redeemed his reputation a few days later by carrying a more sober Rees to victory in the Prix des Drags, which was the only success in his new owner's colours because barely a month later "Low" Lowenstein fell out of his private aeroplane while crossing the Channel.

So, for the second time that year Easter Hero was sold, this time to the American millionaire "Jock" Hay Whitney, who sent him to be trained by Jack Anthony at Letcombe, who sent him out to win the Gold Cup in the following two years.

So now, as the car climbed the hill away from Wantage, even young Bruce was impressed by the sight of the stables where so much history had been made. But he was sad indeed. This bare, rolling downland country was not for him. He would miss the glorious grass fields and fences of Leicestershire and he viewed with trepidation the gallops that now came into view, but when he saw the schooling fences and hurdles on the left, knowing that there was no going back now, he began to feel excited. After all he had been conditioned for the last three years of his life by the headlines about Easter Hero. Now he was to be part of that great sport of steeplechasing.

His parents were also fully aware that the little belt of trees at the top of the hill meant "off with the old and on with the new". Reg and Margery had drunk a little too much at lunchtime in the Bear at Wantage. Reg had become boisterously, almost aggressively exuberant, whereas Margery who, due to her husband's behaviour, had begun to drink rather more than was good for her, was uncharacteristically sullen and morose. Always a woman of violent likes and dislikes, she now thoroughly disliked her vivacious husband with his charisma for women and horses. He had taken her away from her home where she was surrounded by friends and relations, and was forcing her only child into what she considered a fast and dangerous profession.

They reached the ridgeway at the top of Sincombe Hill and turned left to begin the long descent down Faringdon Road into Lambourn.

As soon as a horse leaves its stable in Berkshire, it is automatically working. Training yards were usually built in the valleys, between the succession of downland ridges, those watersheds that stretch from East Ilsley right across to Marlborough. For years this land has boasted the finest natural going in the world, such as the famous White Horse Hill with its virgin downland, which rises in the triangle between Wantage, Ashbury and Upper Lambourn. There are innumerable hills for horses to trot up, steadily, slowly putting on muscle in the right places, building vital condition which should stay with them through the long season ahead.

Reg pointed right. "That's Moss Hill," he said. "Wonderful going for the flat horses through the hard summer months." He laughed. "Jumpers aren't allowed near it, unless we can pinch a gallop when no-one's looking!"

Bruce marvelled at the little white discs and posts that marked the gallops, indicating that racing was becoming more of an industry than a sport. "What are the chains for across the gallops, Daddy?"

"They're for closing gallops," his father replied. "After you have used a gallop a bit, the downsmen will close that one and move over to the next strip so that the first one can rest, allowing the grass to grow again.

"This, on both sides of the road, is the famous Faringdon Road Gallop, Bruce," Reg continued. "Never tells a lie. On the collar, steadily uphill all the way to the top. Seven furlongs up here is as good as a mile and a quarter anywhere else. This is where Fred Templeman trained last year's Two Thousand Guineas winner Diolite. Old Fred trains down in Lambourn, but over there," he pointed right again, "Down in those trees, in the dip, is where our old friend Harry Cottrill trains. That's Seven Barrows, so called because of those little grass pimples, burial mounds or barrows as they call them in this part of the world, alongside the lane there. Harry uses this gallop and so does Ossie Bell, who won the Stewards' Cup last week with Poor Lad. That hill over and above Harry's place is Mann Down where you and I will be working and schooling our horses."

As they entered the little village of Lambourn on that afternoon in

1931, Bruce's first impression was not good. The place was empty. One of the strange things about a stable lad's life is that he is free from about twelve-thirty until four-thirty p.m., a period when his wife probably does not want him in the house and when all the races in which he is interested, and which are the breath of life to him, are being contested. So he is liable to spend his afternoons in and out of the betting shop, or in those days the local bookie's. Meltonian Harry Beeby's son George, a prominent character in this story, once said that Lambourn in the afternoon reminded him of nothing so much as a mining-town on strike!

By the Red Lion at the crossroads in the little village square, they turned right past the old Church of St Michael and wound their way a mile and a half to the turning for Upper Lambourn. On the way Reg pointed to some buildings on the right. "That's the Malt Shovel pub," he said, "and above it is where old Ted Gwilt, the selling-plate specialist, lives. They call it Saxon House." No-one could have known at the time what a part this training establishment was to play, not only in Bruce's life but in the entire steeplechasing world.

They turned right by a little red Chapel of Rest, four hundred yards down to a T-junction and right again until they reached the old manor, a small Tudor house bordering the ditch that runs between Upper Lambourn and the Malt Shovel. Opposite was Ronehurst, the small attractive house that was to be Bruce's home for the next fifteen years. The lane, enclosed by trees that ran uphill beside the house, with its loose boxes below, was soon to be called Hobbs's Lane.

It is really an ideal steep little hill for riding a young horse away loose because it climbs up to Mann Down between high banks, with trees covering its full length on either side so that the young horse has no distractions. He can be led to the bottom behind an old experienced animal and loosed off just as the lead horse starts trotting. By the time the youngster gets to the top, he will have got his back down. A couple more times up the lane and the yearling or young jumper will be said to have been "ridden away".

Within days the boxes at Ronehurst were full with some decent horses, many of which belonged to Ambrose Clark. Reg, Bruce, Len Gregory, and the new lads whom Reg had engaged, collected them from Lambourn Station and walked them up to the stables. Quickly life settled into the racing routine. The first person to open up the sleeping yard every morning was Len Gregory, the head man, who visited each horse with his bucket of oats and his bowl. Half an hour before the lads arrived at six-thirty a.m., he would have given the last horse his breakfast, and noted any that had left some of their feed.

At seven-twenty, under Len's orders, the horses would start pulling out and, when Reg appeared at seven-thirty, they would move off up Hobbs's Lane to the downs.

Like all the good old trainers, Reg insisted that a horse must be out of his box, walking and trotting, limbering up, before he did his first canter. The first day that Bruce, riding a racehorse for the first time, cantered up with the string on Mann Down, he was amazed at what he saw. There, perched high with only the larks for company, was an incredible variety of slopes and natural gallops. Along the top were six straight miles of undulating land, rather like Chepstow. Down in the dip, between Mann Down and Seven Barrows, he saw Mann Down Bottom, a mile-and-a-quarter round in circumference with, then, four flights of hurdles and four fences placed in the circuit. From Mann Down Bottom you could go either up The Back of the Hill, an ideal steady climb for bad-legged horses, or up The Face of the Hill, a little short-slanting gallop which earned the name "Gwilt's" because old Ted Gwilt used it to ready his sprinting two-year-olds, or round the loop and into the straight mile, finishing at the top below White Horse Hill. Horses trained at Lambourn should be able to act on any racecourse anywhere in the world.

After work, they would lead their horses back to Ronehurst in time for breakfast at about nine-thirty. While the lads went out second lot, Bruce would be at his books. "For two years while I was at Lambourn and learning to ride racehorses, I had a tutor," he says, "and then I spent two years at St Bartholomew's, a boarding school at Newbury. While I was still at school, I started riding in races and, before long, my father had decided that it was time for me to leave school permanently.

"From the start he was very successful. Make no mistake, he was a marvellous horsemaster and trainer.

"Eventually the day came when I was to have my first ride in a hurdle race at Stratford-on-Avon. I was fourteen years old and the horse chosen for my first public appearance over hurdles was Thoughtless II, which belonged to our patron Mrs Ambrose Clark.

"I have said my father was brilliant, and he was. He never left anything to chance, either with his horses, or with me. He was very hard on his horses and, although they always ran big, carrying a lot of condition which he had built up on them, they were very fit. They would be galloped flat out twice a week. We use to go a mile and a quarter round Mann Down Bottom. We would set off with our backs to the hill where you come down to the bottom of the dip and we would gallop round; then, coming down the hill, we would let out a reef and as soon as we got into the dip we had to kick them on for the next two furlongs. We would work on Wednesdays and Saturdays and school on Tuesdays and Fridays. Thursday was an easy day and, except for occasional Monday runners, which would be led out, the horses stayed in their boxes on Sundays. They were fit enough and good enough to win first time out. A number fell by the wayside because they weren't tough enough. My father had always had his hunt horses supremely fit, and after all, it is an easy step from there to get any horse racing fit. Placing is the thing that wins races. Placing and jumping. The late Atty Persse used to say, 'The phrase jumping trainer means a man who can train his horses to jump at home so that they don't fall on the racecourses. If they fall, he is falling down on the job.' My father's horses were always splendidly schooled.

"Before anyone got on them they learnt to jump in the loose school which he had already built before we arrived. Then we had two little fences in the paddock, little hurdles, a plain fence and a little ditch which they would jump, and then they would go out to the schooling ground on the top of Mann Down. I have always favoured those three fences in a line – a plain fence, a fence with a pole in front of it and an open ditch. Once he had got them jumping properly, they would have a run and, provided they were foot perfect, that was it. They would just have one school when they came back from grass each year. I can tell you that my father's jumpers were patent safety."

By the time the day came for his first public appearance over hurdles, Bruce was as excited and enthusiastic about the sport as his father. Though he was already over six feet tall, he had learnt to streamline himself and sit into his horse. Like most of the great jump jockeys, he started as an amateur – Mr B. R. Hobbs.

"From the moment that I went into the changing room at Stratford-on-Avon, I knew I was among friends. Even though I was still a boy, I shared the camaraderie of the jumping jockeys. In those pre-war days money was short and the professionals got only three pounds a ride. They used to joke about a pound a mile. The racecourses were not very well looked after and many of the fences were stiffer, blacker and much straighter than they are now. But there was not so much racing and every jockey was keener to ride whatever came along. If you were asked to ride something, you never looked in the form book to see whether it had fallen in its previous races. You just automatically said yes, please. There were not so many runners in a race and you knew your jockeys better. There were fewer boys and such as there were – I was one myself, after all – were frightened into keeping a straight course. As my old friend Fred Rimell said, 'It was easier to ride a race than it is today when half these barbarians don't know where the hell they're going!' You knew where you were going and you knew where to go. There was a grand spirit in the changing-room in those days. All the jockeys were always fooling about and laughing but there was no quarter shown when you went out on the course.

"They used to say that if you looked into a race-train you could tell the difference between the jump-jockeys' compartment and the flat-race jockeys'. The jumping lads would be playing cards, gambling with each other, enjoying themselves, where as their flat counterparts would be just counting their cash!

"I had been well taught by my father and Len Gregory and had been schooling for a long time with our jockeys, Tim Hamey and Freddie Maxwell, as well as Len. We rode all the schooling.

"At Stratford my father asked Eric Brown to look after me and show me what to do in the race. As we turned into the straight for the last time, there were no dolls, markers or anything like that, but suddenly there were rails with the hurdle course on the inside and the chase course on the outside. Eric Brown was on the wrong side of these rails as the field turned into the straight and he jumped back onto the proper course! I finished fourth and my father considered that I had done well enough to ride a horse with a real chance at Wolverhampton. This time he asked one of the finest hurdle jockeys in the country, Staff Ingham, to look after me. I was riding Armida, trained by Fred Pratt, who lived almost next door to us and had four attractive daughters, one of whom, Nellie, was to become my first stepmother. The horse was owned by the late Jimmy de Rothschild, for whose widow I am delighted to say that I train to this day.

"Staff was on the favourite and told me to line up next to him. He took the inside and, as we came into the first hurdle, there was a terrible crash. That was the end of my mentor and guide! I went on to win my first race. It was a wonderful feeling, although of course I was no stranger to success in public. But this was so different from the showring where you relied on the verdict of the judge. This time I had got to that winning-post first, beating first-class professionals after a tough two-mile gallop over hurdles. I can honestly say that through all my riding career I was never to get blasé about it. I was never to lose that thrill and the satisfaction of riding into the winner's enclosure."

After this victory Bruce was much in demand among the Lambourn trainers because he could ride at the minimum weight, claim the allowance and was eligible for amateur events. Despite his height, he weighed only seven stone at the age of fourteen and even the flat trainers were interested in this natural horseman. Marcus Marsh, nephew of the great Fred Darling, was in Lambourn at the time, training handsome Windsor Lad, generally considered to be one of the best of all Derby winners. Bruce says, "I used to ride a horse called Black Tulip, leading Windsor Lad. Jack Dowdeswell's brother Tom, later headman to Arthur Budgett, was there and Marcus's headman was Harry Coventry who had been at Chattis Hill with Atty Persse. After working up Faringdon Road, we had to lead the horses down to the bottom of the hill and then get up un-assisted to go back to the stables. To begin with I couldn't jump up, but I very soon learnt because it was too damn far to walk all the way back to Lambourn!

"One famous morning I went down to canter up Faringdon Road and Marcus, in his beige Morris, drove up the side of the road with us. My horse took off, got right away with me so that I couldn't possibly stop until I reached the very top of the hill, where he eventually pulled up in the trees. That was the end of my flat-racing ventures!"

His first ride over fences, as opposed to hurdles, ended in failure when he fell at the water at Huntingdon. It was at Huntingdon that he was to train his last National Hunt winner in 1950. "I still say that Huntingdon had one of the biggest open ditches in the country," says Bruce.

Now Bruce was riding all over the country, not only at the big courses but at the little ones, of which there were so many before the war and whose passing is so much regretted by all of us – for example Torquay, Totness, Buckfastleigh, Oswestry, Woore Hunt, Cardiff, Cowbridge, Bungay, Hethersett, Derby ... "Freddie Maxwell, who, with Sandy Scratchley, rode for us and looked after me as a boy so well, drove me to Derby one day where I rode a winner for John Goldsmith. After the race a chap came up and gave me a white envelope. I rushed off to the loo, opened it and found a hundred-pound note. I was absolutely petrified. I asked Freddie, 'What shall I do with this?' He took it and looked after it until we got home! Freddie was terribly kind to me, giving me some lovely Lionel Edwards and Snaffles books – all first editions – and he rode for us very well for some time while he lived at the pub in Eastbury, looked after by Old Mother Kelly. But he proposed to his first wife Mary in our drawing-room."

Bruce had his share of falls but the only breakages were his nose twice, his left collarbone three times and his right one once. "I would get it strapped up" he says, "with a tennis ball under my armpit and would be riding with it in under a fortnight. The last time they miscalculated and it finished up set wrong, so that I get quite a bit of arthritis in it now."

Looking after a fourteen-year-old boy must have been quite a job for a happy-go-lucky jump jockey. "Sandy Scratchley took me up to Haydock for the New Year meeting after Newbury," says Bruce. "We booked for New Year's Eve at the big five-star Midland Hotel in Manchester. Sandy saw me up to my room but he was not going to be denied his night out to see the New Year in. He said, 'You'll be all right now, won't you?'

"'Yes, Sandy,' I said.

"'Don't go out and I'll see you in the morning,' and off he went. The next day I rode this horse for Walter Easterby and got beaten a neck. Now I had to go back to Oxford, where my father was meeting me. 'Do you know what train you have to catch?' Sandy asked. I assured him that I did but, of course, I went to the wrong station and, instead of arriving at Oxford at nine o'clock in the evening, I got in at three o'clock the next morning. Father was still waiting for me. Having got beaten a neck and kept him up half the night, I was not the most popular boy in the world, I can tell you!"

Bruce was still an amateur when he went to Wincanton on Boxing Day 1936, the day before his sixteenth birthday. "I had previously ridden eight winners and I rode two winners that day. I was just going out to ride my third race when the clerk of the scales told me, 'Pull up. You can't ride anywhere until you get a permit or you turn pro.'

"So I missed father's third winner of the day and applied for my professional licence overnight. It was granted and the telegram came through to Wolverhampton where I had ridden my first winner as an amateur and where I was due to ride the next day. It was there I had my first two rides as a professional – on my birthday – and I won on both of them. So my last two rides as an amateur and my first two as a pro had all been winning ones. Wolverhampton has very happy memories for me."

At Newmarket, Epsom and other training centres, there have always been touts, knowledgeable men who report gallops to the newspapers and also frequently run tipping services, charging their punters the odds to a pound or so. Lambourn is the exception. The touts at Lambourn have always been the Rodbourne family – honourable, respected men who have never given away information when asked to keep it quiet by the trainer but who have always done a magnificent job for the public. Bruce says, "I was very fond of old Harry Rodbourne and went to school at Newbury with his son John. They used to watch the horses work, through a telescope, and Harry claimed that he knew the identity of any new horse within forty-eight hours of its arrival at Lambourn. From Faringdon Road he could see right across to where the horses used to work at the back of Park Farm, miles away. Weathercock Hill and Mann Down were easy for him. He could tell you exactly what was working there, who was riding and how the gallop went.

"In those days you did not have to declare a runner until three-quarters of an hour before the race and, with no overnight declarations, there was no compulsion to state your plans on the previous day for the benefit of the newspapers and the betting public. Men like the Rodbournes did their best and it was surprising how accurate the lists of runners were, but sometimes there were errors, due to the canniness of the trainers. For example certain betting trainers would ensure that one of the horses appeared in the papers as a runner at, say, Kempton whereas in fact the horse-box was travelling under sealed orders to

Nottingham, where the animal was also engaged and where, unbeknown to the stay-at-home punters, it would romp home to land a nice little touch.

"One day we had a very moderate horse called Edouard entered for a selling hurdle at Wincanton. We were staying near the course and two hours before the first, heard that the race had cut up so badly that no runner was likely to turn up. So father telephoned back to Lambourn for Edouard to be sent down. We walked over. I think that was the only race the horse ever won. He had been gelded only two days before!"

All this time trouble was brewing between Bruce's parents. The danger to her son was one of the factors that finally persuaded Margery Hobbs to divorce her husband. "At first my mother used to come to the races but she would stand with her back turned to the action when I was riding, so that she could not see if I had a fall. I suppose you couldn't really blame her, because there were one or two fairly hairy chance rides. I was riding at near-by Taunton on the day when poor Jack Baxter got killed, falling at the open ditch, which was the fence in front of the stands. We had no proper crash-helmets in those days and when the following horse put his foot on his head, that was the end of him.

"There was the time when a trainer asked me to ride a horse for him and I went over to Bourton-on-the-Water to school the animal, which used to pull like blazes. After a fairly satisfactory school he booked me to ride it first time out at Towcester, where, on the way to the start, I found that I just could not stop. I wasn't going very fast but there was no way that I could pull up. I could just about steer and follow the rail all the way round. This I did for one complete circuit, which was not particularly popular. Nevertheless the trainer didn't take me off the horse and the next time I rode it was at Birmingham in a novice chase. All was going well until the third last, which was an open ditch, and down we came in a clatter. I was all right and got up, only to find that the first man on the scene was the trainer himself. So he must have been down there, anticipating the fall. It was a hell of a long way from the stands but, as I picked myself up off the ground, there he was standing over me at that particular spot!"

Those magnificent professionals, the incomparable Gerry Wilson, Frenchy Nicholson and Danny Morgan, were particularly good to young Bruce and they were extremely annoyed with Reg when he put his son on No Reckoning at Chepstow. "This was a quite unstoppable tearaway horse," says Bruce. "Father used to ride him himself most of the time at home in draw reins, so that he could not get his head up. He had had one or two races in which he had just taken off with the unfortunate jockey, who had 'gone for the papers', as they say, completely out of control. Gerry, the great champion, squared up to my father. With his head on one side and that quizzical look he said, 'We all like you, Reg, and we think – or rather we thought – that you were a decent chap. But if you put that young lad of yours on that sod of a horse, then we think you're a bastard! You've got no right to do it to any boy, let alone your own son, fine horseman that he is.'

"The more they criticised him, the more stubborn he became. What the others never realised was that I had total confidence in my father. I knew that he was the complete master of his craft. So off we went to Chepstow, that beautiful, green undulating racecourse amidst the hills of the Wye Valley."

The boy was led down to the start for that two-mile hurdle. "By the time we had jumped the first and got round that turn on top of the hill, I was about fifty-five lengths in front. I could steer all right but I couldn't do anything about holding my horse. Along the back stretch, round that turn and up that switchback straight, I just sat and suffered. Jumping the last, we were still about four lengths in front and at the post I won by half a length. Father had been proved right. He was jumping with joy as he came to lead me in and spent the rest of the afternoon going round like a turkey-cock. The horse never ran again, but my father had proved his point!"

After he had watched Bruce weigh in, Reg went into the changing-room and told Gerry, Frenchy and the others just what he thought of them. They smiled wryly but said nothing. Reg had undoubtedly been wrong, but the boy was even better than they thought. Then the winning trainer went off to the bar for a celebration drink with his neighbour Nellie Pratt. His friendship for Miss Pratt was another source of concern to Bruce's mother. On the way home they called in at several pubs and it was quite late when they arrived back at Ronehurst.

"I am just going to take Nellie home," Reg said to his wife as he dropped his son, and drove off. Considering that the Pratts lived only five hundred yards away at Waltham House, the journey seemed to take an unconscionable time and it was quite late before he finally put the car in the garage. "Old Fred asked me in for a drink," he said offhandedly.

In his spare time, particularly during the summer months, Bruce, who has always had a fascination for farmyard animals, used to amuse himself with his poultry. "I used to breed turkeys, go into Newbury market and buy a box of fifty day-old chicks for five shillings," he says. "On Saturdays and Sundays I would play tennis with the Pratts or village cricket with Sandy Scratchley and Teddy Underdown, still one of our best friends."

Looking back now, Bruce realises that the break-up of his parents' marriage was inevitable. Reg, right at the top of a tree in his new profession, a superlative horseman, sparkling with *joie de vivre* and a Meltonian polish such as Lambourn had never known, was irresistible to the ladies and made no secret of the fact that he loved them all. Margery, resentful of this success in a fast new world foreign to her, and fearful for the safety of her beloved only son, missed her cosy Leicestershire life, her friends and her bridge sessions. Nellie, born into racing, pretty and vivacious, was always available to go to the races with the dashing National Hunt trainer of whom she was becoming increasingly fond. As their relationship intensified until their attraction was obvious to all, her father, Fred Pratt, an outstanding trainer of high-class horses on the flat, who was friendly with both Reg and Margery, became acutely embarrassed. So Nellie left home in an effort to end the affair and went to live at Stamford-in-the-Vale. But it had gone too far and they could not keep away from each other. Reg made any excuse to visit her and ran more and more horses at the Midland meetings so that he could stop off at Stamford for an hour or so on the way home, leaving Bruce in the car outside.

These episodes brought matters to a head and Margery left Ronehurst to return to Melton. "My mother wanted me to go with her but I was persuaded by my father to stay at Lambourn. I was about sixteen, and was so heavily involved in my racing career, that, much as I loved my mother, I knew that my future lay with him."

Margery went back to Melton, back to the life she knew, back to her friends and to her bridge.

"My mother had a great eye for property and for antiques," says Bruce. "When she left my father she had very little money but, in order to maintain her lifestyle, she dealt in property with considerable success. She would sell the house she was living in, buy another, do it up and sell it after living in it for a bit. So she was always starting again, but always in the same area. Moreover she was marvellous with antiques and succeeded in making a comfortable living for the rest of her life. She was an avid and very good bridge player, who would play for nine hours a day in about three different places. It helped to keep her occupied now that she was on her own and she had some exceptionally good friends, especially Malcolm and Di McAlpine – he was Master of the Cottesmore – and Margery used to follow hounds by car."

Nellie moved back to Upper Lambourn and, when the divorce came through, married Reg. They had two children, Michael, who is now in agriculture, and Susan, a beautiful horsewoman who is now Mrs Robert Leader.

Although he visited his mother as often as possible, Bruce, having made his decision, threw himself wholeheartedly into his chosen profession.

In 1933 Lord Derby's great little horse Hyperion won the Derby and the following year the Maharajah of Rajpipla's Windsor Lad, trained by Marcus Marsh, brought the coveted Epsom trophy back to Lambourn. Between 1932 and 1936, magnificent, brave, power-packed, raking Golden Miller won five successive Gold Cups for Dorothy Paget, the fabulous patron of National Hunt racing, who became a legend in her own lifetime through her dress – that famous, everlasting old grey coat – and her constant entourage of secretaries, her immense appetite, her habit of living at night and her rudeness, which probably stemmed from shyness.

She would lock herself in the lavatory at a race meeting until all the people had left. Then she would emerge to eat a dinner as large as those Henry VIII enjoyed, firing questions at her trainer and her attendants. In 1934, following his Cheltenham triumph, her great horse achieved the coveted double by winning the Grand National in record time, ridden by champion jockey Gerry Wilson. But the following year, after a desperate struggle in which he beat Thomond II three-quarters of a length for the Gold Cup, he went to Aintree a changed horse, disliking every aspect of the Grand National, and screwed appallingly over Valentine's, unseating the gallant Gerry who came in for some very harsh criticism quite unjustly. That race was won by Reynoldstown, who triumphed again the following year in the hands of Fulke Walwyn, substituting for Frank Furlong, his brother officer in the 9th Lancers.

Fulke left the Army to turn professional and his first ride as a pro in 1936 was a winner. A brilliant riding career ended in 1939 with a cracked skull, and his first winner as a trainer, eight days before the outbreak of war, was ridden by young Bruce Hobbs.

Bruce says to this day that two of the finest jockeys he has ever known were Gerry Wilson and Frenchy Nicholson. "Not only were they wonderful riders, but they looked after me so well when I was a boy. Nothing was too much trouble. They were tremendous chaps."

He adds, "I knew Frenchy's wife Di before he did. During the holidays I used to go from Lambourn to Colonel Holman's in Cheltenham to play tennis. His daughter, Di, has been a marvellous wife to Frenchy and mother to my godson David and her other children.

"The National Hunt racing season used to start, as it does now, at Newton Abbot and we all went down as a party for the Devon circuit. This particular year we stayed at a pub in Paignton because we had been a bit naughty in Torquay and Ben Warner, who owned the hotel there, didn't want us because we had made too much noise. When Tommy Carey, Frenchy and I were riding work on the track in the morning before racing, they both told me that they always had trouble with their weight at the beginning of the season. They were supposed that day to ride at ten stone, but they had no chance of doing that weight. We went into the changing-room and they sat on the trial scales. In those days, instead of the modern automatic scales, you had weights which you had to balance, including some big ones of fifty-six pounds. When we tried, it was obvious that Tommy and Frenchy were not going to make it. So I suggested that we should put seven pounds of lead underneath the big weights of the trial scales and also underneath the big weights in the weighing-room. This we did and it worked like a charm. The clerk of the scales never noticed, because the big fifty-six pound weight stayed put, with the result that on that particular day every single jockey rode at seven pounds overweight without anybody knowing! It was perfectly fair for everybody!"

If by the strictest standards, that particular prank was a bit naughty, it must be remembered that racing is a tough game.

The pre-war prize money for jump races was low indeed. The majority were worth under £100. Bruce says, "If the winning prize was £85 or more, you got £5 to ride and £10 for a winner, and if it was under £85 you got £3 a ride and £5 a winner. So in all those races down in the West Country, your jockey's fee was only £3 a time. It was literally a pound a mile!"

In fact, throughout his career the name Bruce Hobbs has been synonymous with integrity. "At Pershore one day," he recalls, "I was riding a fancied runner and the connections had had a big gamble on a horse ridden by Eric Foley. At the second last I was going much the better of the two and he stuck his whip under my horse's tail. Unfortunately for him it had the opposite effect. Instead of stopping my animal, it spurred my horse on and he shot away to win!

"If you let anybody up on your inside in those days, you got a hell of a rocket from your trainer when you came in and quite likely would never ride for him again. As a boy one had to look after oneself. Old Fred Gurney, for example, had only one place in a race – up in the front. As long as there was any breath left in his body, he was going to stay there and nobody would take it off him, either on the outside or the inner. There was no quarter given or taken. One day at Huntingdon I quite unintentionally maimed Charlie Spares who came back to ride for Willie Stephenson afterwards. He tried to come up on my inside at the turn, going into a hurdle and instinctively I shot him off. He went straight through the wing and smashed himself to smithereens. Some people blamed me for his injury but I had done nothing wrong. I had stopped him legitimately, but I was of course so sorry for him that I went to see him an awful lot in hospital.

"I was lucky enough to ride winners on most tracks. I loved it all, particularly down in the West Country where a lot of gamesmanship won races. It was a case of knowing the little courses and making the turn before you got there. I won races down there which I never should have done on bad horses, just through knowing the contours and the bends.

"Then there was my mystery horse. Somebody rang me up one night asking whether I would ride a horse called Inglesent in a selling hurdle at Newbury. Well, taught by Gerry, who never hesitated when asked, I immediately said, 'Yes, I'd be delighted.' When I weighed out, somebody I had never seen before collected the saddle; and, when I went into the paddock, there was nobody to meet me but just a lad leading round a scruffy beast, with a long straggly unplaited mane. In the race we were going well until two hurdles from home when the horse just pulled up.

"Nobody came near me and a few days later the telephone went again. Would I ride the same horse in a selling hurdle at Wolverhampton? I accepted but, although once again there was nobody in the paddock to greet me, the horse looked different. It was on its toes. This time it pulled like a train throughout the race and won by a furlong! I thought this was very very funny, but when I was asked again to ride the horse in a seller at Haydock, in all innocence, I said 'Yes, I'll ride it.' As soon as I arrived at Haydock the stewards got hold of me and I was asked, 'Do you know anything about this horse?' 'No, nothing at all, sir,' I replied. I told the senior steward the story, that I had been telephoned to ride the horse and that I had never met anybody connected with it, but I was a little bit suspicious. This time, although it was odds-on favourite, it did exactly the same as it had done at Newbury – pulled up at the second last. Of course, it had been doped to the eyebrows at Wolverhampton and it turned out that it was owned by a man who was later to be warned off.

"Mind you, in those days, a certain amount of what would now be called doping was quite legitimate. For example, every trainer had his strychnine tonic, passed down from father to son, and you were allowed to tube a horse on the morning of the race. One day at Taunton we had a horse of Mrs Ambrose Clark's that had gone in his wind. So father decided to have him tubed that very morning. The vet used cocaine as an anaesthetic and my father got him to administer just a little more than he need have done, to wake the horse up a bit. He won by six lengths instead of, perhaps, half a length. That was all quite legitimate.

"There was so much gamesmanship in those days too. In selling races, to stop anybody bidding, you would always put bandages on the horses' legs or French clay to pretend that he had broken down, and even smear pig's blood all over his nose to give the impression that he had broken a blood vessel!

"Sure, we had great fun and there was a wonderful spirit of camaraderie but, both trainers and jockeys were real professionals. I rode one of Paul Mellon's horses called Glenmore Lad for Ivor Anthony at Newbury one day. This had been a good timber horse in America where he had won a number of races, and my instructions were, 'You win a neck – no more.' I won by half a length and Ivor was not particularly pleased. When he met me, he said, 'I told you to win a neck!'"

It was not Jack, but Ivor's other brother Owen Anthony who gave Bruce the best advice he has ever received, at a time when he had grown to his full six feet one and a half inches and was having to start wasting. "I was coming home from racing one day with him and we stopped for a drink, which I refused. Afterwards Owen said, 'Look, just one word of advice. All the money in the world and bad health are no good to you. As long as you have got good health, you can always earn a crust of bread. Remember that when you start wasting.'"

Chapter Five

One day recently, on a cold dark January afternoon we stood by the winner's enclosure in front of the weighing-room; snowflakes hovered hesitantly, uncertain where to land, and the jockeys returned from the novices' chase.

Drenched to the skin, their bright colours plastered with grime, they came in, carrying their saddles, wiping the mud from their faces, smiling, protesting, gesticulating, starting the inevitable post-mortems.

I recalled poor Johnny Lehane's description of the start of a modern novices' chase at a little meeting: "Twenty horses you've never heard of and twenty riders you've never met, each with a lethal weapon in his hands!"

Siren wailing, blue light flashing in the gloom, the ambulance carried its cargo from the medical room to the local hospital.

"Disgraceful conditions. They should never have raced on this going," said a young journalist with the supreme authority of ignorance.

The tall figure beside me stiffened, the handsome head went up and the famous jaw jutted. "What on earth is he talking about?" asked Bruce incredulously. Then he relaxed, smiled that gentle smile and said quietly, "Gerry would have called this, 'good jumping ground'."

Muttering to himself, the young reporter left to file his complaints for a million breakfast tables, confident in his belief that the illustrious flat trainer was as out of his element here as a space invader.

A girl jockey passed by, in earnest conversation with her trainer, soaking silks and light breeches clinging to her body, revealing a delightful little figure and leaving little to the imagination.

Bruce's eyes twinkled. "Can't be all bad nowadays," he said. "There are obviously definite compensations!"

He reflected and, ever modest, volunteered with an effort, "I suppose you have to say that I was jumping's young Lester Piggott of the late thirties."

Dick Francis, who was unable to fulfil his ambition of race-riding until after the war, agreed. "Of course he was," said Dick. "I showed against Bruce as a boy, but then he left our world to become a top jockey and he was so young and so good that everything he did was headline news."

Bruce was in fact a wonder boy. Like Lester, he started so spectacularly. He was absolutely dedicated, virginal and abstemious. "Sometimes," he says, "when my father was drinking and playing poker with the boys – he was an inveterate gambler – I would be asleep on the sofa!

"Mind, that was not to say that we didn't have a lot of fun, particularly on that West Country circuit. I remember a party one evening at Ben Warner's Hotel in Torquay when there was a competition for the man with the biggest feet in the ballroom. I am not very good on the dance floor and that was the only prize of its sort I've ever won. My size-twelve feet were always a joke with the jockeys, who are inclined to take a much smaller size in shoes! Frenchy came in when I was lying on the table in the changing-room at Buckfastleigh with my feet towards the window. 'Get off,' he said. 'You're shutting out the light!'

"As I said earlier Frenchy and Gerry, as well as my valet Charlie Stalker, looked after me splendidly throughout the period when, as a growing boy, life could have been so difficult for me. The chief friends of my own age were Mervyn and Hywell Jones, nephews of Jack, Ivor and Owen Anthony. It was a happy, exciting life."

Mervyn Jones's promising career as a jump jockey was halted by World War Two, when he joined the R.A.F. and became a Pilot Sergeant. In 1940, owing to the injury of Eric Foley, he was offered the ride on Lord Stalbridge's Bogskar in the Grand National. His Air Commodore, in giving his permission, enquired whether Jones had passed his navigation exam. On being answered in the affirmative, he ordered, "Well, go and navigate Bogskar round Aintree and if you don't we'll put you through another navigation examination!" Mervyn Jones successfully accomplished his mission, but in April 1942 he was reported missing, presumed dead.

Despite his height and his youth, by the 1937/38 season, at the age of seventeen, in only his second season as a professional, Bruce was already third on the jockeys' list, equal with Fred Rimell, also the son of a professional trainer, but seven years his senior, destined to become champion jockey, champion trainer and to saddle a record four Grand National winners.

As early as 1936 Bruce was getting many outside rides for top-class stables, including a number for J.V. Rank, the milling millionaire who during the thirties set about channelling some of his vast resources into achieving his triple ambition to win the Derby, the Grand National and the Waterloo Cup. Between 1935 and 1938 his animals were second in all three. Scottish Union was second in the 1938 Derby, Cooleen second in the 1937 Grand National and Joker's Resort was second in the 1935 Waterloo Cup at Altcar. For twenty years he was so well known on the Turf that the advertisement, "Bread for Energy", on the hoardings portrayed a horse jumping a fence, carrying his famous yellow-and-blue quartered colours. He owned a number of really good horses, notably Southern Hero who won eighteen chases, including three Scottish Grand Nationals, and one really great one in Prince Regent. His bad luck persisted when he nearly bought Reynoldstown before that horse went on to win the Grand National twice but was dissuaded by a friend who disliked black horses ("Isn't that the colour of the funeral horses?" say the Irish) and, even more ironically, he actually owned Early Mist but died just before that horse won the National in the colours of Joe Griffin. A blunt but immensely kind man, he was one of the nicest of chasing's big owners.

Bruce says, "I won the Welsh National for him on Timber Wolf and towards the end of his career old Southern Hero gave me a fantastic ride in the Cheltenham Gold Cup. I finished fifth. Morse Code won it and Golden Miller was in the race along with all the old-timers."

In the background at home during these formative years was his constant mentor and guide, Leonard Gregory – the same steadfast, loyal Leonard, good looking and smart, who went to Reg first as second horseman, then as chief nagsman and finally as headman at Ronehurst. "A remarkable chap," says Bruce, "a wonderful nagsman, who could teach a horse to jump any obstacle and indeed rode a brilliant school over hurdles or fences but somehow, like so many others, never had what it needed to become a jockey. His great ambition was to ride racing and so Father, just to show him what it was like, gave him four rides in public. On every single one he fell. After the fourth, Len said, 'I am obviously not cut out to be a jockey', and from that moment on he settled down to be the most marvellous headman imaginable. He was a natural gentleman and what a lovely horseman! When my father gave up, he went to Tom Hanbury as headman and he died two years ago. But only a short while before that he came up to Newmarket to stay with Ben Hanbury. One morning on the Heath, although Ben's string was two hundred yards away and I hadn't seen Len for years, I spotted him at once. His polished style was unmistakable. There was the old Len still riding out as beautifully as ever."

Since the horsemastership of Reg and his headman was equalled only by their man-management, it was hardly surprising that Ronehurst was a happy, successful yard for both its human and equine occupants. Later Reg Hobbs was to turn down an offer to go as private trainer to J.V. Rank at Druid's Lodge near Salisbury because he would not have been allowed to take with him the horses belonging to Mrs Marion du Pont Scott.

This wiry little American lady, who died at the end of 1983, was married to the handsome film star Randolph Scott. But, in her own right, she was rich beyond the dreams of avarice, having inherited on the death of her father William du Pont, in 1927, an immense fortune and the glorious five-thousand acre sporting estate of Montpelier in Orange County, Virginia, with its superb eighteenth-century mansion, its own racecourse, stud farm, stables, foxhound kennels, cockpits and game preserves. Possessed of the same tough aggressive character as her legion of Border terriers and fighting cocks, she was dedicated to all horse sports and quite unaccustomed to being thwarted.

Years earlier, when he was with Ambrose Clark, Reg Hobbs had helped a penniless, down-at-heel Irishman called Jim Ryan to find a job with horses in the United States. By 1936 Ryan was America's top racehorse trainer, a charming man with considerable influence, who had become a millionaire. It was Jim, repaying the good turn, who suggested to Mrs Scott that she should send a couple of horses to Reg in Upper Lambourn.

Mrs Scott, who had earlier had a "sighter" at Aintree with a horse called Trouble Maker, was determined to win the Grand National with Battleship. She was later to write, "I had learnt that a high-class horse was needed to win, that while those big English and Irish jumpers looked like the kind of horse you would think a fat man would ride in the hunting field, they were misleading. Very misleading. They could turn it on. They would fool you now and then with their speed. My preconception of them was wrong. They were better than I thought. But once I got Battleship I knew he had enough class for the Grand National. Battleship had proven that, in winning the American Grand National and in our so-called hunter races. So I sent him to England." When Reg saw Battleship, he was equally determined that this high-class, chestnut entire horse would not run in the National. He did not know his owner.

He wrote to Mrs Scott on 6 August, 1936, "Battleship and War Vessel arrived here safely last Tuesday. I personally went up to the London Docks to meet the horses. I was very pleased by their appearance and condition. Battleship is a grand-looking little horse and full of quality. The leg that was fired feels and handles real well and I see no reason why he shouldn't stand training and racing over here ..."

War Vessel was of little consequence, but Battleship, standing barely fifteen hands two inches, had been foaled in 1927, bred by Walker J. Salmon at the Mereworth Stud, Lexington, Kentucky, by the great Man o'War out of a mare by Seasick called Quarantine. He was bought as a two-year-old by Mrs Scott and he had climaxed a successful career in his native land by winning the 1934 American Grand National.

From the very beginning of their association, it is noticeable that Reg's letters to Mrs Scott constantly referred to Battleship as "the little horse", "the old horse", and "a stallion". Like the good dealer that he was, he was making his excuses in advance!

27 August, 1936: "Battleship is a fine mover. I like the old horse a great deal ..."

22 September, 1936: "I schooled Battleship over fences this morning for the first time and he went and jumped beautifully ..."

Now that the future of Aintree is apparently assured, it is high time that the November meeting was reinstituted as an introduction to the Grand National fences for horses unaccustomed to jumping that particular type of obstacle. To take horses straight to Aintree from park fences is unfair, a confidence trick on the animals. They are used to jumping ordinary black birch fences and now they have to jump fences covered in green gorse. Instead of finding the landing on the same level as the take-off, they are apt to find, over the huge drops, that the ground vanishes beneath them. Creatures of memory, they can be completely bewildered by the change.

As Bruce confirms, in his day the fences were considerably bigger, wider and stiffer, as well as being straight up with no guideline – no belly at the take-off. He says, "There was a newspaper picture of two men side by side, walking across the top of the Chair and I can tell you that when the sun is brightly shining on that fence, it casts a most disturbing shadow that has caused a number of falls." Even with the slightly easier fences nowadays, we still need to go back to the Aintree November meeting. One of the oldest military principles is, "Time spent in reconnaissance is seldom wasted."

The correspondence continued. 5 October, 1936: "I am pleased to say that both horses are going on very well in every way, particularly Battleship who I feel sure will be a useful horse here, but the ground is still hard with us so, I can't say a lot about the horses yet ..."

27 October, 1936: "Battleship ran in a two-mile steeplechase at Nottingham, in which he had to carry twelve stone (168 pounds). As the going was firm I told the jockey not to give the horse a hard race, but a real nice school, as he would have had no chance of winning with all that weight on his back, as it was a very good class race. He finished

fifth in a field of eight horses, jumping wonderfully . . . The little horse was a bit troublesome to saddle, also troublesome at the start, but I feel sure he will get over all that. I have not yet decided whether to send him to Liverpool or not, as I would hate the little fellow to get a fall there, as it might shake his nerve and confidence etc., with his being a stallion . . ."

9 November, 1936: "I have decided not to run Battleship at Liverpool, as I have only been able to give him one run up to the present and I didn't think it would be fair to the little horse as it might have been asking him to do too much. I hope to run him next week at Wolverhampton . . ."

Tim Hamey, who had up till now been riding many of the best Hobbs horses, was on Battleship at Nottingham and at Wolverhampton, where, in the race-by-race record kept by Reg, he "Lost rider". In all but one of his remaining races Battleship was ridden by Bruce, who took over as first jockey to the stable and, incidentally, had his first ride over the Aintree fences that year after walking the course carefully with his father.

"It's always amazing how those big fences look to be at an angle as you walk the course," he says, "but when you ride over them, you meet them just right."

He had made it to the top. "I was riding winners at nearly all the tracks in the country," he says. "Three winners in a day at Pershore, Uttoxeter and so on . . . It was a great thrill but I never rode more than three in an afternoon."

He was still only fifteen years old when he won Battleship's first English race, the Pond Steeplechase at Sandown on 12 December 1936. On 28 December, the day after Bruce's sixteenth birthday, Battleship finished second in a three-mile chase at Wolverhampton and a week later won over two miles at Leicester. He won again, this time with twelve stone at Newbury on 24 February and, as time was to prove, should surely have gone on to Aintree that year. But, after he had finished fourth in the National Hunt Handicap Chase at the Cheltenham Festival, where the ground was in Reg's words, "Terribly deep and heavy", Reg took him out of the big Aintree Chase and wrote to his owner:

RONEHURST,
LAMBOURN,
BERKS.

14th March, 1937

Dear Mrs Scott,

I hated to have to scratch Battleship from the Grand National this year as he would have had a real good chance if he was only a bit bigger and had a little more scope, but he is inclined to jump on his head a little when landing over his fences in the heavy going in this country and that is the chief reason for my not running the little horse in the National this year, but it was a very great temptation. However, he is entered in two or three more big races in this country, including the Scottish National and the Lancashire Steeplechase, so I am hoping he will win one of those. I ran Battleship at Cheltenham last Tuesday in the big three-mile steeplechase there of £1,500. There were a lot of runners and the going was terribly deep and holding, but the little horse ran a really fine race and he finished fourth, less than three lengths behind the winner, but owing to the terrible state of the going he did not jump quite as well as usual and made a bad mistake at the last fence losing about four lengths, otherwise I am certain he would have won and all the critics said so too.

War Vessel missed his Cheltenham engagement as two out of the three days there were abandoned owing to the course being flooded. He would also have had a great chance at Cheltenham in the big four-year-old chase. However, both horses are very well and I think they will win more races before the end of the season.

I think that is all the news this time, Mrs Scott. I sincerely hope that you and Mr Scott are fit and well.

Yours obediently,

Reggie Hobbs

The letter is a masterpiece of deception. Did Reg really imagine that he could "kid" a horsewoman of vast experience into believing that her ten-year-old could be "a bit bigger" and have "a little more scope" next year?

Although Battleship did not run in the 1937 Grand National, Bruce had the mount on Flying Minutes for Mrs Ambrose Clark. This was the centenary year of the great race, but that did not stop the criticism. The authorities had decided to revert to a minimum weight of ten stone. Since 1931 the minimum had been ten stone seven pounds, with the declared purpose of eliminating the mediocre horses. The measure as one of several, had been largely successful. In 1934 there had been less than half the runners of 1929 and the result had been a genuine race, brilliantly won by Golden Miller.

The decision to revert brought many protests, including a published letter from the Hon. George Lambton, formerly an outstanding amateur rider over fences, who had become one of the great Classic trainers on the flat. He wrote, "The Grand National . . . is not meant to be won by moderate horses. . . . if the authorities encourage owners to enter them, the race will lose its high tone and quality and revert to the farcical scramble it became some years ago."

There were other points of view. The public liked the race for its uncertainty – and so of course did the bookmakers! The most moderate horse could be "in with a chance", as Tipperary Tim had proved in the year of Easter Hero's fiasco, 1928. Moreover, it cost no less to enter a bad horse than a good one; the more bad horses, the more fees and forfeits to swell the final stake.

Reynoldstown did not try again in the centenary year. The previous year, ridden by Fulke Walwyn, he had won the race for the second time in succession, when poor Anthony Mildmay, with loose reins flapping and unable to control Davy Jones, had run out at the last fence. Reynoldstown's owner, Major Furlong, commented that you could take the pitcher to the well too often. However, the Hon. Dorothy Paget had no such scruples about Golden Miller, who had won the race in 1934 but had failed on other occasions and obviously hated the course. He came back this time with a different jockey. Danny Morgan succeeded Evan Williams and Gerry Wilson in the hot seat.

King George VI and Queen Elizabeth who, thanks to Lord Mildmay, was later to become the greatest patron in the history of National Hunt Racing, were there to watch Evan Williams win on Royal Mail, trained by Ivor Anthony, who had triumphed with Kellsboro' Jack in 1933, from J.V. Rank's Cooleen and Pucka Belle.

Bruce says, "I was lying third at the last ditch, three from home, when I fell off Flying Minutes. I would undoubtedly have been in the first four."

Instead of running in the Grand National, Battleship, ridden on each occasion by Bruce, finished that season by running second in the Holman Cup at Cheltenham and winning three-mile chases at Ludlow and Stratford-on-Avon, earning the princely total of £309 for these three performances!

The following season Battleship again missed the Liverpool November meeting, where Bruce on Flying Minutes was beaten a short head in the Grand Sefton Chase. Nevertheless, Mrs Scott's little horse was fit enough to run fourth at Cheltenham on 18 November and second at Newbury on 2 December before winning the prestigious Lonsdale Chase at Hurst Park on 11 December. The last race, run over three miles and 180 yards, and worth £417 to the winner, was considered to be an important Grand National trial.

By Christmas, Reg, still scheming to avoid running Battleship in the Grand National, had virtually decided that Bruce would ride Flying Minutes again in the race. This horse had a real chance although, admittedly, he was a bit worried about one of its forelegs.

On his seventeenth birthday, Bruce acquired a motorcar, a Rover Ten Coupé. He had already learnt to drive around the Lambourn lanes and up the long stretch to Maddle Farm, so that the driving test was a formality.

He now also had a dog, a little white Jack Russell terrier with black saddle marking which Jack Anthony had given him. "I called him Budge after Donald Budge, the Wimbledon Champion," says Bruce. "He was the sweetest little dog, who went everywhere with me, slept on my bed at all times and was always waiting for me when I came back from the racecourse. One of his pet habits was to sit right in front of the fire, almost on top of it, looking straight into the flames, with the result that eventually he blinded himself. The little chap was to wait for me all through the war and on my return, after five years, he went absolutely mad with delight. But now at this stage, he was only a puppy.

"One Sunday, accompanied by Budge as usual, I had driven off to look at some horses and I was in a hurry to get back to Lambourn, to play tennis up at the Pratts'. At the Challow crossroads I was apparently on the wrong side of the road, hit someone a right wallop and woke up lying on the verge with my dog sitting on top of me. They whipped me off to Wantage Hospital, where the five people from the other car were in a far worse state, with broken arms, legs and other injuries. I escaped with a bruising, but of course there was hell to pay. I was had up for driving without due care and attention but, although it cost my father a fair few quid, I got away with it. Later that year, after all the banner headlines about my success, I received a letter from each individual one of them, congratulating me and apologising for being so rude at the time!"

Reg considered that, in his last two outings before Cheltenham, at Sandown and Newbury, Battleship had become a bit sour. So for the National Hunt Handicap Chase he decided to fit blinkers. On the first day of the Festival Meeting, Bruce was riding the reigning champion, Free Fare, five-to-two on favourite for the Champion Hurdle. "It was a tremendous thrill to ride him because he was such a fantastic jumper at speed," says Bruce. "We would undoubtedly have won but, racing into the second last, he stood off right back in the wing, reached for his hurdle and just got his foreleg caught in the top bar, turning him over and breaking my nose."

His nose was in fact badly broken and the doctors refused to let him ride Battleship in the National Hunt Handicap Chase. So Reg engaged the Irish jockey Tommy McNeil, best known as the one rider who could stay on the tearaway, extravagant, spectacular jumper Airgead Sios. The Cheltenham going was heavy again and Battleship was set to give no less than twenty-three pounds to the very useful Teme Willow, ridden by Fred Rimell. McNeil rode a good race but, not knowing his horse, came just too late and finished third, beaten three parts of a length. It was an excellent performance which completely vindicated Reg's decision to use blinkers.

After the race Johnny Maguire, a Scottish bookmaker who was a great friend, told Reg that Bruce would undoubtedly have won if he had ridden Battleship. "I think you can win the National. In fact I am going to back him." Reg thought that Maguire should have more sense, but the bookmaker had a very big bet at 66 to 1.

Still trying to avoid running at Liverpool, Reg sent a last despairing telegram to his owner at Montpelier: "Battleship finished third big chase yesterday Cheltenham. Ran fine race gave lot of weight to all runners beaten less than length from winner. Has chance in National if he jumps the course. Royal Mail being sold public auction Saturday with Grand National engagement. Horse favourite for race at present. Please cable at once if you would like me to bid for you or any of your friends. Hobbs."

Marion Scott remained unmoved. She made no response to her trainer's suggestion about buying the previous year's winner. Royal Mail was for sale because his gallant owner, Hugh Lloyd Thomas, formerly assistant secretary to the Prince of Wales and a member of the British Embassy in Paris, after announcing that he intended to ride his own horse at the age of fifty following two years of virtual inactivity as a jockey, had been killed a month before the National by a fall from another of his horses, Perrywinkle. Two years earlier Mrs Scott had decided that she would win the Grand National – with Battleship!

Chapter Six

The jockey who tells you that he is not nervous before the Grand National is notable rather for his mendacity than for his courage. At the start, every heart beats faster, every mouth is dry and every laugh is a little forced as you gaze down the Aintree back-stretch and think of the four and a half gruelling miles ahead. There will be loose horses, fallers, injuries. There may even be dead horses and jockeys maimed. You have to be good to get round, but, even more, you have to be lucky. In 1938 the race was watched by a quarter of a million people surrounding that green triangle where the world's greatest steeplechase was being staged.

Bruce says, "Our original entries for the National included Mrs Clark's Flying Minutes, Battleship and two rather moderate horses called Bagatelle and What Have You. Flying Minutes, who would have had a genuine chance, broke down a fortnight before the race and I was asked to ride the second favourite, Delachance, for George Beeby because his stable jockey, Fulke Walwyn, was out of action with a broken wrist. I was also offered the ride on the useful French candidate, Takvor Pacha. However, although I didn't think that the little horse had much chance, my choice was not difficult because I was offered £300 to ride Battleship and only £100 to ride the others. That was quite a lot of money in those days!"

In his final gallop, eight days before Liverpool Battleship went wonderfully well but, on the morning of the day when he was to leave Lambourn for the races, Leonard Gregory reported that he was "set fast". He had developed kidney trouble and could barely walk, let alone run or gallop. They had trouble loading him into the horse-box and so, although it was rather late in the day, Reg had no option. He gave him a Cupiss ball purgative himself, and by the time that Battleship arrived in the racecourse stable, he was right back to his old self.

In those days the famous meeting ran from Thursday to Saturday, with the Grand National on the second day. The celebrated parties in Liverpool's Adelphi Hotel were at their wildest and best in the days when the National was held on a Friday. Then trainers and jockeys, who had been tensed up for the big race, were able to relax for once. They were tough, healthy and fit for anything. Chief sufferers during those glorious evenings of wild excess were apt to be the huge chandeliers so beloved by the hotels, which were constructed regardless of cost in Victorian times by the great private railway companies – the famous glass fountain and assorted items of furniture, so that some of the bills presented and paid on Saturday's hangover morning were astronomical.

Although the Adelphi valeting was second to none, the knowing ones remembered not to put their shoes outside the bedroom door for cleaning. The Adelphi had 284 rooms, many of them doubles. One year in the early hours of Saturday morning, about four hundred pairs of shoes were collected and thrown out of the window higgledy-piggledy on to the pavement of one of Liverpool's busiest streets. A great many people were very late getting to the races!

So the gathering of the clans from all corners of the earth took place in the Adelphi on Wednesday evening. Needless to say, young Bruce was sent to bed early every day of the meeting while Reg sat drinking in the hotel lounge with Jack Anthony and their friends. They were joined by London bookmaker Percy Thompson, one of the most popular members of his fraternity, who asked whether Reg fancied his horse on Friday. "Don't be daft," said Reg, "he won't even be able to see over the Chair!"

Thompson persisted, "I'll lay you 100 to 1 against him," he said.

Reg, unable to resist those odds, took a tenner each-way. He was to tell the press later that he had backed his horse for only a pound at the starting price of 40 to 1, "In case I have to buy the champagne!"

One of his greatest fears about Battleship was that, being so close-coupled and small, he would land on his nose and tip over at the big drop fences. Reg had the reins lengthened by eighteen inches so that they could slip just that vital bit further through Bruce's hands.

Fearful that his son might injure himself before the big race, Reg did not allow him to ride Mrs Scott's other horse, War Vessel, in the Stanley Chase on Thursday, which was a pity, because the horse had improved sufficiently to win nicely. With Bruce safely tucked up in bed, Reg celebrated the victory with his friends who, still dressed in their dinner jackets, decided to walk the course at midnight. Inevitably they tried to jump the sixteen-foot water-jump and landed right in the middle of it!

Early next morning, when they met Mrs Scott on the course to give

Battleship a final pipe-opener, Reg was as usual fresh as a daisy. A little rain followed by a sharpish overnight frost showed him that the going might be just a little bit slippery and so he got the blacksmith to put two little screws into Battleship's hind plates to give him more grip. This was yet another move by the brilliant horsemaster which probably made all the difference between success and failure.

Even now, at the eleventh hour, he tried to persuade Mrs Scott to take her horse out of the race, promising that Battleship would do well again over park courses the following season. The terrier-like little American lady said, "I had it out with him right there on the course. I'd been disappointed that Battleship hadn't run in the Grand National the first year he was in England. Hobbs wasn't going to down me again, a second straight year. I told him Battleship was going home to Virginia the next week. When he heard that, his attitude changed."

In the parade the blinkered pony stallion was dwarfed by horses like the powerful Royal Danieli, the pride of Ireland, ridden by Dan Moore. Battleship seemed even smaller when he was mounted by Bruce, so tall and so youthful that he was described by Jim Ryan as "a hairpin on a telephone-pole". If Bruce and Battleship were to win, they would break three separate records. The smallest horse, the tallest jockey and the youngest jockey. The punters had worked this out. They didn't like those odds either. Despite his record and the usually loyal support of American racegoers, Battleship was easy to back at 40 to 1.

Reg Hobbs had raised his son to hunt in the world's finest country. Now he gave him the orders which have since become so commonplace that everyone else believes they invented them. "Just hunt him round the first time. Then, when you've jumped the water, if you're still in with a chance, you can start riding a race."

Bruce says, "Battleship was classically bred, unlike any of the other runners, and had such a turn of foot that my father always swore, if he had had him as a four-year-old, he would have won an Ascot Gold Cup. The little horse loved to join the leaders at the last fence and from that moment he would beat anything on the run-in. We planned to do just that, knowing that our horse never believed in winning by more than half a length."

Lining up at the start Bruce looked over at Dan Moore and Royal Danieli. It was like David and Goliath, only they were not playing at catapults! The flag went down.

From the start Airgead Sios predictably led from Royal Danieli. Bruce says, "Battleship never made any real mistakes in the first part of the race, although being so small, he landed on his head at all the drop fences and, being a colt, he was inclined to tip up.

"Battleship jumped Becher's perfectly although, of course, I had to slip right back to the buckle as he landed on his little nose but he seemed to find another leg. Then at the next fence, that little one on the twist, our race was very nearly over. He was a bit unbalanced going in, jumped to the right and suddenly came round. I was falling off! No argument! I was gone, when Fred Rimell grabbed hold of me by the seat of the pants and, shouting 'Where do you think you're going, matey?', pulled me back into the saddle. Poor Fred himself fell at the very next fence, the Canal Turn."

Airgead Sios, the early leader, fell at the plain fence after Valentine's where he over-jumped. Delachance now quickly moved ahead of Royal Danieli and they were first and second over the water at the end of the first circuit. When Delachance began to fade – he held on to finish fifth – it promised to be a one-horse race as Royal Danieli strode out in front with the stylish confidence of Easter Hero. Only Workman and Battleship could stay with him and, approaching Becher's for the second time, Bruce allowed the American pony to take on the Irish giant. Workman was about five lengths behind the pair as they jumped Becher's beautifully. So far the pony had jumped everything with courage and skill. So far the boy jockey, coached by his father, had shown the determined calm of a veteran. But three fences out their luck seemed to explode. Battleship made his only mistake and was almost down.

"It was three fences out," says Bruce, "when we were upsides with Royal Danieli, that Battleship made his one real mistake and was just about on the floor. Dan really got the advantage then and had gone a good length up, but luckily there's a good long gap between the third last and the second last. With a sort of unconscious reaction, I gave Battleship a breather and he got on his legs again, so that he was flying. Actually, that mistake was what won the race for him as it turned out. I am sure it was. Because I had to give him a breather. He lost a lot of ground and it fairly knocked the stuffing out of him, poor little mate. But for that mistake I would have been in front at the last and then he would not have gone on, because he never won from the front. He had to come from behind with this blinding speed of his."

Mrs Scott said, "Bruce was real good at not hurrying a horse. When he saw Battleship kind of stuck in that fence, he didn't push him right away. He let him go into his stride right nice. Watching from the stands, I saw Battleship go up and jump the last fence real well, but he still had to make up ground during the long run-in."

Bruce continues his account of the exciting race. "Workman made a mistake two out and we were three lengths behind Royal Danieli going into the last. There was just Dan Moore and a loose horse – and me. Dan chose to stick to the rails, taking advantage of the elbow up that long run-in, but the loose horse, the French Takvor Pacha, worried me all the way up the run-in, causing me to finish under the stand rails. We were so far apart that you could have driven two buses up the course between Royal Danieli and Battleship. My little horse had that tremendous Classic turn of foot and the courage of a giant."

The two horses fought it out stride for stride while the sympathies of the crowd switched from the well-backed Royal Danieli to the youngest jockey on the smallest horse. With one hundred yards remaining, the Americans still did not visualise victory. They were ready to settle for gallant defeat. But Battleship really had the supreme courage of which Bruce speaks. The little horse gave all he had but, nearing the finish, was still half a length behind. He reached into his reserves and found something more, and was in front for the first time in the final strides.

"There was a long delay before the official verdict was given," Bruce recalls. "Dan thought Royal Danieli had won and the Irish thought he was right. For me, there was never any doubt. I thought I'd won half a length."

Perhaps it only seemed a long delay. Certainly the packed crowds stood in stunned anticipation while seconds ticked as slowly as the traditional silence of Armistice Day. Finally the judge placed Number 5 in the frame. He had given the race to Battleship by a head. Third, a long way back, was Workman, who was to frank the form by winning the race the following year. Battleship had won, carrying 11 stone 6lbs., giving three pounds to Royal Danieli and eighteen pounds to the third.

The Irish were furious but a great cheer went up from the bookmakers! Reg, immaculate as ever in bowler hat and overcoat, ran to lead his son in, flanked by the traditional mounted-police escort. Bruce says, "In the last ten yards, I was convinced I'd won. We simply got to Royal Danieli and beat him. There was no great controversy. Most people were quite satisfied with the result. Right up to his death Dan maintained that if there had been a photograph, the result would have been different. 'By Jesus,' he would say, 'if there had been a photo-finish, I think there would have been a dead-heat.' Well, you know, if I had been second, I'm sure I'd have said much the same thing," added Bruce generously.

Even as they returned in triumph, professionalism was still paramount with Reg. "What was that trouble after Becher's first time?" he said, looking up. Bruce explained that Fred Rimell had pulled him back into the saddle. "Battleship didn't make a mistake," he said, "it was my mistake because I'd got the angle wrong. The little horse jumped, turned and I wasn't ready for it. I was just slipping off. You see, after you jump Becher's, unless you pull out to your right a little bit, you meet that next fence wrong; you must get the Canal Turn just right. Battleship jumped the fence all right and turned five degrees. Well I didn't turn with him!"

Reg was a little subdued during the first part of the victory dinner at the Adelphi. His smile was a trifle forced for one who had just achieved his life's ambition as he fiddled with his smoked salmon, sipped his turtle soup and took somewhat larger gulps of his champagne. He said afterwards, "I didn't know who was going to pay for it. Mrs Scott headed straight back for London and the trip home. I knew the party was going to cost at least a thousand quid. It wasn't until after the main course was served that I received a telegram from her, 'To extend all the hospitalities'. I enjoyed the rest!"

Marion Scott said, "Some people couldn't understand why we didn't stay for the dinner. The truth was I hadn't nerve enough to bring along a special dress for such a party. We hardly expected to win. I remember having had tea with Mrs Ambrose Clark under the stands after the race and when we got back to London to the Berkeley, there already was a stack of mail at the door, so you could hardly open it. There were congratulations, plus some charity hospitals trying to make a touch. The Berkeley had a special cake ready with two horses jumping on top. I'll always think that Battleship would have won by a greater margin if he'd been right in the thick of things through the final yards. He was the kind of horse that likes competition. He did better if you could keep him right up against his opponent. As for Bruce he rode just a wonderful race.

"But I'll say this for Reg Hobbs. Once Battleship won, he didn't change his tune. He continued to say what he'd said before the race, that he hadn't wanted the horse to start. Not many trainers do that in that situation. He was a fine trainer."

Reg's anxiety about Battleship and the drop fences was completely vindicated when Bruce rode back into that famous, shabby, dusty winners enclosure to unsaddle. The little horse was streaming with blood from his nostrils and his trainer thought at first that perhaps he had broken a blood vessel, but the blood was only from scratches where he had landed and slipped along on his rose. As Bruce had said earlier, "He's got five legs, Daddy, not four."

"I was much more confident", Bruce says, "in those days than I am now. As far as I was concerned I'd won half a length and when my father came rushing up and asked 'Did you win?' I said 'Yes!' It was announced before we got back to the unsaddling enclosure. The police escort came straight up to me anyway. It seemed that they knew!

"The first time I ever saw Mrs Marion Scott was when the horse was cooling down after the race. She couldn't get into the paddock beforehand; she hadn't even arrived in time! I changed quickly, in order to go back to the stable-yard to see Battleship. A blue suit, blue coat, bowler hat and gloves. My father insisted that I was always turned out like that for all London meetings, let along the Grand National. I had a terrible rocket one day after the war when I was living at home and went to Cheltenham at one of those early meetings. I'd been staying with Frenchy and I'd been riding schooling and I arrived at Cheltenham in jodphurs. I never thought anything about it. My father said, 'Don't you dare go racing like that again, even though you have been in the army!' I suppose he was quite right.

"When we got home, we had to parade Battleship through Lambourn and I received a whole heap of fan mail. I may have been a hero but I didn't get romantically involved with anybody! I was chased but still strictly chaste! A dreadful pun, but so true at the time.

"Every year when the Grand National comes round, there is still something special, something magic about it for me and I have to be left alone. I won't go flat-racing on that day, even if I have runners, and I just sit in front of the television. Even though the fences are so much smaller, it still has that air about it; and as long as it remains at Aintree, the magic will still be there. If they ever take it away, then it will be finished.

"I read the other day that the owner of a really good horse said that he would never run it in the National. I can understand that today because there are so many other good races to win. After the war there were two really good jumping races in the year, the Gold Cup at Cheltenham and the Grand National. Everybody wanted to win both. All the good three-mile chasers around went for those two races. Nobody thought about cruelty to horses and even less cruelty to jockeys! Of course I'm all for safety, but I think we are so safety-conscious nowadays that very soon you'll have to wear a crash helmet to cross the road!

"People are not willing to risk their good horses at Aintree and I am afraid that the National has now become a spectacle and little else. The way they're going, it will become even more dangerous. If they soften those fences still further, they're going to have some real carnage. I remember immediately after the war the fences had not been completely rebuilt when they ran the National, and I think it was old Fred Gurney who went straight through the first open ditch, leaving a whole which you could have driven a bus through. Next time round everybody went for this hole, crashed into each other and came down. That's the sort of thing that'll happen.

"Of course I knew Aintree well by the time of Battleship's National, but I discussed with Gerry Wilson before the race the way to ride the course and still today my advice to any young jockey would be to go straight down the middle to Becher's. It is a bigger drop on the inside than the outside, but if you're in the middle going to Becher's you're right for the fence after. Those fences were precision built, sited absolutely right and, although now they have been bellied out to make them more encouraging, even when they were straight up, that big rail about three foot off the ground made horses look at it and it used to make them stand up. You don't want to stand back too far anyway. You have to fiddle those fences and a bold, carefree natural jumper has no chance round Liverpool any more than a horse that shies at things and peeps at things in the hedge. Red Rum used to fiddle those fences, climb up and climb over rather than stand back and use all his energy. There's nothing worse than the intelligent racehorse who tries to think when he's going to take off. Just the same on the flat, an intelligent horse has one hard race and he says, 'Not on your nellie! I get my butt smacked to get my head in front. Not likely!' People call him soft, a pig, a swine. He's just too intelligent. That's his trouble.

"There were several personal appearances at cinemas and I remember one at the Elephant and Castle, of all places, when my escort was an actress called Avril Angers, a most attractive blond girl, who subsequently came out to the Middle East with a concert party. It was father who got the birds, not me!"

One of the many postscripts to the 1938 Grand National came to me personally ten years later when I was home on leave, travelling from the West Country up to London. At Sherborne the train was boarded by the late Lord Digby, a lovely, popular, portly man, wearing a red carnation in his button-hole and eating Charbonnel and Walker chocolates throughout the journey. He told me that he had had the only ticket on the first leg of the Tote Double at Aintree that day. That one ticket on Battleship had paid him £5000. As we drew near Paddington Lord Digby stood up and removed a small box from the rack. Inside, carefully wrapped in tissue paper, was a white carnation. With this he replaced the red one, which went back in the box ready for the journey home. The white one was for London!

Chapter Seven

One of the few horses to win the Grand National in blinkers, Battleship was also, at that time, the only National winner bred and owned in America and ridden by an American-born jockey. Bruce explains why an entire horse like Battleship is inclined to land on his head over the National fences. "He was frightened of scratching his undercarriage on the gorse," he says. "He was a very good racehorse who would, as my father had stated, undoubtedly have won top-class staying races on the Flat in England if he had come over earlier. As it was, he won at all distances from four furlongs to four and a half miles but, surprisingly, remained a maiden over hurdles. Overall he had fifty-eight foals from fifteen crops, including thirty-three winners of many races and eleven stakes winners. The total earnings of his progeny were nearly a million dollars. He sired four individual sons who went on to win the American Grand National. The interesting thing was that he sired several two-year-old winners. Of course it's worth remembering that his dam, Quarantine, was a French Classic filly. He went blind before he died."

Mrs Scott was determined that Battleship would never race again and she kept her word. After the victory celebrations in Lambourn, the little champion remained at Ronehurst until the end of the jumping season in June when, at the invitation of his owner, Battleship, Reg and Bruce travelled to the United States together on the *S. S. Manhattan*. Bruce says, "They built a special box for him down in the hold, fourteen feet by fourteen feet, a magnificent affair, and established a lucerne patch so that he had fresh lucerne each day. On board we were feted the whole way over. It was very embarrassing now I think back on it. There was a conducted tour for passengers to go down to see the horse all the way across – ladies had to be asked to wear trousers going down the companion-way ladders! This was a trifle difficult because women didn't wear trousers in those days, so they had to borrow or put old pyjamas over their skirts. We had to hold court down there several times a day.

"When we arrived in New York there was a band waiting for us, sirens blaring and the traditional fire-hose welcome. The water squirted out, flags waved, the horse came up in a special crate and there was I, the National hero, frightened to death while my father stood there with tears streaming down his face.

"One of Mrs Scott's horse-vans was at the docks to meet us but first we were met by La Guardia, Mayor of New York. He was very nice to us, and Randolph Scott came in from Hollywood just to greet us. He took time off from making a movie, *The Texan*, just to be there when Battleship arrived.

"Battleship was whisked through customs and the huge crowd to the station, where he went by rail to Mrs Scott's home at Montpelier, Virginia. We went first to Westbury, Long Island to stay with the Ambrose Clarks in their summer residence. The only thing that I can remember about that stay was that we had to change for dinner every night, and that I fell asleep on two occasions. Very bad form, but I was being kept up too late. Moreover I was riding work every day. Then we went to a dinner at Meadowbrook Polo Club where I was the guest of honour. I had to make a speech, which I wasn't particularly good at but it was taken in good spirit and then we went down to Montpelier to stay with Mrs Scott. It was a fascinating experience, because, although she was a very, very shy woman, she had this glorious, enormous house and my father and I stayed in the guest wing, with our own staff looking after us. Of course, we had our meals with Mrs Scott and it was a great pleasure to see the Grand National trophy taking pride of place in her famous trophy room."

The house at Montpelier, a wonderful example of mid-eighteenth century architecture, had been modified by William Thornton, architect of the Capitol in Washington, so that it achieved, in his words, "simplicity, but symmetry of proportion and faultlessness of taste." It had been the home of James Madison, known in the United States as the Father of the Constitution who retired to Montpelier after serving two terms as President, from 1809 to 1817. He lived there until his death in 1836 and was buried there.

Bruce says, "It was a fabulous estate where she kept her racehorses, had a pack of foxhounds and, of course, the cock-fighting pit. Vast sums of money changed hands there and my father, who was a great gambler at horses as well as cards, enjoyed himself immensely.

"I had taken my riding kit with me and I rode at four different meetings while I was in the United States. The first was a little hunt meeting at a place called Rosslyn Park. The changing-room was a tent.

I can see it now. There was a fellow sitting over on the other side from me and, when he took his jacket off, he had a revolver in the pocket. He just hung it up naturally on his peg and I asked Mrs Scott's jockey, a real flashy little guy who used to go about in white suits, 'Why does that chap have a revolver? What goes on?' He said, 'He got held up in a bank robbery last week.'

"I rode two winners there, one over hurdles and one over fences. The fences were growing privet hedges on a bank of about two foot six inches high and then on top the privet hedge was faced up with birch. Well spread, but in fact very soft and all you had to do was just bend your knees. The hurdles were more or less the same as they are here but a little bit flatter, so that you could roll them as you galloped. The track was sloppy and I came in from the last race, covered in mud. I asked Mrs Scott's jockey where I could find a shower. Without changing expression he said, 'Well, you could go outside and grab the last of the rain!'

"Instead of going off in front, I did what I'd been taught in England, sat behind and gave the horses a chance to get on their legs before asking them to go on to win. As a result I got a very good press. Then I went to another hunt meeting to ride for Louis Stoddard, one of our friends from Leicestershire, in a race which was called the Cedarhurst Grand National on Long Island. My horse didn't just win but won by half the track and so obviously he'd been readied up for the race and for me to ride. That was quite a thrill!

"Although I didn't fancy riding over the timber fences, I obviously would have done if I'd been asked. Luckily I wasn't. But I did ride at one of the bigger tracks, Delaware Park, which was owned by the du Pont family and, although I didn't win on this particular day it was a great experience to ride round one of their top tracks. I went to Belmont, looked after by another American jockey, Reagan Mackinney, and was taken into the dressing-room where I had to stay. Because I was a licensed jockey, I wasn't allowed out again until the end of racing. All jockeys, once they had gone into the weighing-room had to stay there for the rest of the afternoon, except to race. Mind, everything was laid on for you, with changing-rooms, Turkish baths, etc., but that was it. You stayed in until you'd finished work.

"We were made very welcome over there and feted all the time. My father was a tremendous boxing fan and I too was fired with enthusiasm, particularly when we were given ringside tickets for the World Championship fight at Madison Square Gardens, between Joe Louis and the German Max Schmeling, who had beaten him on their previous meeting. Mrs Scott laid on an aeroplane to fly us to New York, which was a great thrill because neither of us had ever flown before. Hitler had built Schmeling up as the great white champion who would establish his dominance over the Negro. Louis was going to see about that! You could see the fixed determination on his face as he came up the aisle past us to get in the ring. The fight lasted under two minutes and the end came in the corner above us. The punch only went a foot and Schmeling dropped like a stone. Louis had avenged his defeat and won the world title but he left the ring with exactly the same expression. There's no doubt he was the greatest of all time and he was still world champion at the age of forty-one.

"We returned home on the *S. S. Washington* and I was still feted all the way back. The film of the National was shown every night and my father and I were the hosts."

When the famous comedian Jack Benny was presented with an Oscar, he stood for sometime holding the award, looking at the assembled guests. Then, with unusual modesty, he said, "I don't deserve this." He paused. "But then I have arthritis, and I didn't deserve that either!"

In the autumn after the Grant National seventeen-year-old Bruce did not deserve his fall or the arthritis that was to follow. But, on the other hand, he was very fortunate to be alive, even luckier perhaps not to have been paralysed, crippled and confined to a wheelchair for the remainder of his life. He says, "Of course I have arthritis in my back. Professor Girdlestone, that splendid tall thin man with the half-moon glasses, scraped bone off my shin, so that it came off like a bit of paper, and grafted it on either side of my broken spine, living tissue which grew onto the other bone and strengthened it up. So that much of my spine, I suppose, is fixed because, instead of being straight, it has bone on either side and undulations in it. That is why I have a hump on my back and I cannot sit in a chair in quite the same way as other people. Now I have arthritis in the bottom end as well but that is only through compression from the top for a number of years. I went through the war with it. It aches all the time, particularly when I think about it, but more than forty years on, I have learnt to live with it."

In one way that break in hospital was a blessing because, for the first time in his life, Bruce was away from horses and able to read. Up until this time he had never read anything except the form book and the back pages of the papers. Now he was able to read books of all kinds and was becoming absorbed in the news, appreciating in a way that he would never have done before that war was imminent and inevitable.

Bruce says, "I was on my back for twelve weeks and the day came when I was taken out of this plaster and I was told that I had got to lie absolutely still because I had to learn to walk again. They were going to teach me. So, when the plaster was removed, and I was left alone on a bed, I started to move about. Then, although I wasn't supposed to, I sat up. I began to feel a bit funny, slightly wuzzy, but I threw off the clothes, put my legs over the side of the bed, stood up and walked a couple of strides. I came back fairly sharply, but I was happy because I knew that I could walk. The nurse came in and caught me, threw her hands up in horror and pushed me back into bed, pulling the clothes over me again, saying, 'You shouldn't have done it. You are not supposed to move.' I said, 'Nurse, I can walk. I can walk!' That was probably the best day in my life.

"Through all the forced Christmas gaiety in hospital and my eighteenth birthday, they had been preparing me, telling me in the most tactful way possible, first that I would be crippled for life and then that I would never ride again. By April, a year after I won the Grand National and five months after the fall – and a month after that first walk – I was back on a horse again, riding exercise. I didn't ride again that season but by August I was raring to go again. During that summer I had my first experience with a girl. I had never been 'birding' until Frenchy initiated me in London. I took to it rather well after that!"

As that last uneasy summer in the aftermath of Munich drifted by, racing people, Bruce's friends with whom he had spent the last eight years of his life, prepared for the new jump season; but Bruce, who knew more about the outside world than the rest of them, made preparations for war.

"I realised that I had to go eventually and I wanted to go in my own time, wherever I wanted to go. I thought that I would love to fly but the R.A.F. turned me down because of my back. Then, since it was obvious that I would be better employed with horses, I talked to Hector Gordon, who was an amateur rider, one of our owners and an officer in the North Somerset Yeomanry. Although they were already full up, Hector and his brother-in-law, who was also in the same regiment, got me in and I went to Newbury to sign on as a Territorial."

The little racing circus drifted down to the West Country as usual at the end of July and it was in Torquay that Bruce met his first decent girlfriend. "I had never been romantically involved with anybody," he says, "but I did start having a walk-out with Bill Rees's daughter Peggy. We corresponded all through the war when she was a WAAF, but we just drifted apart. I had not seen her from then until the Saturday of Goodwood forty years later, when a woman came up and said, "Bruce Hobbs, you don't remember me, do you?' I looked at her and said, 'Yes, of course I do,' and there was Peggy, who still lives in Lewes with her husband."

On the day that war was declared, Trooper Hobbs was called to the colours. "In my own MG 1½-litre coupé I was driven down to the Drill Hall at Bath," says Bruce. At eleven o'clock that morning, crackling over the ether, we'd heard the declaration of war announced in the sad, resigned voice of the Prime Minister, Neville Chamberlain, who, only a short while earlier, had been waving that infamous piece of paper, firmly convinced that he had secured 'Peace in our time'.

"After reporting, I signed on, was issued with my kit and drew the King's shilling. They all seemed to know me. The adjutant was Sir Peter Grant-Lawson, a member of the National Hunt Committee, who was delighted that I had joined the North Somerset Yeomanry, and my first troop-leader was Hugh Hobhouse, who wasn't in racing himself but whose brother John had horses with my father at Ronehurst. After all, it was only eighteen months after Battleship's National and, although I had had the usual trouble coming back after a long lay-off, I had already ridden four winners by the day war was declared. One of these was Fulke Walwyn's first ever as a trainer. For me to get the ride my father had to buy half the horse! He paid £50 for our share but I never received any prize money when he won!

"And I had established, I suppose, a certain reputation for integrity among the powers that be. All the time I was riding I was never once up in front of the Stewards for anything.

"People were coming into the Drill Hall at Bath the whole time to sign on – all a terribly nice lot of people, but mostly bank clerks, professional men, who knew very little about horses. With the approach of war the Territorial Army had become popular, particularly the North Somerset Yeomanry, and I was surprised to find how many part-time soldiers there were. These were the men who had given up their peacetime leisure for their regular drills and annual camps. We spent the first ten days digging trenches. At night I had my army blankets on the floor of the Drill Hall.

"The first evening, while I was lying on my improvised bed, a figure in uniform approached. 'Trooper Hobbs,' I heard in a loud voice of authority. I answered 'Sir!', jumped to my feet and gave him a sloppy civilian salute. 'You don't salute me. I'm the Regimental Sergeant Major.'

"'I'm sorry, sir,' I said.

"'Come and have a drink.'

"'I don't drink, sir.'

"'You're in the Army now, boy. You do as you're told!'

"So RSM Bird and I went out for a drink in a local pub. I had half a pint of beer, hating every drop, but I had to have it."

Apart from his introduction to alcohol, Bruce, raised in an atmosphere of discipline, which he had always appreciated, took to the Army "like a duck to water". Moreover, brought up as he had been to be impeccably turned out at all times, he found no difficulty in making himself the smartest soldier in the regiment. The stiff khaki cap, with its silver cap-badge, gleaming leather chin-strap and little brass buttons; the tunic with larger brass buttons, collar badges and blancoed white lanyard; breeches, puttees wound as smoothly round the long legs as you would expect from someone who has known how to bandage a horse's leg all his life; superbly polished black boots and spurs – over all was the leather bandolier, reflecting always the glories of dark tan Kiwi Boot Polish and Brasso. After a few days he drew a sword and a sword belt, but no rifle as yet.

Before the whole party moved down to Weston-super-Mare, where the regiment was being assembled, Bruce took a short leave back to Lambourn to collect his car, which he drove down to one of the disused hotels on the seafront where the North Somerset Yeomanry were now to be billeted. During those late summer days Bruce learnt to drill, to march, to salute and, perhaps most important, to live with young men of his own age instead of with the much older top jockeys.

"I adored every single minute of it," he says. "Dismounted sword drill is one of the funniest spectacles for the uninitiated. The squad, well spread out, stand with their legs apart in a riding attitude. The thumb of the left hand is held in the top of the breeches, keeping that hand in roughly the right position for holding the reins. Now the recruit, sword in right hand, must imagine that he is mounted, facing an enemy who may jump from the ground, assault from either side on the same level as himself or come in from above. He must be prepared to thrust, parry and punch. The sword is resting on the right shoulder in the 'carry position'. 'Cavalry right, engage!' The sword flashes down, pointing to the front.

"'Point!' The recruit lunges forward, locking his arm as he does so, imagining that he is galloping, thrusting, killing his enemy.

"'That's the stuff! Put some venom into it. You have to kill him before he kills you. You'll find that a sword goes through a human body like a knife through butter! Now, let your sword go back so that the body can drop off and you're ready for the next one as you gallop on.

"'Infantry left, engage! Ah, Trooper Hobbs, what are you trying to do, cut your horse's head off? You didn't lift your sword over his neck, did you? Now this time, over you go. Infantry right, engage. That's it. Point! Out after it! Cavalry left, engage. Infantry right, engage. Cavalry left, engage. Point! Out after it again! Don't fall off there, Trooper Brown.'"

In addition to the drill and the basic training, the North Somerset Yeomanry were preparing to receive their horses. In retrospect it is easy to ridicule the overall strategy of 1939 when England was hardly ready for war. We were pitifully short of aircraft, tanks, anti-tank weapons, every sort of vehicle, armoured and otherwise – all the paraphernalia needed to oppose the might of the Wermacht. But, although slightly muddled after twenty-one years of peace, memories still persisted of the German threat to the vital Middle East through the Balkans and Turkey. Britain and her far-flung empire, standing alone against the might of Nazi Germany, needed at least a presence in this area to thwart the threat, and there were still men in high places who had served with Allenby. So it was decided to send out to Palestine, as it then was, a Yeomanry Division fully equipped as horse cavalry with six thousand horses and men.

We should give someone in the higher command the credit for appreciating that, although the horses would probably never be used in anger, at least top-quality trained men would be on the spot, all ready for speedy mechanisation when the necessary equipment became available. After all, the ordnance stores were still bursting with cavalry equipment turned in during those twenty-one years since 1918 as regiment after regiment had been mechanised. Only the Household Cavalry, the Royal Dragoons and the Royal Scots Greys of the regulars had retained their horses. The last two famous regiments had already been in Palestine for a year, policing the country and keeping the peace between Arabs and Jews with considerable success. So they were now to be joined by a fully horsed Yeomanry Division.

At Weston-super-Mare, the North Somerset Yeomanry made preparations to receive their horses, who were to be picketed on the rugby-football ground. While civilians, now equipped with gas-masks, were filling sandbags, digging trenches, erecting air-raid shelters and building beach fortifications, the Yeomanry were establishing forage centres, putting up water-troughs and digging in posts between which to tie the strong ropes, three to four feet high, that formed the breast lines for tethering their horses. Bruce says, "Every day we used to form up outside the billets in the morning to march down to the horse lines to get things ready, through the station, over the bridge and there was the football ground. A lot of us had our own cars and Hugh Hobhouse would say, 'Fall out the car party.' There would be two or three poor chaps left panting behind and we would offer them a lift. So in the end no-one marched!

"Then the day came when we had to go and find all our horses. It was great fun to me because, since there were very few who knew anything about horses at all, I was on every single horse party and we went all over Cornwall on trains, rounding up our horses. They had been commandeered for us in advance. £60 was the top price the Army was paying for horses. We had to go down and collect them at the addresses which we had been given. They were all sorts – thoroughbreds, show-horses, well-bred hunters, hairy-legged cobs. Having assembled them, we had to load them into cattle trucks, nose to tail, eight to a truck, packed in so tight that they couldn't kick each other.

As they were on permanent standing lines, each horse had one heel shackled to a heel line on the ground to prevent him from kicking his neighbour. Horses were fed in nose-bags and each animal had a haynet attached to the rope in front of him. For watering, one man would normally lead four horses at a time to the trough. Picket guards were posted to look after the horses day and night. We already had our rifles and now came the great moment when every man was issued with a saddle, bridle and the full equipment for a cavalryman. Then everyone was given a horse. Needless to say, as I had selected and collected all of them, I picked a particularly good sort for myself!

"My squadron leader was Major Spence whose widow, Judy, is now a great friend of ours. We used to exercise and school the horses on the beach, where one day I heard a roar from Peter Grant-Lawson, 'Let those bloody stirrup-leathers down, Hobbs. You're not riding in a race!' As it happens, I was riding a perfectly respectable hunting length but it didn't suit him. He was rather apt to pick on me, perhaps because he knew I had ridden a little before!

"One of the funniest happenings of my entire life was our first squadron parade. When a cavalry horse appears on parade, the rider's sword is already strapped to the saddle behind the flap on the near, or left, side of the animal. On the right side in the same position is the rifle bucket, a long polished leather container, in which the trooper's rifle is carried."

Now remember that the Lee Enfield ·303 rifle, that magnificent weapon designed to stand the stress of all active-service conditions, which stood the test of time so well, was large, long, heavy and cumbersome. It was hard enough to teach mounting and dismounting with the rifle to regular recruits with well-trained, steady old troop-horses in an indoor school. The yeomanry instructors were faced with the task of teaching raw civilians to perform the same exercise with ordinary part-trained horses, on the grass, in the open, whipped by the sea breeze at Weston-super-Mare.

The Army *Manual of Horsemastership, Equitation and Animal Transport* gives explicit but confusingly complicated instructions. For example:

"To Mount

"Prepare to Mount

"Transfer the rifle to the right hand, grasping it at the muzzle, turn three-quarters right-about and take up the reins as described in paragraph 1, i, above; place the rifle on the off side of the horse, magazine to the front, and then grasp it with the left hand about three inches below the muzzle.

"Mount

"Mount as usual, raise the rifle with the left hand, seize it with the right hand in front of the magazine and throw it backwards to the full extent of the arm, lower it into the rifle bucket and push it home."

Bruce says, "When we had our first squadron parade, all four troops lined up and the squadron leader ordered '*Mount*'. It was the funniest sight I have ever seen – sheer pandemonium! There were horses up trees, up lamp-posts, in the gardens of seaside villas, galloping back through the streets to the rugby pitch with everything flapping ... Soldiers falling off or hopping round with one foot in the stirrup, trying to get their rifles into the right position, hitting their horses over the heads, on the flanks, everywhere ... Talk about the Crazy Gang! Even they were never so good!"

From now on the North Somerset Yeomanry progressed until it was time for the Yeomanry Division, strengthened now by the Household Cavalry – the Life Guards and Royal Horse Guards (Blues) – to assemble in the Dukeries.

Bruce says, "I was in 'A' Squadron, stationed at Ollerton where the officers' mess was in the Hop Pole Hotel. My troop was in the village hall just by the railway line and our horses were billeted in farm buildings on various farms.

"All of a sudden a familiar face appeared on the scene. Hugh Hobhouse was replaced as my troop-leader by none other than Lieutenant Neville Crump, formerly of the 4th Hussars, who had been called back on the Regular Officers' Reserve. At thirty, Neville, who was later to train three Grand National winners, was the same splendid, fearless, upright extrovert that he is today. I had already had a few rides for him before the war and now, as my troop-leader, he appointed me as feeder and clipper. At first we had a hand machine to clip the horses with. As you can well imagine, the blades got blunt and the chain was always breaking. From that we graduated to a more sophisticated clipping machine which worked off the battery of a motor-car. When I told him that, feeding thirty-two horses and keeping them all clipped, I had too much to do, he said, 'In that case you'd better be my second servant.' A cavalry officer had a first servant, the equivalent of an infantry batman, and a second servant, who looked after his horses. This meant that there were basically two horses for the officer and one for his servant, but as long as the regiment was in England, the odd hunter was apt to be added. Naturally horses and tack had to be perfectly turned out at all times. For this job I received the princely sum of five shillings a week extra. That was all right for a while but eventually I became bored with Neville returning from hunting with filthy horses at five o'clock on a Saturday evening. So I returned to feeding, about which I had learnt so much all my life from my father and Leonard Gregory."

Living only a mile away at the time was a pretty girl called Betty Winder, who used to see the yeomanry soldiers exercising their horses as she walked through the fields with her mother and their dogs but never met them in that uneasy cold-war winter of 1939.

Bruce says, "The training up there was only very basic. Apart from firing rifles on the range, we did very little real troop-training. No manoeuvres with the horses. Foot drill and mounted drill, yes. More sword drill, by now graduating to mounted dummy-thrusting. That is, charging with our swords at straw-filled dummies in different positions, representing the bodies of our enemy. Our instructors told us gruesomely that they were much tougher to pierce than humans! Although the drill hall where we were supposed to feed was about a mile away, we and our horses were billeted in a farmyard that kindly produced plenty of fresh milk. Add a little café in the village, where I could get a magnificent bacon-and-eggs breakfast for just 1s 6d, and I was more than happy. Every Saturday morning I used to salute for my pay, which was fourteen shillings a week. 'Trooper Hobbs, sir!'

"Christmas passed, and then in January 1940, the Yeomanry Division started to move to the Middle East. Officially, of course, we had no idea where we were going. The Fourth Brigade of the First Cavalry Division included ourselves, the North Somerset Yeomanry, and the Household Cavalry. We had travelled up from Somerset by train and now we had to be organised for the big move to the south coast for embarkation. We were sorted out into those who were going to be in charge of the horses and those who were going by troop-ship. Naturally Neville Crump and I were chosen for the horse party and our vet was Frank Cundell, a wonderful man, who was later to become one of the most successful and outstandingly popular jump-trainers. Riding one and leading two, with no saddles, just ordinary jute rugs on the horses, we went from Ollerton to Tuxford to entrain for Dover.

"Although normally very fit, I had chosen this occasion to contract a bout of flu and I really thought I was going to get pneumonia. I felt like the wrath of God but I was determined to travel with the horse party. So I went into the pub and bought my first ever bottle of whisky to keep me going – two halves, one for each pocket, 12s 6d in all. Cattle trucks, eight horses to each wagon, watering at different stations en route and stopping occasionally because a horse had kicked out the side of a cattle wagon. Rattling through snow covered fields. A hard winter as a nation prepared belatedly for war. Every different kind of uniform, tin hats, gas-masks, the still unusual sight, for me, of women in uniform. We didn't appreciate that we were an anachronism as England struggled to mechanise."

On arrival at Dover they somehow succeeded in embarking all their horses onto Channel steamers and down into the holds.

"It was a hell of an operation. I was tremendously excited and I remember our boat steering round a mine while we fired our rifles at it. Perhaps fortunately it did not explode. When we got to Dunkirk, there was a scene of complete chaos, because all these horses were arriving and they had to be loaded with no proper ramps into those enormous great metal French wagons with two double doors in the middle. We had to put eight horses into each wagon, four on each side facing inwards, tethered to a rope with four men in the gangway between them. The loading went on all night long, under flood lights. It was ghastly because, although our horses were well shod, there was no straw and the floors of the wagons were absolutely smooth. Our manpower consisted not only of inexperienced Yeomen, but all sorts of French dockers and assorted helpers who knew nothing whatsoever about horses. Slapping, pulling, pushing, encouraging, we somehow got all the animals onto the train and set off on the four-day journey down to Marseilles."

The advance party had done its job well. There were Army kitchens and forage stores at various halts along the way where the train stopped for the English soldiers to water and feed their horses and themselves. "We were able to mix feeds in their individual nose-bags for the horses, but we ourselves had only haversack meals – never a hot meal on the four days' trip."

They finally arrived at a little halt just outside Marseilles called appropriately Chateau Renard. "It was an enormous castle and there were horses everywhere," says Bruce. "The weather was exceptionally treacherous. It was lovely and warm when we arrived but it had been so wet beforehand that the horse lines were flooded. We ourselves were sleeping in bell-tents but the duckboards were, for the most part, floating ! Our horses were once again on breast lines but on the second night the weather changed and it froze so hard that I saw four big black Household Cavalry horses standing stark and stiff, frozen to death on the lines. We stayed at Chateau Renard for four nights and then were on the move again, riding and leading into Marseilles. As soon as I saw those cobbled streets, I dismounted quickly and so advised the others around me. But of course, I was only a trooper and was in no position to give orders. So, as they had not been warned in advance, many of the party did not appreciate the danger, and horses were going down like ninepins. A number of them cut their knees badly. When we arrived at the docks we loaded the horses onto a boat which had previously carried mules. They had to go right down into the hold. There were wings on either side of the gangway and the only way to get the horses on was to let them loose, aim them at the opening, crack a whip behind them and say 'Go on!'. There would be somebody at the other end to tether them up. The pens were built for mules, so that, although they were fitted in fairly tight, each horse had its own little partition. There were horses from the hold right up to the top deck, as many as three hundred to a boat.

"We had all our saddlery, personal equipment and kit – sacks and sacks of it – on board. I had my racing breeches, boots, whip and goodness knows what else strapped onto the underneath of my saddle, on the old Army principle that 'A good soldier is never parted from his kit'. Neville Crump and Frank Cundell were on our particular boat. We slept in hammocks on the horse deck, more cramped than the animals in fact. The crew were Lascars and it was quite interesting, in a gruesome sort of way, to watch them making the bread, kneading it with their feet and spitting on it. However, we never got any tummy bugs, but two horses died.

"During the five-day voyage, poor Frank Cundell and his veterinary assistants worked flat out the whole way, chiefly because of the Household Cavalry horses, many of whom were so soft from living indoors all the time that they were constantly sick with colic and every other sort of illness. One mare gave birth to a foal.

"We had to wait until dark until we could manhandle the two dead horses into slings, slit their bellies open to make them sink and let the cranes put them overboard. It was vital that enemy submarines should not find the trail of blood. As we had set out, Lord Haw Haw announced on the radio that the Fourth Brigade of the First Cavalry Division were setting sail for Marseilles and would be the first convoy success for the Fuhrer."

Nevertheless, at this stage most of the German war effort was concentrated on the impending invasion of the Low Countries and France, with the result that the North Somerset Yeomanry's voyage through the Mediterranean was without incident and they arrived safely at Haifa five days after leaving Marseilles. The regiment had been brought up to fighting strength by the addition of a number of reservists from regular cavalry regiments, some of whom were old sweats but others, excellent men by any standards, were to prove a tremendous asset. Bruce became friendly with several of these men, including "a cracking chap" called Dusty Dewster, and began to learn some of the ways and means of Army life.

The saddlery issued to the yeomanry was, for the most part, unused and contained bits and stirrup irons made of steel, which had to be burnished to keep clean. No such chore was required of the Household Cavalry troopers because all their bits and irons had been chromium-plated.

"It seemed unfair," says Bruce, "that they should have all the best tack. Four of us decided that something would have to be done about it and, somehow or other, by the time we came to disembark, our troop was fully equipped with chrome bits and irons. Nothing dishonest. Nothing stolen. Just a few members of the Blues having to work a little harder than usual – like the rest of us!"

Chapter Eight

After the austerity of wartime England and the blackout at home and on the ship, Palestine seemed like another planet, particularly to nineteen-year-old Bruce, whose only venture abroad following the family's return to Britain had been that heavily escorted trip to the United States nearly two years earlier.

Haifa, in those days, although capable of taking ships of fairly considerable draught, was more like a seaside resort than a port, perhaps a modernised Mediterranean version of Deauville/Trouville. The bright lights shone at night, the shops were full, good food and drink abounded, the girls were pretty and childhood Biblical concepts of Mount Carmel were shattered by the discovery that there were nightclubs at the top and bottom and brothels half way up!

Outside the towns many parts of the Holy Land in early spring were sheer joy, with the citrus groves, terraced olive trees and, in the hills, the most glorious wild flowers in the world. "Haifa was a revelation," says Bruce. "It was like a holiday town."

The North Somerset Yeomanry assembled and reorganised at Hadera, a short way from Haifa. After a few weeks they moved as a regiment to the permanent barracks at Jenin. "It was only half a day's march, but we did it as our first regimental exercise, with leading section, leading troop, squadron, flank guards and so on."

There is no doubt that modern cavalry tactics of caution allied to dash, when adapted later to mechanised warfare, were responsible for considerable success and lack of casualties in those formations which had been trained in their use. With the notable exceptions of the Greys, Royals and Household Cavalry, many of the other cavalry regiments, who had been mechanised for some time before the war, suffered badly because they believed that dash was the chief characteristic of a cavalryman, even when it was patently foolhardy.

They had never experienced the naked feeling of the leading section and troop of a horsed cavalry squadron, who used to advance led by one man with a drawn sword to deal summarily with any attacker. He was covered from just behind, round every corner and over every rise, by a man with a drawn rifle; he in turn was covered by the leading section who were covered further back by the remainder of the troop and so on to the squadron and regiment on longer bounds. So they moved like a caterpillar, covered at every stage and ready to deploy immediately into attack or defence at the first sign of danger. This conception of tactics, which is surely the right one, was to pay handsome dividends and save many lives in the years to come.

Moreover, it is worth remarking here that horse-training produces the finest NCOs imaginable. From the word go a man has to control something other than himself, the horse. As a humble trooper, he may be given a message to take to another troop or squadron. He has to find his own way, across country, directing his horse and thinking fast how best to get there. When he comes to commanding a tank, it is second nature. He has an advantage over his counterpart in a wholly mechanised regiment, who has spent his early days cooped up in the bowels of a tank, as a driver, gunner or wireless operator, unable to look all around him and develop an eye for country.

On an ordinary routine march, the leading squadron leader had to be as good a judge of pace as the best flat-race jockey. The march table worked out at exactly six miles in the hour, provided that you stuck to the rules. Trot fifteen minutes, walk ten, trot fifteen, dismount and walk ten, halt ten, in each hour.

Many of today's trainers do not realise that, whatever the pace the leading horse is going in front of a long string or column, those in the rear will be going twice as fast trying to catch up. So it is essential when trotting, for instance, that the leader go no faster than a slow hound-jog, otherwise they will be cantering behind in order to keep up. Similarly a lot of nonsense is talked about horses being made to walk out. This is the greatest possible mistake. Animals lose condition so quickly by walking and trotting too fast.

After a pre-arranged halt for lunch, refreshment for horse and man, the regiment would be on its way again and would arrive at the appointed place at exactly the anticipated time. There the advanced party, who had left in vehicles the same morning, would have selected the site for the night, erected horse-lines and made all necessary arrangements.

An officer's first duty was to see that his animals were correctly groomed, watered, fed and secured, fore and aft, for the night. Then he must see that his soldiers were equally well cared for. The food would already have been prepared and would be waiting for them. Then he could see to himself and, if his first servant was any good, he would find himself well organised. The squadron sergeant major was normally in charge of the advance party.

In March 1940, when Trooper Hobbs and the North Somerset Yeomanry arrived at Jenin, they were fortunate to find a fully equipped, permanent camp with hutted accommodation for the men and well-drained lines on concrete base for the horses. Jenin was an ideally situated station, close to Haifa and within easy distance of both Jerusalem and Rehovoth, lying in the plain with the hills as an attractive backdrop to the east.

Now the regiment was able to get down to some serious training and, for the first time, to adopt a normal army routine. The yeomen were issued with tropical kit, KD (khaki drill), lightweight breeches, shirts and tunics with the addition of solar topees. Riding, exercising and drilling, they looked supremely fit as, stripped to the waist and all as brown as berries, they strapped their horses on the open-air lines at evening stables.

Bruce was still troop feeder and was horrified to find that, instead of oats, the stable diet was barley, which was always considered to be very blood-heating, tiffin, a kind of chopped straw chaff, and particularly rich hay called dreis, which was almost entirely sainfoin or lucerne. He need not have worried. For many years the British cavalry had been accustomed to feeding their horses in hot climates and he discovered that the heat counteracted any bad effects which the rich forage might have had.

With Captain Neville Crump as the officer in charge of the riding school, the recruits quickly became capable horsemen. To an outsider it was obvious that tall, impeccably turned out, highly efficient Bruce would not remain a trooper for much longer. Even the social aspect was becoming a trifle embarrassing. He says, "Officers and men were not allowed to mix socially. For instance, while we were at Ollerton, if we wanted to go to the Hop Pole pub at night, any officers who were there would reluctantly have to tell us to depart. But, very soon, by arrangement, we had a little corner of the dining-room curtained off so that we, as other ranks, could go and have a little nosh as well!

"One night, while we were stationed at Jenin, Neville Crump, Frank Cundell and Hector Gordon decided to go to Tel Aviv for a night on the tiles. They had to have an armed escort and asked me to go with them. Off we went to the luxurious Gat-Rimon Hotel, where they wanted me to join them. However, as armed escort, I was lumbered with a rifle and a bandolier containing ninety rounds of ammunition. 'That's all right,' said Neville. 'Give it all to the barman!' That's exactly what I did."

By May a Cavalry OCTU (Officer Cadet Training Unit) had been formed at Karkur and Bruce with two other yeomen, Noel Palmer and Tony Dufosee of the famous Wiltshire hunter-chasing farming family, were selected to do the six-month course which should make them into officers. Bruce's selection was opposed by his squadron leader, Major Jimmy Spence, and second-in-command Hector Gordon, on account of his age – he was still only nineteen – but they were overruled by his commanding officer.

"There were nineteen of us on the course, including my old friend Bill Payne from the Staffordshire Yeomanry and Tom Pettifer from the Warwickshires. I have never enjoyed six months in my life as much as I enjoyed that. We worked hard, played hard and generally had the greatest fun. It was at Karkur that the foundations were laid of a friendship between Bill, Tom and myself which was to last for the remainder of our lives."

This was the same Bill Payne, who, at the age of seventeen, had been so unlucky not to win the Grand National on Great Span. Son of an excellent trainer for whom Bruce had often ridden, Bill was so tough that he had nearly become a professional boxer instead of a jockey. All three enjoyed life to the full but perhaps little Tom was the most mischievous.

The commandant and chief instructor at Karkur, which became known as the Middle East Cavalry School, was Major "Doodle" Stanton, an enormous man, one of half a dozen officers of six foot four inches or over in the Greys at that time. The equitation officer was also a Grey, Major "Tubby" Martyr, assisted by Sergeant Major Fountain from the KDGs and Sergeant Whalley from the Greys. Ferris St George and Peter Herbert came from the Household Cavalry. Neville Crump soon found his way to Karkur with Frank Cundell accompanying him as veterinary instructor.

Concurrently the Middle East Cavalry School ran a course for officers which I was lucky enough to attend while Bruce was at the OCTU, and so I can appreciate the excellence of the training he received. "I learnt every branch of horsemanship and horsemastership," he says. "For the first two months we never put a saddle on our horses but rode them in just blankets and surcingles. This taught us balance in the most amazing way. As a lifetime professional I could do plenty of things to and with a horse, but now I learnt to shoe, rasp and extract teeth, deal with all minor ailments, groom, trim, feed and subject the horse to every form of indignity, such as giving it a physic-ball, washing out its sheath and, when necessary, backraking it. Tactics, bookwork, arms drill, every sort of training in the class room and in the field. Into those six months, Doodle Stanton, an officer of extraordinary intelligence, and his instructors condensed the entire eighteen-month course from the famous Cavalry School at Weedon plus so much more that was required to turn young recruits into capable officers, fit for the war that was already upon us."

Bruce became a very proficient swordsman. Hitherto he had done little more than the dismounted sword drill and thrusting at the occasional dummy. Now things were very different, "The dummy course, mounted and galloping, was something else," he says. "A dummy is meant to represent a human body. It is made of straw, tightly packed into sacking, and it was always cunningly situated on the course at the most awkward places, just when you'd be taking a jump, for example. It might be an infantryman on the left or a cavalryman on the right or vice versa. In each case you had to deal with it satisfactorily and, believe me, those dummies can be hard if you just happen to be holding your sword in slightly the wrong way. Another complication of the full dummy course at Karkur could be very painful. It consisted of a large padded knob like a hard boxing-glove which would spring out at your head just as you had stabbed the dummy on the ground and as you were jumping an obstacle. You had to learn to parry this new attacker by punching it with the hilt of your sword – or pay the consequences!"

There were few dull moments for "The Three Musketeers" as Doodle Stanton had christened them. There was hunting with the Ramleh Vale Foxhounds, racing, shooting and, in the evening, when they could afford it, drinking and "birding", usually in Tel Aviv.

When my regiment, the Greys, was stationed at nearby Rehovoth, the most attractive girls were to be found in the Yemenite quarters, which was strictly out of bounds to all ranks. Imagine the surprise of one of my brother officers when, driving past this part of the town one morning, he saw two grey horses which he suddenly recognised as his own chargers tied up outside one of the little houses. Rupert Milburn was surprised, but nothing like as much as his second servant when his officer burst in and discovered him in the arms of a Yemenite girl!

As the end of this wonderful course came in sight and it was clear that all three of our heroes were passing out with flying colours, they were given the choice of which regiment they would prefer to join when they were commissioned. Nine horsed regiments remained, the Greys and the Household Cavalry being the only two regular units; the others were the North Somerset, Warwickshire, Cheshire, Staffordshire and Wiltshire Yeomanry and the Yorkshire Dragoons and the Yorkshire Hussars.

It says a great deal for Bruce, Bill and Tom that Doodle Stanton wanted all three to join the Greys and Ferris St George was equally keen for them to go into the Household Cavalry.

"We decided," says Bruce, "that, if it was humanly possible, we three wanted to be in the same unit, preferably with horses. After sitting down and thinking about it, we thought that, on our army pay, we could not afford either the Greys or the Household Cavalry. So, as we had heard good reports of a very sporting regiment called the Yorkshire Dragoons, we decided to plump for that and put it at the top of our form as first choice."

They were granted their wish and, when "The Three Musketeers" emerged from OCTU as second lieutenants Hobbs, Payne and Pettifer, they had something to celebrate.

They had a fortnight's leave in Jerusalem in order to get themselves kitted up as officers, for which purpose they each received a uniform allowance of £40, compared with £30 for an infantry subaltern. "We spent the money all right," says Bruce, "but not on kit! We were young, supremely fit and ready for anything. The girls seemed sexier and the beer tasted better than ever before. We had a whale of a time!"

The King David Hotel was one of the best in the world, meriting a rating of about ten stars by modern standards. From the moment you entered those cool, high marbled pillared halls, you experienced a sensation of absolute luxury and you were never disappointed in any department.

They got an Arab to make them some boots and somehow acquired the rest of their new uniforms – Sam Browne belts, caps, cap badges and so on, persuading cavalry officers – who were leaving to go back to England – to lend them various items of vital equipment, such as officers swords, beautifully engraved creations with leather scabbards instead of the burnished ones of the other ranks.

The Yorkshire Dragoons were stationed at Acre, another well-built permanent cavalry camp on the coast near Haifa. When they finally left Jerusalem to join their regiment for the first time, Bruce and Bill were a little nervous but in tremendous form.

The officers mess at Acre, like that at Jenin, was a large wooden building on brick foundations, very well equipped and furnished. "When we arrived, the ante-room was empty except for three subalterns who had recently arrived from the Inns of Court Regiment, an officer-producing territorial unit from London, comprised mostly of young solicitors and stockbrokers. They had been with the Yorkshire Dragoons for about a month, of which it appeared they had hated every minute. They told us, 'This is a terrible crowd. You won't enjoy it at all. Unless you're hunting, shooting and fishing people, you've got no chance!'

"We were billeted right next door to the colonel and, before dinner that night we were introduced all round. Everyone was smartly dressed and, to the obvious fury of the Inns of Court chaps, we were very well received from the start. At dinner Bill Payne, the senior of our threesome, was put on the colonel's right; I was on the colonel's left and Tom was opposite. In the middle of dinner the mess sergeant told me that I was wanted on the telephone by Captain Crump. Covered in confusion, I excused myself and went to the telephone to find Neville offering rides for all three of us for the next day's race meeting at Sarafand.

"'Two winners for you, me boy!' he said. I told him that it was extremely awkward because we had only just joined the regiment and that I would ring him back a bit later. During dinner the conversation turned to racing and I muttered something to the colonel about the meeting the next day. 'Oh yes, I heard about that, Hobbs,' said Colonel Stephenson. I gulped. 'That telephone call was from Captain Neville Crump,' I said. 'He trains horses back home and I was with him in the North Somerset Yeomanry and he's asked me if I could go as he has a couple of rides for me and a ride for Pettifer ...' I was bright red and sweating with embarrassment.

"The Colonel laughed. 'Of course you can go!' he said. 'We'll all come and have a bet!'

"So off we all went the next day to Sarafand, where I rode a double and Bill rode a winner. From that moment we were in. Thereafter we started having races of our own on the sands at Acre – three-and-a-half furlong scurries, which were good for a bet. Then we had regimental sports, athletics, boxing, riding with show-jumping competitions and one of our more dangerous pastimes was keeping the verminous jackal population down by galloping across the plain after them, carrying polo sticks with the heads removed and a piece of lead put on the end. It was the greatest of fun, but, because of the cracks in that awful cotton soil, there were one or two frightful falls.

"But we were not idle. The training was so severe and serious that we were fast becoming a very efficient regiment and we were employed a lot on policing duties. We would receive a report that a bad man, wanted by the authorities, was in a certain village. Following the example of the Greys who had been doing this successfully since 1938, we would send out a troop to cordon and search the village. The procedure was to get as close as you could to your objective before sending the horses back, and then enter the village on foot. You would then conduct a house-to-house search – nearly always in vain because obviously the warning had gone well ahead on the Arab grapevine — and protocol then demanded that you should be entertained by the Mukhtar, the head man, sitting down on your haunches around the whole lamb, steaming in its bed of rice, helping yourself to portions which you ate in your hands and always dreading the fact that you, as troop leader and guest of honour, had to consume the ultimate delicacy, the eyes of the beast.

"Then, because the Arabs always respected a mounted man, you would summon the horses and get up on your charger before shaking hands with your host and departing. Throughout the Palestinian troubles, this respect for a man on a horse, coupled with the efficiency of the British cavalry and the manoeuvrability of the horse as compared with any other form of military transport in the hilly country, had somehow prevented any casualties.

"One of our squadrons was temporarily posted to an outpost at one of the Jewish colonies, a kibbutz. These colonies were successful experiments in complete communal living. For example, all the children were left under one supervisor in the 'baby farm' while their mothers went out to work in the fields. You owned nothing. Everything was the property of the community and everything was done for the community. There was one very awkward evening when the head man of this particular village was invited to dinner in the tiny squadron officers mess and cannot have helped recognising the huge fish which was served up so scrumptiously for dinner as the stallion from the communal fish farm which had been proudly caught by the mess corporal!"

During the troubles it was easy for young soldiers, lonely on stable guard at night, to feel nervous and trigger-happy as they patrolled the horse-lines under the stars. One misty night with a Greys squadron on outpost, a young Glasgow soldier saw a white figure with flowing robes approaching. He called out, "Halt, who goes there?" No response, but still the slow approach. Terrified, he screamed as he had been taught, "Halt, or I fire!" With trembling hands, he raised his rifle and shot at the stranger. It had no effect and he thought his last day had come when this mysterious stranger advanced right up to him. It was just an old grey troop horse with his jute rug hanging round his neck, which had, of course, fortunately absorbed the force of the bullet.

The troop horses thrived in Palestine and Bruce discovered, to his delight, that about one horse in thirty (one in a troop) would eat oranges off the trees, just as about the same proportion of animals will swim even if they cannot see the opposite bank. Bruce says, "Fortunately I have always been a good swimmer. I got medals as a boy and have always loved it. We did quite a lot of swimming horses in Palestine. It's great fun."

There are two ways of swimming horses. Either you can swim alongside your horse, if you are a very good swimmer, giving light pulls on the rein if you wish the horse to come towards you and splashing water in its face if you wish it to go in the other direction; or, if you are doubtful of your own prowess in the water, you can drop behind the animal, seize its tail and allow yourself to be dragged across. This is a perfectly effective method and, although perhaps a little alarming in prospect, does not result in kicks in a vital place.

The Sea of Galilee, however, is very large. There is no possible chance of a horse seeing the other bank, and recruits, particularly young officers, could have their legs pulled mercilessly when their troop went horse-swimming. The newcomer would be alloted one of the few horses that swam happily for pleasure when it could not see the other bank. Suddenly, like the Apostles, the young man would find himself in the middle of the Sea of Galilee, completely out of his depth and terrified. The horse would seem to be going on and on just like a motor-boat. He would let go of the horse's tail and start to swim back, even more conscious of the fact that he had let the side down badly by allowing a valuable horse to go to its death. He need not have worried. The horse invariably turned round and came back too. On the bank the older soldiers would be laughing themselves silly.

Of course, with the horses, sickness and occasional injury took their toll. It was normal practice to "cast" horses at the age of fifteen. In peacetime it had been possible, when a horse reached that age, for him to be bought out if required for £60, or if he were, say, a fit, high-class show jumper, then he would be reprieved. Now in wartime, fifteen was the arbitrary limit for hard-working horses on semi-active service. The casting parade resulting in the shooting of old stagers was a common occurence in regular regiments. Fortunately, the yeomanry had obviously requisitioned younger horses but there was still a number of animals that had to be put down. Each squadron had its own farrier-major, a senior warrant officer of remarkable toughness who had been a farrier all his soldiering life, working harder and drinking harder than any, and acting as the vet's representative.

The toughness of regular farriers dates back to the days when, as fourteen-year-old boys, they started work in the forge at six a.m., slaving and sweating in the heat until they enjoyed the farriers break of a quarter of an hour. During that fifteen minutes, even at that early age, they were expected to drink at least three pints of strong ale.

One day in Palestine the squadron farrier-major had to shoot five horses. That evening the officers were entertained at a particularly successful sergeants mess "smoker" at which, as was customary, the officers had had their drinks properly spiked, and had, for the most part, gone to bed in a fair old state. The squadron second-in-command, already doomed for an imperial hangover, was called early next morning by the farrier-major, who knocked on the door of his room and woke him with the words, "Good morning, sir, I have brought your early-morning tea." He presented a bucket containing horses' guts to the recumbent officer, who leant down and was promptly sick on the spot!

This period saw the staging of the largest race-meeting in

Bruce aged 4 with Bombo (1925).

Three generations of Hobbs at Olympia — *left to right* Reg, Bruce on Lady Marvel and Captain Tom Hobbs (Bruce's grandfather).

above left Bruce on Fisherman with the Quorn (1928). *above right* Bruce on Lady Marvel and the Hon. Lavinia Strutt (now Lavinia, Duchess of Norfolk) on Mischief, first and second in a children's jumping competition. *below* Reg, Battleship and Bruce at Lambourn in February 1938 before Aintree.

attleship and Bruce
ımping Becher's for
ıe second time in the
ad.

left Bruce being led into the winner's enclosure on Battleship.
below The triumphant homecoming to Lambourn.

Presentation after Bruce had won the Cedarhurst Grand National, Long Island, USA with Blackcock in 1938 (on the right Reg, Louis Stoddard, Bruce).

327184 Trooper Hobbs, B R North Somerset Yeomanry.

Four Grand National winners: F. Walwyn (Reynoldstown, 1936), F. Furlong (Reynoldstown, 1935), Bruce Hobbs (Battleship, 1938), and T. Cullinan (Shaun Goilin, 1930).

Bruce on Agility, the winner of the Palestine Grand National (2½ miles).

Bruce rides another winner in Palestine with Captain Neville Crump (*left*) and Hector Gordon (*right*).

Bruce and Margery Hobbs outside Buckingham Palace in 1945 for the investiture.

above opposite Last ride in a chase as a professional in February 1945 — The Old Windsor Novices' Chase at Windsor with Bruce (*right*) on Field of Gold.

below opposite John and Eileen Rogerson, Bruce's first owners.

Hobblette and Betty.

War Risk (grey) with Bob Turnell up. This was Bruce's first good winner as a trainer.

Bruce's string on the sand.

HM The Queen on a rainy day with Captain Charles Moore, Prince Charles and Bruce (on the grey) at Newmarket.

Henry Cecil, Arthur Boyd-Rochfort, David Cecil and Hobblette.

The fillies' triple crown winner, Meld.

Below The late Mrs John Rogerson with Absolved having won at Newmarket in April 1972.

The Group 1 Cheveley Park Stakes winner Jacinth (J. Gorton) in the unsaddling enclosure.

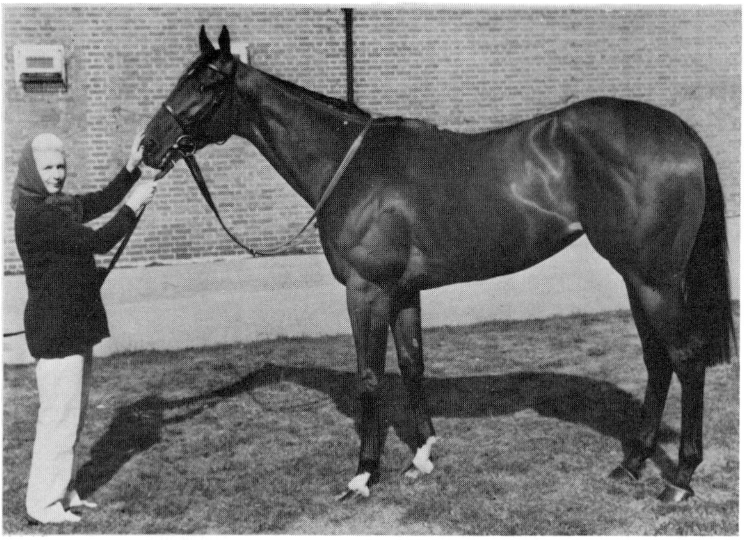

Betty and Stilvi.

Bruce with the late George Cambanis, Mrs Lenior Cambanis and their daughter Marina.

Mrs Betty Fyfe-Jamie and Tony Villar, the owners of Hotfoot, w had just won the Play Wills Stakes at the Curragh 1970.

Tromos (Busted - Stilvi) winner of the Group 1 William Hill Dewhurst Stakes in 1978 photographed at Palace House.

above Tyrnavos winning the Irish Sweeps Derby in 1980.

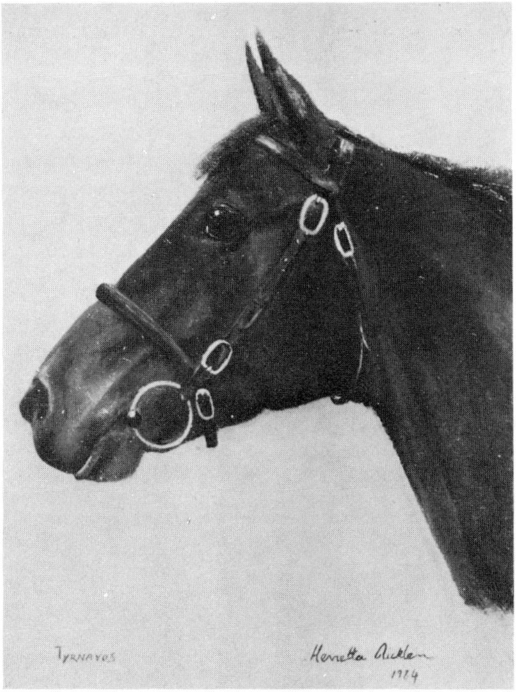

Tyrnavos head by Henrietta Micklem.

right Bruce with the Late Tom Blackwell at Palace House.

left Three Musketeers 38 years on — Tom Pettifer, Bruce and Bill Payne.

below
Jocelyn Hambro, MC, photographed at his Waverton Stud where he has bred some of Bruce's best winners, including Acclimatise.

In June 1984 Bruce and Betty had the great honour of driving down the course at Ascot in the Royal Procession.

Charles and Hobblette with their children Georgina, Tana and Rupert.

Now in their Ruby Wedding year, Bruce and Betty nearly 40 years on.

Palestinian history. The programme contained the Palestine Grand National and our own regimental event, the last Grey Horse Race. This, in happier days, had been one of the Greys' three annual races, and was for officers on grey horses. Onlookers said that it was a wonderful sight as, dressed in topees with our silver eagle cap-badges surmounted by white hackles on the left-hand side, we set off in a charge that must have resembled the famous picture, "Scotland Forever". I rode the favourite and fell at the second fence!

The Palestine Grand National was won in superb style by a good-class English thoroughbred called Agility, ridden by the hero of the Aintree Grand National, Second Lieutenant Bruce Hobbs.

Simon Lycett-Green, who now has horses with both Bruce and Neville Crump, had been in the Yorkshire Dragoons virtually since leaving Cambridge. He had been appointed to command 'C' Squadron shortly before Bruce's arrival after a great mock battle between the Greys and the Yeomanry Brigade, to which the Yorkshire Dragoons belonged. In this tactical exercise the Brigade was defending a pass through the hills to the plain, which had never been taken, even back to the days of the Bible.

My regiment, the Greys, the last of the cavalry to lose their horses, had reached a higher standard of proficiency than had ever been achieved by the cavalry in military history. They suceeded in outwitting the entire Brigade and taking the pass. 'A' Squadron of the Yorkshire Dragoons had been in a vital position. The squadron leader, however, not suspecting the nefarious plans of his professional adversaries, was somewhere at his headquarters playing bridge when the Greys launched their surprise attack on the pass. Soon afterwards, Simon took over.

The Yorkshire Dragoons had been immensely strengthened when they were joined by the late Colonel "Babe" Moseley, formerly of the Royals, that chubby-faced, much-loved character of wit and authority, who had been an amateur rider of distinction and was later to play a great part in the organisation and conduct of the Badminton Three-Day Event. Babe had been sent to the regiment as understudy to the commanding officer, Francis Stephenson, who was thought to be getting a little old for the job. Babe disagreed and typically said so and remained to give Stephenson the recruitment of those two top professional jockeys, Hobbs and Payne.

When Bruce, Bill and Tom joined in December 1940 the officers' wives, including Gladys Lycett-Green, had just been sent back to England. Peacetime soldiering was finally over.

The Dragoons spent Christmas at Acre and in March 1941 moved up to Rosh Pinna, with the job of patrolling villages and guarding part of the Syrian frontier. Simon Lycett-Green says, "We had to stop the

Arabs from smuggling kerosene and eggs over the frontier, and were given the order to set up a prisoner-of-war camp." His officers in 'C' Squadron now included Captain Peter Wood, his second-in-command, uncle of the present Lord Halifax, that fine natural horseman John Shedden, and Bruce.

Bruce says, "My great friend Peter Wood was convinced that he was going to be killed during the war. He would tell me, 'I shall never get through this, never get through the war.' He was right."

Plenty of recreation including racing, jackal-hunting and wild-fowl shooting at Lake Huleh, one of the most famous shoots in the world. I had not been long with the Greys when I first went up to Huleh and found myself waiting in the marshes for the morning flight as dawn began to break, standing behind a rush hide with a little Arab boy of about twelve years old, who had been detailed to act as my loader. It was still practically dark and my teeth were chattering with cold as we waited, so that I was not severely tempted when my companion asked me, "You like my sister?"

One day the Yorkshire Dragoons found an even better place which nobody else knew about. Five of them were out when a snowstorm came down and, as the birds came in over the marsh area, they bagged two hundred and fifty duck.

Guarding the frontier one day, Simon and Bruce heard the sound of horses' hooves approaching, and in came about forty Spahis in full flowing robes, mounted on white stallions. Simon says, "They wanted to join us, so we agreed and told them to put their horses on the horse-lines. When ordered to hand over their arms, including their long swords, they refused, considering it to be dishonourable. Eventually they agreed to put all their arms into a hut, with one of their men and one of ours on guard outside. While discussing other details, there was another uproar. Their stallions had pulled up the lines and we found them all mounting our mares as they stood in their stalls!"

'C' Squadron had now moved to a camp at Al Malakaiya, at a time when that messy little Syrian campaign involving the Free French was starting. Simon says, "I claim that Bruce was the leading figure in the last mounted action ever fought by the British Army. We were informed that on the western flank of south-east Syria, there were two thousand French Colonial troops, those great big black fellows, the Goums – no-one knew whether they were hostile or not, because they were sitting in their fort at Soueida. We had to sally forth from Al Malakaiya on horses, riding down to cross the Jordan north of Tiberius and up onto the Golan Heights. It was rough country, all stone walls and boulders, which was particularly tough on the pack-horses who carried the Hotchkiss guns, a First War automatic which was the forerunner of the Bren and far less efficient. At one place where we had to slither down a rock, take two strides and then hop over a little ditch, one of Bruce's pack-horses slipped, fell over the ditch and lay there. We sent for the farrier who decided that the only thing to do was to despatch the animal, but the poor chap who looked after it was so upset that, in desperation, he pulled out his water-bottle and poured water into the horse's ear, whereupon it sprang to its feet.

"We marched on to Quneitra, which had fallen to the British and Free French after quite a battle. My squadron was positioned six miles away on the road to Soueida, where there was an old French fort, with orders to patrol the villages between there and Soueida as the outpost squadron. It was known that there were a lot of Vichy French Druse cavalry. They wore red and white turbans – those who had joined the British wore black and white headdresses. We were told to carry on our duties and, if we came across any of these red-and-white hatted gentlemen, we would make friendly signs to them and try to persuade them to come over to our side. It was like a game we used to play at prep school called French and English. My colonel told me to go out and find these chaps. So I took two troops, one of which I placed on the high ground behind some rocks where we could see into these villages and cover Bruce's troop as it entered them and inspected them."

Bruce carries on the story. "In one village, after watering my horses, we had just remounted when we were surprised by the crack of rifle shots and bullets pinging around us. We dismounted and I sent the horses back while we got down behind cover and engaged the enemy. As I had been given strict orders not to get involved in any armed combat and we were obviously hopelessly outnumbered in any case, I said, 'Come on boys, out!' and, summoning the horses, beat an orderly retreat."

His squadron leader up in the hills heard the shots and saw Bruce's troop emerging. "Then we saw some of the red and white hats following," says Simon, "then more, then more ... they seemed to have turned out a whole regiment for us in an encircling movement. Some of them got within range of us and so we shot at them but, not wanting to get involved in the armed combat, obeying orders, I told Bruce to make his way back. The last section to come out returned minus one man and, when I asked where Miller had gone, I was told, 'He put his head up over a rock and a bullet went slap through his head.' He was wearing one of those ridiculous topees. So I had to report one soldier missing, presumed dead.

"We had a scruffy, High Church padre, who had come to dinner in the mess on his first night wearing shorts, who now asked to hold a memorial service for Miller which was duly organised on a voluntary basis, which most men attended. When the Vichy French surrendered, after cleaning ourselves up 'C' Squadron led the victory march into

Soueida. The actual march in was all arranged under the white flag. We formed up in the square and the French marched out – all with a sort of tin-whistle band. Suddenly there was Trooper Miller, hatless, waving like mad to us. He had only had his topee shot off!

"Then it was reported that two very suspicious, scruffy-looking individuals, armed with strange guns, had been arrested and locked up. They turned out to be 'pigeon shooters' with twelve-bores who had been despatched from headquarters in Jerusalem to shoot the French carrier-pigeons!"

The Syrian campaign had started on 6th June and the Armistice was signed on 10th July. The victory march to take over Soueida and the Djebel Druze, took place on 20th July.

For the next five months the Yorkshire Dragoons remained in Syria, garrisoning the Djebel Druze, a hotbed of political intrigue, from the old Crusader fort at Soueida and from Salkhad, twenty miles away. Soueida was one of those old stone-walled forts so beloved by makers of films about the Foreign Legion. The French had maintained "maisons de tolérance" or brothels. "Our Commanding Officer thought they were a good idea," says Simon, "so he kept them on and ordered a medical officer to examine and pass the girls."

The happiest soldier after entering Soueida was an officer's servant who was discovered in the vaults, having attached a tube from one of the enormous wine-vats to his own bed, where he was lying blissfully unconscious!

After Christmas 1941 the Yorkshire Dragoons moved back to Palestine, to Azzib. They were now training to repel any form of German advance down through Syria, but clearly, at this crucial point of the war, all help was needed in the Western Desert. In February the regiment was visited by the former commanding officer of the Royal Scots Greys, "Touche" Gaisford St. Lawrence, who now commanded the Yeomanry Brigade. All the officers were assembled and, when Touche arrived a little late, which was most unusual, he apologised saying that he had received a cable from Cairo saying that the North Somerset Yeomanry and the Cheshire Yeomanry were to be turned into signallers but he did not yet know what was to happen to the Yorkshire Dragoons. So the exercise planned for that day was called off.

Three days later Colonel Francis Stephenson was summoned to Cairo to see General Auchinleck, who wanted him to operate dummy tanks for about six months (three months' training, three months' operational) until there was enough weaponry in the theatre, when the division would be given armoured cars or tanks.

At the end of February 1942 the Queen's Own Yorkshire Dragoons had their final regimental parade at full strength at Azzib. It was an historic occasion because it was also the last regimental horsed cavalry parade in British military history. Simon Lycett-Green arranged to photograph the regiment and each individual troop of 'C' Squadron, with Lieutenants Bruce Hobbs and John Shedden on the right of their respective troops. He treasures those pictures today. Major-General Clark, commander of First Cavalry Division, wrote to Colonel Francis Stephenson saying, "I have never seen a better mounted regiment."

Bruce was, of course, in the parties that took the Yorkshire Dragoons' horses down to the remount depot at Nathaniya, where, for the first time, he met Ted Molyneux, who was later to be his headman. Now that the decision had finally been taken, they had to move fast. The situation in the desert had deteriorated and Auchinleck needed men.

The officers were allowed to keep sixteen horses, mainly polo ponies, classified as chargers for recreation during the training period. These animals were sent down to the racing and sporting club at Gezira outside Cairo.

Then the regiment was transported by train to Cairo and settled at Mena by the pyramids for mechanisation training. All the soldiers had to be taught to drive old trucks with just a driving seat and chassis and carrying a few boards, and diabolical brakes, known as "three-ton flats". Bruce says, "We had quite a few prangs in the canal!"

For recreation they played polo and raced at Gezira, and in the evenings they were still able to enjoy themselves in Cairo and Alexandria. The luxury hotels, Shepheard's, the Continental and the Cecil, were as good as ever and did a roaring trade. The girls, food and drink were of a high standard, or so they thought, and they made the most of them, knowing that they were unlikely to enjoy such delights for some time to come.

One of the better ploys on a riotous evening was to tease the Arab drivers of the gharries, the horse-drawn taxis which thronged the streets of Cairo. As the driver slept, waiting for his next passenger, the well-trained cavalry officer would surreptitiously unharness the old horse standing in the shafts. Then he would leap into the gharry, wake up the drive and shout, "Shepheards, quickly. Yallah!", whereupon the startled Arab would pick up his whip and lash the horse's rump, causing it to leap forward and vanish at a smart pace into the night, leaving behind the furious coachman!

Mena was quite a good introduction to the ways of life in the Western Desert and to the gravel-topped sandy terrain of which it was comprised. But now time and Rommel were pressing. The great German general was making his final throw which so nearly succeeded in getting right through to the Delta. At all costs his advance had to be halted. Equipped with these canvas screens on trucks, and some static dummies too, Simon, Bruce and the other Yorkshire Dragoons were sent up to the Knightsbridge line. Simon says, "The higher command hoped that the enemy would think we had masses of tanks and, in fact, the German records have subsequently shown that the ruse succeeded."

Bruce says, "The trouble was that as soon as a tracer hit the canvas of the dummy tank, the damn thing went up in flames. If you happened to be sitting behind it, it was too bad. When the German attack came in, luckily we didn't lose anybody, but we scarpered pretty sharpish."

Simon says, "Kenneth Parkinson had the static dummies and, when the Germans advanced on him and fired, a shell hit one of the connecting wires and his whole squadron of tanks collapsed! In the great retreat we were all spread out when an enormous German bomber swooped on us, dropping the biggest bomb we'd ever seen, which landed right in the middle of our formation but didn't go off. Edward St John very bravely crawled up to inspect it and discovered that it was made of wood. The Germans had dropped a dummy bomb on the dummy tanks!"

When Bruce got back to the Delta, he learnt that his father had achieved one of his ambitions by winning the Gold Cup with Lord Sefton's Medoc II, ridden by Frenchy Nicholson. He was surprised at his own reaction, surprised in particular to find how little he cared that he had missed riding this winner of the steeplechasing classic which would have made him headline news once more. Good old Frenchy, he thought, and hoped that they had had a nice touch at 9 to 2. But Rommel's forces had been so nearly, so very nearly, through to Alexandria, Cairo and the soft underbelly of the British war effort, of which he was a part, that the racing world which had been his whole life now seemed insignificant.

Instead of the Earl of Sefton's white, yellow sleeves and black cap over his own light racing breeches and polished boots, he was happier now to be wearing battered suede desert boots, pale khaki stockings, faded shorts and a shirt with two pips upon it and his Yorkshire Dragoons officers cap. In a rare moment of self inspection he realised that just now he felt no nostalgia, no longing for the green turf and the slopes and fences of glorious Cheltenham racecourse set beneath Cleeve Hill and the scarp of the Cotswolds. That would come perhaps.

But, as he penned a belated letter of congratulations, dating it three weeks earlier because no-one at home would know, he understood that Bruce Hobbs belonged here, with the heat, the dirt, the desert sores and the flies.

He smiled as he handed the letter to his driver to send back with the ration trucks. "We belong here now, Robinson, don't we?" he said.

Trooper Robinson, slight, quiet, brave and possessed of a nice sense of humour, was on the same wavelength as the officer whose second servant he had been from the time that Bruce had first joined the Yorkshire Dragoons. This was the same Noel Robinson, who had served his apprenticeship with the great Fred Darling at Beckhampton and was later to train racehorses in Northumberland until his recent death.

The regiment retrained at Minuf, just outside Alexandria, and then joined the brigade of the Bays, the 10th Hussars and the 9th Lancers as their motor battalion. Each armoured brigade had a motor battalion of infantry in trucks and armoured carriers to scout for it and to guard the tanks at night when they were at their most vulnerable. The Yorkshire Dragoons were delighted to be associated with three of the most famous mechanised cavalry regiments, who spoke the same language as themselves.

There had been dramatic changes. General Auchinleck had gone and the new commander of the 8th Army, that little terrier, Montgomery, had made his determination and will to win known right down to the lowest ranks. No-one knew better than Monty the truth of Napoleon's dictum, "The moral is to the physical as two is to one." The morale of the Yorkshire Dragoons was high as they advanced towards their first real battle at Alamein in late October 1942.

Simon says, "On the opening night of Alamein we went through the first minefield behind the armour, but we could not get through the second and were stuck between the two. On the second night the tanks managed to get through the minefield, so we had to follow to look after them. Everything was dropped on us – even the British reconnaissance planes came over, dropped flares and lit us up so that we had tracer-bullets from the enemy flying over us."

Bruce had often wondered about his own reaction to death. He had not long to wait because Alamein was one of the most fiercely fought battles of the war. His friend Peter Wood, who had known all along that he would not survive, was one of the first to go, as he stood near Bruce, leaning on the sprocket of the tank.

"There was a hell of a lot of stuff coming at us and suddenly Peter, who was talking to Colonel Barclay of the Bays, was gone. We picked him up in bits, poor fellow. I felt then, as when other friends were killed later, that it was just a very sad part of our life as professionals. But professionals we were now and it made me all the more determined to keep going. As a life-long Christian who has always loved and prayed to my God, particularly in times of stress, I felt that my faith was strengthened, knowing now at first hand that the soul had gone on and that the body was just a useless hulk. As we advanced and I saw the dead bodies of Germans and Italians lying where they had fallen, bloated and blackened by the heat, I felt no reaction except one of hate."

Once through the Alamein defences, the Yorkshire Dragoons pursued the retreating enemy, trying to cut them off until a combination of torrential rain and shortage of petrol conspired to slow them down.

Life was strange. There were wonderful sunrises and sunsets, divided by heat so intense that you could burn yourself on the metal of a vehicle. Bacon, beans, soya links (tinned American sausages that really reminded one of bangers at home), "bully" (corned beef) which was inevitably the staple diet, tea, condensed milk, and so on – the rations reached the front line under cover of darkness. Was it Napoleon who said that an army marches on its stomach? If so, then Monty was following the precepts of the Master again, because the 8th Army rations were by no means bad. During a week that I spent as a prisoner of Rommel's crack 90th Light Division at about this time, I discovered that the Germans were far worse fed than the British and New Zealanders.

The cooking procedure was simple. Each vehicle carried two halves of a four-gallon petrol can, usually peppered with holes to enable the breeze to get in. When told to brew up, the "cook", who might be the driver or the lap-gunner in a tank, would put sand in these containers, mix in petrol (high-octane aviation in the case of tanks!), set fire to the mixture and boil water for tea on one stove and the main meal, be it bully-beef hash or stew, on the other. It always surprised me that more cooks were not burnt to death! The tinned stew was quick and popular.

Bruce remembers the old 8th Army concert-party song, based on "Give my regards to Broadway": –

We're going to brew up on Broadway,
We'll show La Guardia how
To stew up the old way
We learnt by the sweat of our brow.
We're going to brew up on Broadway
McConachies will be wow,
And on that stew we'll fatten
Bronx, Harlem and Manhattan.
We're going to brew up on Broadway,
Stew up on Broadway,
Brew up on Broadway now!

For most of the time water was rationed at half a gallon per man per day and this included shaving. The discipline of what in retrospect was a crack formation was, naturally, excellent. You very rarely saw an unshaven soldier, whatever his rank.

When beer was delivered, in pint bottles, usually an excellent brew from Canada, it was far better not to drink it during the day. The best plan was to make a little hole in the ground at night and leave it there until the morning when you could drink it really cold. Officers were entitled to a bottle of whisky on ration periodically, in addition to the beer, and this was often described as the cause of jaundice, which seemed to affect officers but not other ranks.

Each vehicle carried at least one shovel, which was used not only for digging trenches but also for natural functions. When the opportunity presented itself, you would walk off some way from the vehicles and dig a hole in the ground to relieve yourself, covering it up with sand when you had finished.

Bruce says, "If you had to fight a war, there's no doubt that the Western Desert was the place to do it. It was nothing like as frightening as the close country we were to encounter later on. In fact shot and shell never really worried me. I was frightened, however, of aerial strafing. Somehow you felt that you couldn't get away from it. There was a sort of fixation and I suppose that, above all, there was the feeling that you could do nothing about it. If you could shoot back, you felt so much better."

The incidental characters of the Desert War were the black-robed Bedouins who, in some extraordinary way, managed to carry on their lives as the gypsies of the Middle East, regardless of hostilities, in their shabby sprawling tents north of the main coast-road. The "props" were the vehicles of war, British and enemy, either burnt out, crippled or still burning and exploding under a column of black smoke that rose into the blue sky and created a firework show at night, which were as common as red coats at a meet of the Quorn. All too often, perished therein, lay the hopes and dreams of mothers' sons who would never see Melton or any other part of Britain again.

The Yorkshire Dragoons, after this baptism of fire, now followed on to Tmimi, where the entire First Armoured Division had stopped to refit and retrain. The shoulders of their battledress and their vehicles now carried the divisional insignia of a rhinoceros. They stayed at Tmimi from 17th November, 1942 until 1st March, 1943, paying fairly frequent visits to Alexandria on leave.

Simon Lycett-Green and his squadron spent a happy, if somewhat uncomfortable, Christmas sleeping in holes in the ground and by March, after the fall of Tripoli, which they briefly entered as part of the Victory Parade, the Yorkshire Dragoons motored up to Medinine, twenty miles short of Mareth. The Battle of Medinine had taken place and it had been secured. "So," says Simon, "we took up a position there and waited for Monty's attack on the Mareth Line."

Bruce says, "At this stage, before the final big assault, we were inspected by the army commander. Simon introduced me as the steeplechase jockey who had won the Grand National. Little Monty never smiled. He said, 'Lieutenant Hobbs, there'll be many more bigger fences to jump than you've ever seen before this is over.' I'll remember that to my dying day."

Simon Lycett-Green takes up the story. "We had to send numerous patrols out across a plain about ten miles wide. It was a thankless task and Bruce, on one of these ghastly patrols, had to go up into the hills with about ten men. They could go only so far in their truck, leave it to do the patrolling and find their way back by compass. Unhappily they ran into an ambush and were very badly shot up, but somehow Bruce managed to fight his way out and, after walking about twelve miles, came back to us. It was a wonderful effort because the rest of the patrol had either been killed or taken prisoner.

"Monty's first attack on the Mareth Line failed and we were moved up onto a flank in an infantry role. Then, in preparation for the second attack, all squadron leaders were told that the attack was going to take place further up the mountainside, on the west side of the Mareth Line. The Yorkshire Dragoons were told that because the sappers had had such a bloody morning, they were to lift the mines instead. We had had some instruction as to how to do it but were obviously not particularly thrilled about attempting it! This was at mid-day. Four hours later all squadron leaders were ordered to report back again and informed that the mine-lifting was off. The Yorkshire Dragoons would now be withdrawn from their positions and would rendezvous with the 2nd Armoured Brigade for the now famous Left Hook. We were back in our old role when we formed up at six o'clock that evening and Bruce had his carriers.

"At six o'clock in the evening we formed up and started the Left Hook. We drove all that night and all through the next day until we reached the rendezvous at about four o'clock in the afternoon and we just had time to eat.

"As the sun was setting the New Zealanders, who were wonderful soldiers, attacked a force composed mainly of Italians and were, needless to say, one hundred per cent successful. Now on the heels of the Kiwi infantry attack, the armour was going through during the night, following the line of a road. The main body of the 10th Hussars now commanded by Tony Wingfield, was to go down the road with one squadron on the left and another on the right. We stopped and waited for the moon. The 10th Hussars did not want to go first because if there had been mines on the road which could blow off the tracks of their tanks, it could have halted the whole plan. So the Yorkshire Dragoons advanced (we had sandbags under our trucks to protect us from mines). As we passed a wadi on our right, I was in the fourth vehicle when something shot past me at about sixty miles an hour. I shouted to him to stop but we heard him yell back, 'Achtung!' We knew that if the Germans could go through, so could we. There was no need to worry about mines. So off we drove through the night. It was at this stage that we missed Pettifer."

Bruce says, "Tom had lost radio contact and we had no idea where he was. At first light we were streaming down the road and there suddenly was Tom on our flank with six hundred Italian prisoners and, more important, an intact 88-millimetre gun, the most feared German weapon of the Desert War, with its anti-aircraft and deadly accurate anti-tank capability. Tom was given an M.C. for this escapade. But his Italians were quite an embarrassment. We didn't know what to do with them. We had to find someone among them who could speak English and eventually we discovered an Italian who spoke perfect English with a broad Yorkshire accent. He had been an ice-cream merchant in Bradford!"

They then moved on to El Hamma and swiftly on to the outskirts of Tunis where the Germans held a very strong position, the Djebel Mournine. Simon says, "This mountain completely surveyed the area where we were lying, so that they could see nearly everything we were doing. Our armoured advance checked on the plain below and we were stuck there for at least three days. If we got close together, we were shelled. We had to go out in fairly good strength in patrols in front during the night and, as soon as it was daylight, we would withdraw and the tanks would move up to a ridge where they could wait hull-down – that is, with just the top of the tank peeping over. It was at first light on the third night, when we had just got back to our leaguer area and I was in the middle of shaving, that an enormous tank recovery vehicle drove in amongst our vehicles. I bellowed, 'Get out of my leaguer area or we will be shelled!' Of course, at that very moment the shells started to rain down on us. I dived behind the wheel of my vehicle and left my foot sticking out. A bit of shrapnel went through my boot and I was whisked off to hospital."

It was on one of these patrols – this time in daylight – that Bruce himself earned a magnificent Military Cross. The 10th Hussars were held up behind a ridge, being shelled by some Germans over the other side. Bruce drove his carrier up under the ridge, dismounted and, equipped with a wireless transmitter, climbed to the top, where he could see the enemy, and proceeded to direct the fire of the 10th Hussars tanks onto the target. It must have been one of the only occasions when armour-piercing shells were used indirectly – without the gunner seeing the target – with considerable success.

Bruce says, "I was scared stiff because the Germans could see me and soon appreciated that I had established a little forward observation post on my own. So they kept shooting at me and I had to dodge, bobbing about on the ridge. I was on the side of the hill, with Gerry just the other side, and he could hear me yattering away on the wireless. Occasionally I could hear him. His forward troops and I were so close together. I could see so much and in a role that was entirely new to me, as an observation officer, I was lucky enough to be able to direct the 10th Hussars' guns so that they knocked out so many German tanks that the 1st Armoured Division were able to move on through. It was a decisive action."

In July Bruce received two letters. The first, from Lieutenant Colonel Tony Wingfield who was commanding the 10th Hussars and was later to be the Queen's Racing Manager, read: –

My dear Bruce,

Very many congratulations indeed on your M.C. from myself personally and the whole regiment. We know how damned well it was earned and on our behalf too! In fact we feel we can claim a portion of it as one of our decorations!

We miss you all very much but we shall fight together again before this miserable war is over!

Again many congratulations.

Yours,

Tony.

The second letter came from the late Geoffrey Ford North, who was commanding the forward squadron of the 10th: –

Dear Bruce,

I am delighted to hear that you got your Monkey Charlie alright. If ever anyone deserves it you do and I congratulate you most heartily. I wouldn't have been in your shoes at Kournine for all the money in the world when you were sitting up by that bloody OP (observation post) all day. Two minutes was enough for me – and damned glad to get away again!

I have never really thanked you for all the help you were to us both there and on other occasions. Without your help we would certainly have lost some tanks and missed a lot of good targets. No-one could have done your job better than you did, and not many could have done it half as well. So I am absolutely delighted that you have collected the gong that you did such a lot to earn. I would have been really angry if you hadn't got it.

I wish to God we were going to have you, and all of 'C' Squadron, with us for the next battle – it's a damned shame what they have done to you and bloody for us losing you. We have told the unfortunate 60th that they have got something to live up to! I hope you're not having as bloody a time as I am, afraid you are at the moment. We have sweet f.a. to do but quite a pleasant place to do it in. I hope we'll see you somewhere soon.

Yours ever,

Geoff.

About this time the Yorkshire Dragoons met the Americans, who had come in from the west of Tunis with the 1st Army to link up with the 8th Army advance from the east. Even at this stage the Americans were souvenir hunting!

"Who are you?" asked the GIs.

"We're from the 8th Army."

They looked inside the trucks and saw sandbags on the bottom. "Say, what have you got in there?"

"Those are sandbags."

"Is that Alamein sand?"

"Yes."

"Can we have some please?"

Bruce says, "We were the first troops into Tunis but the Germans had all left and scattered up the mountains. As soon as the campaign was over, we were withdrawn from the 1st Armoured Division and, changing our role to lorried infantry, became part of the 1st Infantry Division. During a period of rest and refitting outside Tunis, which consisted of relaxation and training, we were allowed into the city and were able to enjoy ourselves considerably. The Majestic Hotel right in the centre of town became the officers club. Ten years ago when we went on holiday to Tunis, I told Betty that we must stay at the Majestic and found that it was exactly the same as it had been in 1942. It had not altered one little bit. The dining-room and the ante-rooms were just the same and they even had the same carpet on the floor!"

The official glory of capturing the city of Tunis went to the Americans and the Yorkshire Dragoons were soon moved on into Algeria at a place called Quatre Chemins, about ten miles from Algiers.

Bruce says, "This time some of our soldiers were billeted in a large wine-storage depot and were bedded down on the first floor of the building above the vats. We wondered why most of them were in such a blissfully happy state until we discovered that, by removing the bungs from the vats and loosening the floorboards above, they could lower their pint pots down and drag them back up to drink the very rough red wine. That had to be stopped!"

The war was virtually over for Simon Lycett-Green who was sent back to England by a medical board after he left the American hospital, in which he had been treated for more than a month. He says, "The American nurses knew very little. One lovely girl asked, 'Can I give you a back rub?' So, as I lay on my stomach, she would massage my back and then say, 'Turn over'. To which I had to reply, 'Can't, nurse!'

"In the next bed to me there was a Scotsman who had been wounded in the leg. In common with most military hospitals you would be woken up very early with a basin of warm water in which you were supposed to wash and shave. This officer, Captain Tannihill, stayed fast asleep one morning. When breakfast was brought in, the nurse said reproachfully, 'Captain Tannihill, you haven't washed yet. Now you have your breakfast and you haven't even washed yet. Do you ever wash, Captain Tannihill?'

"He said, 'Och, yes! On Monday I started at the top and washed down as far as possible. On Tuesday I started at the bottom and washed up as far as possible. Then on Wednesday I washed possible!'"

Algiers, like Tunis, provided its fair share of wine, women and song for the Desert veterans, who now found themselves being shipped to Italy, to Anzio, where, although a beachhead had been established, a bitter battle and an ugly situation had developed. "We had an uneventful trip and got in all right without being unduly shelled," says Bruce. "I was in charge of unloading our vehicles and, as they came off, I fell over one of the bollards on the ship, hurt my knee on the back of a lorry, became 'walking wounded' and was sent back after we landed to hospital north of Brindisi. While I was there, word came back from other casualites that the Yorkshire Dragoons and the 1st Infantry Division had been badly smashed up. So I got back to the regiment as quickly as I could. I had felt bad about leaving them, but our MO, one of my greatest friends, a young sporting doctor called Geoffrey John, had insisted that I went to hospital to get the crushed knee treated."

He passed through Naples on the way back to Anzio. "See Naples and die" had become "See Naples and catch venereal disease". The British and American troops occupying the town had soon discovered that "a good time" with a luscious signorina could be bought for only a few cigarettes. The results were so disastrous that the Americans had erected enormous hoardings around the town, screening in huge letters, "Hurry or worry – VD!" "Soon or sorry – VD!" and "If she does it, she's got it – VD!"

When he arrived at Anzio, Bruce found that it was just as unpleasant as it had been painted. "It was a wooded area and, because of all the artillery fire, the trees were stunted, but the moment that the guns stopped firing, the nightingales started to sing. This was our only experience of trench warfare. Even at the base line, three miles from the front, we had to live underground, in trenches formed from dried-up river beds, and our mess was a hole in the ground. We were literally eight feet under. Up at the front we were dug into the side of the river bank, in positions with code names like Lobster Claw and Crab. There we sat within lobbing distance of a grenade from the Germans. It was unpleasant and very frightening for us who had come from the open Desert. The Desert War had been mobile, exciting, even sporting and enjoyable. This was a static, dirty form of war, which gave us an inkling of the horrors of 1914-1918. When the time came for you to be relieved, you crawled back on your hands and knees in the dark. When you were in the line, you were constantly going out on patrol at night to make good the approach trenches.

"Out of the line my good corporal mechanic and I were always trying to improve the armament of our carriers by going out at night to take the ·5 Browning machine-guns from knocked-out American Sherman tanks. One night we discovered too late that the tank we were looting had been bobby-trapped by the Germans. There was a violent explosion that blew us back with a bump onto the ground, a bump that jarred my whole spine which had been so badly injured in those far-off days at Cheltenham. Only later was I to realise the extent of the damage. Just now I knew that I had to carry on, even though my back gave me a lot of pain at times.

"Eventually the German resistance collapsed and we broke out, driving straight on to Rome without any opposition and arriving on the day of the Normandy landings. The dead bodies lying around as we drove away from Anzio showed us that we had been up against the Hitler Youth, the six-foot blond boys specially recruited and bred for the job. Enormous, wonderful specimens, all as blond could be with blue eyes and about twenty years old, stretched out dead in their uniforms.

"Poor Bill Payne, too, who had shown himself a magnificent officer and a tower of strength throughout this period, had not got off without doing in his ankle when he dived into a shell-hole during some heavy shelling. I have a picture of him on the beach at Ostia Lido, where we used to bathe, wearing his plaster after a swim.

"Camped just outside Rome, we had a great time in that wonderful city. Birds and booze and no VD there!"

Now, having rejoined the 1st Armoured Division, the Yorkshire Dragoons, reinforced, went on to Florence and the River Arno, only to be ordered once again to join the 1st Infantry Division who were assembling at Ariona for an attack on the Gothic Line. Having arrived at Ariona, an LOB (left out of battle) camp was established at Naples for the Python Scheme, organised for repatriating to England soldiers who had been abroad for more than four and a half years. Most of the other ranks who qualified had gone back and been replaced by reinforcements, but there was a shortage of officers and Bruce knew that he would have to stay. Tom Pettifer, on the other hand, who had been married in Algiers, had an ulcerated stomach and was ordered home. "Tom decided that he was going to get himself down to Naples and then home. So we had the most tremendous party – a veritable piss-up – to see Pettifer off. We hurled him into a truck with a driver to take him back, and in the confusion all fell in a heap. When I got back to my bivvy, I collapsed on my bed but, when I woke up, the pain in my arm was so bad that I could barely move it. I went down to Geoffrey John who told me that I had broken my wrist, and put it in plaster. As soon as my colonel saw me he said, 'You'll have to go home.'"

Bill Payne, the only one of "The Three Musketeers" to be left behind, told Bruce that he had better hurry back to the camp or he would miss the boat. There was no transport but Bruce was able to persuade some American airmen to fly him down to Naples. "I actually stood on the airstrip, waving my thumb like a hitch-hiker!" Eventually the pilot of a DC3 told him to get in, so that he arrived in Naples in time to join up with his friends who were returning to England. "The regiment moved up into the Gothic Line and the fellow who took my place was killed on the first day," he says.

When they went on board at Naples, Bruce and Pettifer discovered that it was a dry ship. They dumped their kit, having found somewhere to sleep, and although they were not supposed to get off, they managed to wangle their way back to the town to remedy this appalling situation. "We somehow managed to smuggle a large quantity of booze back on board without letting too many people into the secret and we became very popular while it was flowing! Unhappily it was all finished about two days out!"

By September 1944 when he arrived back at Liverpool after an uneventful eight-day trip, the Allies were advancing on all fronts. German resistance was crumbling.

"I had only been home for about five days and met Bill Payne's father at Ascot races. He had just heard that Bill had been seriously wounded and was so disfigured that when he got back to the regimental-aid post, our great friend Geoffrey John asked his name. That was how Bill got that frightful scar on his face."

After a month's leave, Bruce reported to the regimental depot at

Dunbar. But now the pain in his back had become so unbearable that he was sent for treatment to the spinal hospital at Gillingham. The medical authorities lost no time in making up their minds. First they gave him indefinite leave, then invalided him out of the Army.

For Captain Bruce Hobbs, MC, the war was over. He wanted to ride again but he weighed fourteen and a half stone!

Chapter Nine

Bruce was determined to ride just one more winner before retiring! But now, twenty-four years old, six foot one and a half inches tall with size twelve feet, he was no longer a stripling but a big man. Furthermore, although he was learning to live with the pain in his back, it tended to be a constant deterrent. Nevertheless the resolution never wavered. He must get the weight down and ride another winner.

He wasted as only an old-fashioned jump jockey could. In the winter of 1944 through sheer guts and dedication, this magnificent horseman set about reducing his weight in a way which could have affected his health for life. Ferocious laxatives, dehydrating pills and Turkish baths can get your weight down when you are fit. But your system is bound to suffer in the long run.

The old jumping jockeys' crash diet was one of the best. The only things that passed their lips in the twenty-four hours were:- 7.30 am, one cup black coffee; 11.00 am, one chunk of cheese and one glass of port. 1.00 pm, one grilled steak; 4.30 pm, one chunk of cheese and one glass of port; 8.00 pm, one grilled steak.

No other liquid at all, and nothing else of any kind was allowed. Keep that up for a few days and you will not lose strength, but the weight will come tumbling off – I once took off a stone in four days – but try to maintain that sort of intake over long periods while earning your living through violent exercise and it will not seem so funny.

Yet trainers and the public will never forget that one pound makes the difference of a length over two miles and will be the first to complain if their horse carries overweight and is narrowly beaten.

"I wasted like hell," says Bruce, "and in six weeks I was down to 11 stone 7. Nothing else but Turkish baths and physic, and how that physic purged me!

"National Hunt racing had only just started again, but there was still a war on and the sport was confined to Cheltenham, and Windsor in the south. Seven races were scheduled for the first Cheltenham meeting and I had a ride in every race. Thank goodness racing was abandoned because of the weather. Just as well because I was so weak that I couldn't lift a cup of tea, let alone ride seven races. Frenchy Nicholson was riding for my father, who, although apparently very proud of me and my war record, was too much of a professional perfectionist to put me up on his horses. So it was left to my old friends, Jack Anthony and Jack Colling, to give me the rides that I craved. Alas, both these fine, sympathetic men are dead. Jack Anthony, who was fifty-five years old at the time, that tough, fearless little Welshman, who had ridden three Grand National winners, was then training at Letcombe Regis and helped me more than any other man. Jack Colling, tall handsome, debonair, a lovely quiet horseman, who trained so successfully on the Flat for the Astors at West Ilsley, introduced my great friend, the Royal trainer, Dick Hern to the big-time.

"Jack's father Bob Colling was a famous trainer in Yorkshire and, when he retired, he asked Jack to buy him a yearling. Jack told me, 'I was terrified of what my father would think of the one I bought him. We had just finished dinner when we were told that the horse-box had arrived back from the sales. In fear and trembling I accompanied the old man down to the yard to inspect my selection. He stood still, saying nothing at all, while it was led round and round him. Eventually I could stand it no longer and blurted out, 'Well, at least you must admit he's a good walker, father." He replied, 'They don't have walking races,' turned on his heel and went back to the house!

"In all," says Bruce, "I had five rides including Typhoon, and Time Step twice, a top-class miler on the Flat whom Jack Anthony trained for Jock Whitney, former owner of Easter Hero, and Portobello for Jack Colling.

"It was on February 10th, 1945, that I rode Portobello into eighth place in a field of twenty-five in the Bray Novices Hurdle at Windsor. The winner of the £136 prize was Ursulus, ridden by Frenchy for Fulke Walwyn. I had ridden at 11 stone 7 pounds and, after that two-mile gallop I was feeling not only as weak as a kitten, but physically sick. I watched Frenchy, Matt Feakes and Ron Smyth ride the placed horses into the winners enclosure and rode off to the parade-ring under the trees at the Thames-side course, where Jack Colling was waiting to greet me. I dismounted, took off the saddle and was about to walk disconsolately back into the changing-room after a few words about the horse to Jack, when he called me back. 'Bruce,' he said, 'You can't go on like this. The same thing happened to me on the Flat, you know. I'm afraid this is it. You really will have to give up. You're fighting a losing battle.'

"I knew in my heart that Jack was right. That afternoon I had tested myself with three rides, Field of Gold for my father, Time Step for Jack Anthony and Portobello. As I walked back to the changing-room, I knew that it was the last time. I had failed the test and I suddenly realised that, at twenty-four, I was a has-been in the only world that I knew. For the first time I tasted defeat and the future looked bleak."

Owing to strict petrol rationing, men and horses had to travel to the races by train. It was dark and the village was still blacked-out as Bruce, with the aid of a pocket torch, started the two-mile walk back from Lambourn Station to Ronehurst. In his distressed state it seemed like a marathon and he was immensely grateful when a small Morris 8 pulled up beside him and Fulke Walwyn gave him a lift home. "What are you doing?" asked Fulke, who was then still an officer in the 9th Lancers. Bruce said, "I don't know. I can't go on trying to ride. This wasting is too much and I had better start training." Fulke said, "Come and see me tomorrow. I think I have a proposition for you."

The next day Fulke told him that, as he had been posted to France for three months, he would be glad if Bruce would help his wife Di with the horses. This was the same beautiful former Diana Carlos-Clarke, who had been his kindergarten girlfriend in Melton. "So", Bruce says, "for three months, I was a trainer. I saddled several winners for him and it gave me an insight into the profession.

"Di was not only the most beautiful woman that most of us have ever seen but she was also a brilliant horsewoman, schooling with me or riding work. I remember one day when she was riding fast work on a nasty hard pulling horse whose girth snapped after a furlong. Of course the saddle went, but far from panicking, she went the full mile and a quarter, never looked like falling off and pulled up as though nothing had happened. She was brilliant.

"I was not actually discharged from the Army until July 1945. So, apart from training the small string of Walwyn horses, I was living at home, unmarried and unhappy. Every morning at eleven o'clock my father would be off to Wantage or Abingdon, frequently taking me with him, for a drinking session with Jack Anthony and his other friends.

"Much as I liked Jack, I hated the life and I put an advertisement into the *Racing Calendar* for a job as a private or assistant trainer. I received a reply from a Mr and Mrs John Rogerson and arranged to meet them at Newmarket, where the wartime substitute Derby was being run. The previous night I went to Letcombe to stay with Jack Anthony, who had offered me a lift up to Newmarket to save my petrol. I never went back home again. The Rogersons took me on as their private trainer. I searched all round the country, particularly Sussex where they lived, but eventually bought a place right next door to Jack, Dunston Lodge, Letcombe. A lovely, little white seventeenth-century thatched cottage with a nice cosy yard. While staying with Jack, I met Betty, whose family were great friends of the Anthonys."

To say that this was the most important happening in Bruce's entire life might seem trite, but it is absolutely true. Dark, petite, so attractive, Betty Winder, who had ridden from childhood, had been brought up with a polo background at home and on the Continent. Her mother was Scottish, a niece of Willie Bailey, a pioneer in glass and founder of the famous Rockware glass, and Major "Pop" Winder was a delightful Yorkshireman of great character. The son of Colonel Aston Winder of Sheffield, "Pop" Winder had, by coincidence, also been in the Yorkshire Dragoons at an earlier date. He had spent some years in the United States and, at the beginning of the 1914-1918 War had come over with the Canadian Army. In the trenches he had a wonderful Alsatian dog, who was eventually buried in Paris with full military honours!

When Bruce first met Betty, she had been a VAD nurse, about to go to India. "We met and she didn't go," he says, smiling. "She married me instead." Jack Anthony was their best-man.

Through all the troubled times ahead Betty has been at Bruce's side, as steady as a rock, full of comfort and inspiration. A splendid hostess, excellent with owners and staff, she is the perfect wife for a trainer – or for any other man for that matter.

Meanwhile back at Ronehurst, Upper Lambourn, Reg Hobbs's fortunes were declining. He was stubbornly and perhaps stupidly tactless with even his best owners. He lost Lord Sefton after a row with the handsome Earl's Flat trainer Atty Persse and even fell out with the highest National Hunt owner of our time, the late Lord Bicester. Reg would say, "I'm not having that old man coming here on a Sunday. I won't see people on Sunday." This was hardly the way to get on in racing, and all those glorious Bicester horses left Lambourn to return to George Beeby.

Bruce says, "It was such a pity. My father just drifted out of racing and eventually, in about 1950, handed in his licence and left Lambourn for Lockinge, where he became friendly with the then Lord Burghley, who was Master of the Old Berks Foxhounds. He became Marquess of Exeter and went back to Stamford, taking Reg with him as Master of the Horse. Then Exeter, helped by Reg, started the Burghley Horse Trials. At the same time Reg ran an excellent branch of the Pony Club and taught many well known people to ride."

I spoke to Reg many times afterwards when he came to the races to watch Bruce's horses running. He was very proud of his son. He died in August 1978. Bruce says, "I saw him on his eightieth birthday in February but he was too ill to come down to the party. He looked awful, went to hospital in Peterborough and did not come out again, going downhill steadily."

From the moment that he met John and Eileen Rogerson at Newmarket on the day that Dante won the Derby for Matt Peacock – the last Derby winner to be trained north of the Trent – Bruce felt an affinity with them. Eileen, tall, vivacious sister of Stanhope Joel, was as sympathetic, popular and keen on National Hunt racing as her husband, a squadron leader in the RAF.

"Once Betty and I were engaged, I asked the Rogersons whether they objected to me getting married," says Bruce. "They were delighted, even more so when they had met the bride. Shortly after we were married, when we went to see them we met their daughter Valda, then a little girl in a red blazer, who was later to become Mrs Embiricos and with her husband Nick, to own the Grand National winner Aldaniti, joint hero of the Bob Champion story.

"Dunston Lodge with its sixteen chalk-floored boxes was an ideal place to start, just behind the Sparrow pub in Letcombe and, as I say, next door to our best-man Jack Anthony, who always called his friends 'mate' and specialised in having 'just one for the road'. That went on for two hours! I took up all the floors of the boxes with a pick and put them back down again by myself. My schooling jockey was Paddy Murray, whose son Tony, after a valuable apprenticeship with Frenchy Nicholson, was to become a top-class Flat jockey and play an important part in this story.

"The Rogersons never had more than fourteen horses and, although they never paid much money for them, we had a lot of success. In five years training for them at Letcombe I saddled over a hundred winners. They were marvellous people to train for. The first decent horse I ever had was War Risk, whom I bought from Maurice Kingscote, then Joint Master of the Meynell Foxhounds. I saw the horse, who was still a maiden, turned out in a field, liked him and, despite opposition from my father, bought him for £1,000. He was my first decent winner, won the Grand Sefton for me over the National fences at Liverpool and started favourite for the National with Bob Turnell riding. He was a good jumper and completed the course.

"After War Risk I had quite a few Rogerson horses from the Flat. Dick Perryman used to train for them on the Flat in those days, and he used to send me their horses, as well as some of Stanhope Joel's, which were suitable for jumping. Bob Turnell was my stable jockey and we paid him the princely sum of £300 as a retainer. We became great friends. He first rode for me in 1946. Believe it or not, Bob had held a licence since 1928 when Jack Anthony was still riding, but, as he still needed fifteen winners to lose his allowance, he was claiming the allowance until 1946! That was the kind of grind Bob had to make the grade, but what a marvellous jockey he was. A beautiful horseman. Maybe he couldn't ride a strong finish from the last, but he could get them over that last fence safely. One night, when we arrived back together from Newton Abbot, his twins were born and I was immediately made Godfather to Robert, brother of Andy, the fine jockey who has now taken over the horses at Ogbourne since his father's death.

"John Rogerson, although aged forty, was a tremendous enthusiast and insisted on riding a horse called C-in-C, whom they had bought through Frank Cundell, in an amateur race at Fontwell. Mrs Rogerson wasn't very keen about it. Neither was I because, although the horse was a perfectly good ride for a professional, he had a habit of missing out one fence. He wouldn't fall over but he would make a proper hash of it and the last thing I wanted was for my owner to get hurt. Nevertheless he got his way. C-in-C duly missed out and fell so heavily that John Rogerson hurt himself badly. It was very embarrassing because neither his wife nor I had wanted him to ride but, fortunately, that was the end of that."

During those immediate postwar years the Rogersons' Flat trainer Dick Perryman had won the 1946 Derby, the first to be run again at Epsom since the war, with 50 to 1 outsider Airborne. In 1948, the year when I arrived in Lambourn as assistant trainer to Atty Persse, Keith Piggott had been training for some time at his little yard on the Eastbury Road and this was the year which saw his son, Lester, who had been riding in gymkhanas during the war, having his first long-awaited ride in public. He had been riding a racehorse in his father's string since he was ten, but it was not until his twelfth birthday that he was officially allowed to be apprenticed to Keith. They lost no time. Only a fortnight after the opening of the new season Lester rode a three-year-old filly called The Chase at Salisbury. But the first winner did not come until The Chase had been downgraded to a Haydock seller, with only 6 stone 9 pounds on the 18th August. Lester won by one and a half lengths and "The Golden Boy" was on his way.

That same year Bruce's old friend from Army days, Neville Crump, won the first of his three Grand Nationals with Sheila's Cottage and a young Irishman called Vincent O'Brien won the first of his four Cheltenham Gold Cups with Cottage Rake, who was to score a hat-trick in the chasing classic.

Bruce says, "I didn't find that the racing scene had changed all that much when I came back from the war. The familiar faces were still there. Frenchy Nicholson and Fred Rimell and the new one, coming to the fore, was Bryan Marshall followed by Tim Molony, who was almost as tough as old Gerry Wilson, who had given up to start training. Then for a while we had the artistry of Tim's brother Martin."

So many of the racing fraternity had returned, expecting to carry on exactly the same as before, just as though nothing had happened. So many could not or would not understand that the ten years, which included the holocaust, had shattered the whole structure of British society. By 1950, when I started training on my own at Lambourn, life for the small professionals with little capital behind them was becoming very difficult indeed, although this fact was still unrecognised by those at the top. The cost of everything connected with training, wages, transport, forage, fuel, and so on, had risen astronomically but prize money had not only remained static but in many cases was lower than it had been in the 'twenties!

After fifty years at the very top of his profession Atty Persse, the man who had produced the world's fastest racehorse, The Tetrarch, told me that in 1950 he was losing £1 a week on every horse in his stable on his training fees, which were, of course, the highest. The Royal trainer too, Cecil Boyd-Rochfort, who had learnt his job with Atty, was losing at the same rate. Of course, I should have seen the danger signs, if I had not been blinded by the tinsel and excitement. Atty had always been a rich man and he was saving a lot of money by employing too many apprentices at the lowest possible cost, barely short of starvation. His tack was apparently almost as old as he was and much more decrepit. Some of the rugs and exercise sheets had been patched so often that they weighed a ton. Yet he was still losing money.

Atty told me that, before the war, you could keep your horses well and enjoy a modest living, even in a bad year, on the training fees. That was your bread and butter. The ten per cent of winning stakes and betting were the jam. Now, with training fees barely covering the cost of keeping the horses, you had to try to live on the jam.

When I asked Atty how most trainers without much capital behind them managed to keep going, he answered without any hesitation, "They cheat in one way or another. They're forced to do so in order to live and educate their children."

A man of Bruce's unswerving integrity was not prepared to cheat in any way, either with his horses on the racecourse or in his dealing. There are so many ways, particularly connected with buying and selling horses, in which a trainer can make his living, some of them ways which would land him in jail in any other walk of life.

In 1957, following my father's death the previous year, I had to give up training. Bruce had done so six years earlier. We had both been successful and had lasted about the same time as each other before, through lack of money, we were forced to give up the profession that we loved. Bruce says, "I lasted at Letcombe until 1950, but then prices started going up and up and the Rogersons found that it was just not paying them to keep all those jumpers. So they let me open up as a public trainer. I had a few winners but, charging what I believed to be the maximum, £7.50 a week, I was making so little money that I told them I could no longer make a living and I had better try to get into Flat racing.

"My father's contemporary, George Beeby, son of our great Melton friend Harry, was just beginning to expand and I went to him as assistant at Compton in 1951. We got on tremendously well. Harry Carr was riding for George at this time when brilliant Grey Sovereign was a three-year-old.

"Although I still had the Rogersons and about fifteen horses in my yard, there was no way that I could make it pay. Everything had to go, tack and all, the whole lot. I had a marvellous headman called Percy Hammond who had lived all his life in Letcombe. He was left high and dry when I went to George until Bob Turnell persuaded him to go with him to Marlborough, where he stayed until he died.

"By now we had the joy of our baby girl, who has always been known as 'The Hobblette'. But we had nowhere to live."

Chapter Ten

Compton and East and West Ilsley lie in downland country on the Oxford side of Newbury. Since time immemorial the wonderful gallops have made these villages an integral part of Britain's racing heritage. George Beeby, charming and attractive, had been particularly successful with the superb chasers of Lord Bicester and, in that year 1951, had won the Cheltenham Gold Cup with Silver Fame, ridden by Martin Molony. He was enjoying an excellent time on the Flat when Bruce went to him at Compton as his assistant trainer.

Searching for somewhere for their little family to live, Betty followed the advice which Mr Tebbit was to give many years later and 'got on her bike'. She pedalled to the Royal Oak at Yattenden, outside Newbury, to make enquiries and was recommended to Sir Arthur and Lady Rucker, delightful people, who lived at Eversham House. Sir Arthur had been Private Secretary to Neville Chamberlain. Bruce says, "Thanks to Betty, we were very lucky. She did a little cooking for them and in return we had very charming rooms and the use of the garden. They made us very welcome and became great friends. I used to have my breakfast in the pub, the Swan at Compton, where John de Burgh, at that time Ken Cundell's assistant trainer, was living. He was riding as an amateur for Ivor Anthony and joined the Curragh Bloodstock Agency. When Johnny went back to his famous Oldtown Stud at Naas in County Kildare, I started doing little jobs for the CBA and have ever since maintained a very happy relationship with them, particularly now with their English boss, David ('Minty') Minton.

The star of the Beeby string at that time was Grey Sovereign, a three-parts brother by that great sire Nasrullah, to the Derby winner Nimbus. Bruce describes him as an "all-quality grey colt of brilliant speed and a temperament which he inherited from his sire. Contrary to popular misconception, he was never kicked at the start but, when I arrived, he had just returned to Compton after injuring a rib. He was just a very bad-tempered horse who would do anything for you as long as you took him quietly. But, if it came to a fight, I'm afraid that he was sure to win. On the gallops, if he was in the mood, he'd go well, but if he wasn't, he would 'plant' – stand stock still and refuse to move. One day when I was riding him, he did it with me. I gave him a crack with my stick and he just lay down. Lay down and tore lumps out of the ground. If I had given him a chance, he would have torn lumps out of me. But, in the box, he would come to the bars and put his tongue out for you to take hold of. Then he would stand there like a sentimental old idiot, with his head on one side as though butter wouldn't melt in his mouth. Because he was so difficult at the start, Harry and I agreed that it would be better if I went down to the gate and we persuaded George to let me do so. It worked well except at Ascot, where, for some reason, if he was not allowed to start the first time he was ready, he wouldn't go at all. Now the other jockeys knew that and in the King's Stand Stakes at Royal Ascot for which he was favourite, just as he was going into the gate, the boys turned their horses round. That was the end as far as Grey Sovereign was concerned. There was no question of him going in again. He backed towards me fast and kicked me as I was trying to get out of the way. My top hat went flying! He was left and Harry Wragg's Royal Serenade won.

"But in the Festival of Britain Stakes at Birmingham he beat Royal Serenade on a tight rein. If you were ever to 'let him down' and started to drive him, he would go backwards. You just had to sit still and let him do the rest. Harry Carr was brilliant on him.

"While I was there, George Beeby had those marvellous jumpers of Lord Bicester's, Silver Fame, Roimond, Finnure and the others which Dick Francis used to ride or, in his absence, Martin Molony. George's wife Eileen had just left him and he was in a terrible state, wanting someone to help him. I arrived at just the right time and, as we got on very well together, I was able to do so. I used to drive him to the races after he had got rid of his chauffeur.

"Harry and Joan Carr, Betty and I became great friends and saw a great deal of each other. Unhappily, towards the end of the 1952 season, things began going badly for George. Lord Bicester had become very old and his horses had gone elsewhere. There was clearly no room for me at Compton and George told me that I must find another job. He would not push me out, but I felt that I must go and was looking around for a job as a starter when, at Windsor one day in September 1952, Harry, who was riding one for us there, told me that Captain Cecil Boyd-Rochfort would like to talk to me. I couldn't think why but fixed a time to meet him and he offered me a job as his assistant trainer. I was to get £10 a week, a fiver a winner, free coal and electricity. I pretended not to be too keen but, after discussing it, accepted gratefully and, entirely thanks to Harry Carr, Betty, the Hobblette and I came up to Newmarket in November 1952. During this period our marriage had gone through a very difficult patch, as many did during these early post-war days.

Bruce laughed. "George Beeby was broke and so were we while we were at Compton. Absolutely skint! Everything at Dunston Lodge, the whole show, had belonged to the Rogersons and it all had to be sold."

That year Neville Crump had won his second Grand National, with Teal. Lord Bicester's magnificent big chaser Finnure, described by Dick Francis as the best horse he ever rode, was brought down, hurt his hock very badly and was declared never likely to race again. Bruce remembered this 17 hand 2 inch character with tremendous affection and it was not long before Finnure was to join him at Newmarket.

It was at Baldoyle in 1900 when Atty Persse, the great hero, leading amateur in five countries, was going out to ride that Mrs Hamilton Boyd-Rochfort came up with her twelve-year-old son. "Cecil's been longing to meet you, Atty," she said.

Atty said the appropriate things one says to a twelve-year-old and turned to go into the paddock. Suddenly he felt a tug on his coat. He looked round. Mrs Boyd-Rochfort was walking away but there was little Cecil. "Can I have a bit on yours?" the boy asked.

"I knew that boy would go a long way!" said Atty. As usual, he was right. Cecil, who grew into a towering imposing man, went a very long way indeed. Six years later he was to learn his job with Atty as pupil-trainer at the Grately stable in Wiltshire and more than half a century on was to write to me, "Not only do I have to thank him for giving me my start in life but also I can truthfully say that without him I would never have been heard of. He taught me everything I know about racing and a better tutor for a young man never existed. Although he was a hard disciplinarian, who would tolerate no nonsense from owners, pupils, jockeys, lads or horses, he was the kindest and most generous of men. He was a great judge of a horse and no-one could produce an animal in better condition ... He was one of the bravest men I ever knew and the most loyal friend. He always insisted on the highest standard of performance and behaviour in horses, in men and in himself. I cannot thank him enough for the start he gave me in life. He was one of the greatest trainers in my time."

After wartime service in the Scots Guards, during which he was wounded on the Somme, Cecil started training at Freemason Lodge in 1923. Constantly maintaining the exceptionally high standards which he had learnt from Atty Persse, "the Captain", as he was universally known, headed the trainers' list for a second time in 1938 but, with the outbreak of war the following year, he was obliged to make drastic reductions in his string and the staff at Freemason Lodge. Among the twenty-five horses in the stable in 1941 was Lord Portal's Sun Castle, who won the St Leger. At that time the health of Willie Jarvis, who was private trainer to King George VI and a few friends of the Royal Family, was beginning to fail and he was soon unable to carry on his duties. In the wartime economic circumstances, it was decided to close the private stable and Captain Boyd-Rochfort was asked to train the King's horses at Freemason Lodge. Although the Royal Studs were going through a lean period, the highlights of this association were Hypericum's victory in the One Thousand Guineas in 1946 (the King's only home-bred Classic winner, Big Game and Sun Chariot being leased from the National Stud) and a triumphant runaway success in the 1950 Cesarewitch with Above Board.

On her accession to the throne in February 1952, the knowledge and enthusiasm of Queen Elizabeth II inspired both stud and stable. Among the races that the Captain won for the Queen during the first year of her reign was the Acomb Maiden Stakes at York with the two-year-old Aureole, a very highly-strung white-faced bright chestnut with three white socks and a wall eye, standing 15 hands 3 inches. Bred at the Royal Studs, he was by Hyperion out of Angelola, a daughter of the wonderful mare Feola.

Boyd-Rochfort always reckoned that the best Hyperions were high-mettled and difficult, and Aureole was no exception to this rule. He was excitable, a difficult ride, with a mind of his own.

Bruce, who had driven George Beeby to York to watch Grey Sovereign finish second in the Nunthorpe Stakes, took a great deal of interest in Aureole, whose only remaining start in 1952 was the Middle Park Stakes at Newmarket in which he finished sixth behind the following year's Two Thousand Guineas winner Nearula.

So, at the time of the December Sales, when Bruce, Betty and the Hobblette moved into The Tyler's Cottage at Freemason Lodge, the star of the stable was Aureole and the Captain had high hopes of winning the Derby for the Queen in Coronation Year.

Nevertheless, all was far from well at Freemason Lodge. Newmarket with its famous Heath, its broad High Street, graced with gems of classical architecture, and its great tradition going back to 'the Merry Monarch", Charles II, delights and thrills the casual visitor. But the Headquarters of Racing has always been a town of high tension, because, with so much money at stake all the time, individual dramas are constantly being acted out behind the proud, bland facade of each stable-yard. As you leave the famous Clock Tower and drive towards Bury St Edmunds, there are famous training establishments on either side of the Bury Road. On the left before you get to the open heath, red-brick Freemason Lodge guarded its secrets well. Once inside, however, Bruce, who had always loved discipline, soon discovered the reason for the decline in the Boyd-Rochfort fortunes over the past few years. No one knew better than he how much the well-being of a trainer and his staff is reflected in the performance of their horses. Moreover, in every branch of the horse world, despite all the arguments of the unions, discipline has always been absolutely essential.

Bruce says, "I was horrified to find that there was none. In fact, it was a scene of near anarchy. The headman, James Barnett, who had been with the Captain for years, had just retired at the age of eighty. He was surrounded by what seemed to me a lot of bolshy apprentices living in the hostel and there was very little organisation. The travelling headman, old Frank Perry, had also been with the Captain for so long that he had no apparent wish to enforce discipline. When they went to the races, our horses' manes were never plaited up because Frank Perry had eczema and couldn't do it. Ironically we were the first stable to run animals unplaited and it caught on! Imitators invented their own specious reasons, such as that plaiting a horse's mane over-excited him.

"I had to do things when I first arrived that I never thought possible. In order to restore discipline I had to box the little boys' ears time and again. They had become a bunch of uncontrolled little hooligans and so I had to take them into a box now and again just to discipline them. The hostel had become a filthy hovel and some of those boys were like dead-end kids. Something had to be done. I did it and, far from going to the police about me, they seemed to thrive on it, as though they appreciated that things had gone badly wrong. They had never had any time off and so I persuaded the Captain to let them have weekends every so often. It paid dividends because, when the very first Newmarket strike started, the ringleader, the chap I always thought was certain to go first, came to me and said, 'I promise you all your men will be here in the morning.' And they were. The Captain, who was away on holiday, had sent me a cable saying, 'Whatever you do, don't give in, even if the horses have to stay in their boxes for a month.'

"I immediately tried to entice two or three different lads into the yard and the breakthrough came when Frank Holmes, who had been travelling headman to the late Bob Jones, applied for a job. He was a super-smart horseman and we got on like a house on fire. I was able to give him Aureole to do, which relieved Harry Carr who had cut short his holiday and taken on full responsibility for this horse who, I promise you, could really perform!

"He wasn't savage, but he used to throw himself all over the place because he was terribly highly-strung and had a mind of his own. Although he was perfectly all right in his box, he would either refuse to start on the gallops or he might go a hundred yards and then suddenly whip round, dropping his rider. But Frank, with his lovely hands, was as good with the horse as Harry Carr – and that's saying something.

"The Captain never minded about my disciplining the lads. Nor did he object to their having more time off. 'Do it your way, Hobbs,' he would say. 'As long as I can have my horses out for two hours.' He always called me Hobbs throughout the time I was with him."

One of the greatest of all human qualities is loyalty, and this Bruce has always possessed to a marked degree. To the Army, to his employers, to his owners, to his staff and above all to his family and himself, Bruce has always remained intensely loyal. So he would never hear a word against Captain Boyd-Rochfort. As the discipline improved at home, the combined efforts of Bruce, Harry Carr and Frank Holmes produced Aureole in good condition for his first outing, the Two Thousand Guineas, in which he showed considerable promise to finish fifth behind Nearula. He then confirmed that promise by winning the Lingfield Derby Trial. In the Derby, despite getting very hot and bothered during the Epsom preliminaries, heightened by the Queen's presence in her Coronation Year, he ran extremely well to finish second, four lengths behind the mighty Pinza who was giving the newly knighted Sir Gordon Richards his first and only Derby winner. The other Freemason runner, Brigadier Wyatt's Premonition, was preferred in the betting. He started co-favourite with Pinza but ran poorly.

Aureole developed a slight cough in the summer and was not at his best when third to the French challenger Argur in the Eclipse Stakes. He ran much better in the King George VI and Queen Elizabeth Stakes at Ascot but again found Pinza, who was trained for Sir Victor Sassoon by Jack Clayton in the name of his assistant Norman Bertie, too good for him.

Bruce says, "I soon realised what a tremendous interest the Queen was taking in her horses and what a fund of knowledge she possessed. She used to come down to Newmarket on her way to Sandringham or on her way back from Sandringham to London and it would be quite a scene on the Heath with the Cecil twins, Henry and David, and Arthur Boyd-Rochfort who rode his tiny pony."

As the St Leger drew near and Pinza was scratched from the final Classic with leg trouble, Aureole was naturally established a hot favourite for the race by bookmakers and public, who did not know that he was becoming most uncooperative at Newmarket.

There was a London neurologist called Dr Charles Brook, who

could regulate the nervous impulse of human beings and animals by laying on of hands. By this means he had quietened the temperaments of several awkward horses due to take part in the Coronation. He had, of course, started by treating people but had found that he could help animals as well and, after discussion with her racing manager, Captain Charles Moore, the Queen suggested that Dr Brook should come down to treat Aureole, as long as the Captain did not object. Boyd-Rochfort approved because he felt that something could be gained and nothing lost and anything which could help his horses found favour with him.

Bruce says, "I think one of the turning points in getting Aureole to improve was the laying on of hands by Dr Brook. During August this little bearded gentleman would come down twice a week to treat the horse. He was a man who took great trouble and wanted to be alone in Aureole's box with the colt. He was not an easy horse in his box and, to start with, I was worried for the doctor's safety. He liked a haynet to be hanging up and within a few minutes of arriving he would get Aureole to relax. He would put his left hand on Aureole's withers and his right under his tummy near the girth and his head against the horse's shoulder, and he would stand quietly there with Aureole for about twenty minutes. At the end of that time he would come out of his box looking ashen white and completely spent, pouring with sweat, but over a period of time he taught the horse to relax and I am sure he had a beneficial effect on him.

"He would never let us drive him down to the station but would just go wandering off on his own. He would come down twice a week from London. I don't know who deserved more credit for Aureole's improvement. I think I would really give it to Frank, but between them they made him into just about the best horse I have ever seen. He was brave and as tough as hell, although not everyone realised it. He was a horse who had confidence in those who knew him and that is why I think I helped him when I went to the start every time Aureole ran as a three-year-old and gave him confidence at the gate."

Bruce underestimates his own part in the making of Aureole. He, Harry Carr and Frank Holmes shared the worry in those days before the St Leger. "You would not believe it, but in his last seven furlongs' work before Doncaster it took Frank and me three-quarters of an hour to get him up the Limekilns. We surrounded him with other horses, but he would always dodge out. Another morning we spent half an hour at the bottom of the Limekilns getting the horse launched off. Harry Carr showed endless patience with him. He would let his leathers down and ride like the true horseman that he was. I had already discovered that a man can be an ace Flat-race jockey without being a horseman. It may seem a contradiction in terms but Harry, a great Flat-race jockey, rode like a jump jockey. He was the sort of horseman I have known all my life who had true understanding and that God-given gift of hands."

At Doncaster, in the presence of his owner, Aureole was cool and well behaved until he got onto the racecourse, when he became restless and temperamental, refused to stay in the parade and went off down the course for a furlong, fighting for his head. Harry Carr, however, patient and firm as always, managed to keep control and got the colt back to the St Leger start, to the right of the stands by the main road. In the race Aureole refused to settle down, pulling hard, with the result that he came to the end of his stamina far too soon and, although he appeared to be going well on the bit in the straight, immediately he was asked to go on and win his race he swerved to the right and found nothing, scrambling to keep third place behind his stable companion Premonition. Harry has always maintained that one and a half miles was Aureole's best distance.

Aureole had one more outing in 1953 in the Cumberland Lodge Stakes at the Ascot Heath October meeting in which, since Harry was unable to do the weight, Eph Smith, who had won the Leger on Premonition, was given the ride. Aureole won easily because the opposition was way below his class and Captain Moore, quite against the wishes of the Captain, insisted that Smith got on better with the colt and must in future be his jockey.

Bruce says, "It was quite unfair. Harry nearly threw up the job and I wouldn't have blamed him. He had given everything to that colt, only to see Smith reaping the benefit of the work which had been done by Frank, Harry and myself."

The following year Aureole had developed into a great horse and, after being beaten in the Coronation Stakes at Sandown by the Irish Derby winner Chamier in a deplorably rough race, he won first the Victor Wild Stakes at Kempton, then the Coronation Cup at Epsom and Hardwicke Stakes at Royal Ascot before a triumphant victory in the King George VI and Queen Elizabeth Stakes.

But even these last two races were not without incident. The Hardwicke Stakes was on the final day of the Royal meeting and the Captain was staying away for Ascot. On the day before the race Aureole was cast in his box and somehow got a severe blow in his left eye. Bruce says, "We had to get our vet, Fred Day, to come to examine the colt's eye, which was nearly closed. He said he had not damaged the eyeball and that it was all right to send him to Ascot to run. I telephoned the Captain to ask whether I should send the horse and he said, 'Let him come to Ascot and we'll decide when he gets here.'"

When he returned to Ascot in July, Aureole was not on his best behaviour and dropped Smith before the start. However, he allowed himself to be caught and, although slowly away, held on to win by three-quarters of a length.

Bruce says, "My word, that horse was a good doer. There is a lot of nonsense talked about feeding. Feeding is a science. If I can get a colt up to fifteen to sixteen pounds and a filly up to thirteen to fourteen pounds of oats a day, I reckon I'm doing well. But Aureole, when racing, ate twenty pounds of oats a day, licked out and would have eaten more if I had given it to him. Fred Day said, 'For God's sake don't give him any more!'"

So Aureole retired to stud, where he was a great success, although, in general, his colts were more successful than his fillies.

Meanwhile at home, while Betty and Bruce were settling into Newmarket life, which is no easy task, and making friends, which for this delightful couple was considerably easier, Betty was having additional trouble because their daughter Hobblette, who was not quite seven years old, suffered from nephritis, a particularly nasty kidney disease, with which she was in bed at hospital and at home for four months.

Bruce says, "She was dragged around with us and bounced from one school to another until we came to Newmarket, when she went to her first proper school, a good kindergarten called Fairsted House. One day after the summer holidays, the children were told to write an essay about autumn and what it meant to them. Hobblette's reaction to that season of the year was, 'This is the time when the yearlings come in and Daddy starts breaking them!' She was given a rocket by the teacher for not writing about autumn tints.

"Of course, she rode from an early age but she was never really pony-club minded. It didn't amuse her. She used to ride with me occasionally and at Freemason Lodge she would often ride the lead pony in front of the Classic horses round the paddock. The Captain didn't mind because he loved children and he was amused to see her sitting on his wife's skewbald pony. Hobblette went to a pony-club camp once and hated every minute of it. The Captain and his lovely wife Rohays were charming to Hobblette, who had so much fun playing cowboys and Indians with his son, Arthur, and with his stepsons, Henry and David Cecil.

"It took me about six months to lick that establishment into shape. The Captain was wonderful with his horses. The forage was the best in the world and nothing was too good for them. But, as I said, the actual running of the yard was chaotic until I arrived and was given a completely free hand, in charge of hiring, firing and all discipline. I was tough with those boys all right but the Captain always backed me up and, having risen from the ranks in the Army, I felt for them. I was the assistant trainer and everyone of those boys called me sir. By degrees I got them into shape and got their respect. I wasn't popular but, when I told them to do something they did it.

"As it was difficult to get decent lads, I started employing some girls and was lucky enough to get the best. Really bright, educated girls who had done their secretarial courses and wanted two or three years with horses before going on to better things. They were a lovely lot too. I was accused of picking them for their looks! In the first running of the Miss Newmarket beauty contest we had six runners and provided the first four places. The girl who was champion that night used to do the Queen's top-class colt, Doutelle. An Australian girl took charge and got all the others to follow her example. Whenever they took their horses racing, they wore cavalry-twill trousers, dark-blue cutaway hacking jackets and a hairband in the colours of the owner."

Brigadier Willie Wyatt's Premonition, having won the St Leger, remained in training as a four-year-old with the Ascot Gold Cup as his objective, and his owner bought a seven-year-old middle-distance handicapper called Osborne to lead him in his work. Both horses ran in the Yorkshire Cup, which Premonition won by three lengths. They both appeared again in the Winston Churchill Stakes at Hurst Park, that course by the Thames near Staines which has now sadly departed and whose turf now lies on the jump course at Ascot. Osborne was ridden by Royce Burrows, the thirty-year-old lad who looked after Premonition. He was told to make the running and finish second if he could. Unfortunately he interpreted these orders absolutely literally. After Osborne had made the running from the start, Harry Carr challenged a hundred yards out but found Premonition wanting. Now, instead of riding out Osborne to maintain his advantage, Burrows, serving what he honestly saw as the best interest of his employers, made no effort to drive his horse and Premonition was able to win by a short head. At the inevitable enquiry by the Stewards of the Jockey Club, the maximum fine of £100 was imposed upon Captain Boyd-Rochfort for failing to give his jockey concise orders. Poor Burrows's licence to ride was withdrawn for three weeks. The outcome, with its undertone of reflection on his professional ability, was perhaps a far greater blow to the Captain than the disqualification of Premonition in the previous year's Irish Derby.

Bruce says, "Nothing like this had ever happened to him before and I felt really sorry for the Captain when he came storming home from London, ranting and raging, and said to me, 'They're not going to treat me like this, Hobbs! I will give you Freemason. You can have it. I've finished.' So I went home and told Betty, 'We are the proud landlords, property owners. The Captain has just given me Freemason Lodge.' Betty said, 'That won't last long.' And the next morning he'd changed his mind. But I was the owner of Freemason Lodge for twelve hours!

When I said good morning to him, he looked at me and said, 'I feel better this morning, Hobbs. Dreadful thing to do, don't you think?'

"Perhaps this was the reason for a strange incident when we were galloping the horses on racecourse side, next door to the Rowley Mile course. This and, in hard weather, the Limekilns were his favourite gallops. Three days a week were 'workdays' when we galloped the horses. The previous night the Captain would give me the list of which horses were to gallop and I would work out the riding-out lists. That morning the first lot of horses to gallop went down while the remainder walked to the stands and circled round until the galloping horses came back. Then we would change the jockeys onto the next lot of work horses and away they'd go down. The Captain had gone off in his car to his point of vantage and I had just got back on my pony when Premonition's owner Willie Wyatt turned up. I should add that he lived at Dunchurch Lodge Stud in Newmarket. 'Good morning, Hobbs,' he said.

"'Good morning, Brigadier Wyatt.'

"'Is my horse Tudor Era working this morning?'

"'Yes, Brigadier, he's just gone down.'

"'Thank you very much, Hobbs.'

"I handed the work-list over to Frank Perry, the travelling headman, and went down to the start, where I stayed until the work was over. Then I hacked back, only to be met by Harry Carr who said, 'God, there's a devil of a row.'

"I asked, 'What the hell has happened?'

"'You told Willie Wyatt that his horse was working, didn't you?'

"'Yes.'

"'The Captain has gone off his nut. He's absolutely furious.'

"The Captain never said a word until I got back at breakfast time. Then he said, 'Hobbs, there will be a horse-box here to pick up Brigadier Wyatt's horses at ten o'clock.' He had turned them out and they went to Marcus Marsh. Brigadier Wyatt had broken the stable rule by coming down, without permission, to watch his horses work. Only the Captain, and no-one else, was master of Freemason Lodge.

"So, when Brigadier Tony Wingfield, who had, when commanding the 10th Hussars, recommended me for my MC, took over as the Queen's racing Manager from Captain Moore, I asked the Captain, 'Is that Brigadier Tony Wingfield who used to be Colonel of the 10th Hussars?' The Captain said, 'Yes.' And I told him, 'I know him very well.'

"'How do you know him?'

"'I served with him during the war.'

"One morning on racecourse side several owners (with permission!) were watching work, including Tony Wingfield and his wife. I was standing away from the Captain on my hack, when Tony Wingfield turned to me and said, 'As a matter of interest, Bruce, which of the Queen's horses is working?' The Captain whipped round and said, 'I'm training these horses and not Hobbs. You ask me those sort of things!'

"The Queen, Queen Mother and occasionally Princess Margaret would sometimes come over for second lot at about ten-thirty, watch the horses work and come round stables. When the Queen Mother went round, I would walk three yards behind her and she would hang back to ask me, 'Who is this boy we're going to see now?', and I would tell her how long he had been with us, what his name was and so on. Then she would have a word with him. She liked to talk to all of them. One morning we were approaching a real little shocker, a drop-out hooligan who did everything wrong. As we neared his box and she asked as usual, I told the Queen Mother, 'This is an unfortunate child, a victim of a broken home and he's very unhappy, finding it extremely difficult to accept discipline.' She stopped and talked to this child for four or five minutes. From that day onwards the boy was completely different. For the first time in his life he felt wanted. He is in Newmarket to this day, an excellent chap. It was that talk with the Queen Mother that did it.

"On another occasion when the Queen Mother came down I was riding my new hack and she said, 'Mr Hobbs, I think I know that horse, don't I?'

"'Indeed you do, Ma'am,' I said.

"With her immense knowledge of, and enthusiasm for, the jumping game, she had immediately recognised one of the greatest chasers of our time, Finnure, whom Lord Bicester had given to me after his retirement.

"In his autobiography *The Sport of Queens*, Dick Francis wrote, 'Of all Lord Bicester's great horses I enjoyed riding Finnure most . . . He was a big chestnut of high quality, beautifully proportioned and very intelligent. It gave me great pleasure just to sit on his back and look forward between his alertly pricked ears. In addition, he jumped with tremendous power and his speed from the last fence was deeply exciting. Urging him home along the straight was like pressing the accelerator of a high-powered car; he passed everything in sight.'

"Finnure's successes had included the Champion Chase at Liverpool and the King George VI Chase at Kempton, when he beat the triple Gold Cup winner Cottage Rake, trained by Vincent O'Brien. In the Grand National of 1951 when he was probably the most likely of all his horses to achieve Lord Bicester's life-long ambition, Finnure jumped the first fence magnificently but landed into an eleven-horse pile-up and, gallantly trying to avoid being brought down, twisted his hock so badly that he never regained his old speed and brilliance. The great old fellow was a perfect hack. I rode him in a little double bridle and he would love to stand and watch the horses work. In those days the schooling ground was Waterhall and, on the topside, where you turned the corner facing the wood, there were three little fences and an open ditch and three big fences and an open ditch. One very cold morning I had been down with the last lot and, as I was hacking back, I couldn't resist the temptation. I clicked the old horse and went sailing into the open ditch when suddenly I saw the Queen's racing manager, Captain Charles Moore, sitting on his shooting stick. There was no way I could stop. I was committed and so was Finnure. So I yelled, 'Look out!', and luckily he got out of the way. Captain Moore was delighted and there were laughs all round.

"Fergy and Judy Sutherland, who became our great friends, had arrived in Newmarket with a very good hunter-chaser. One day Fergy asked me to come out with the Cambridge Drag, so I told the hack-man at Freemason Lodge who had worked in the Belvoir Kennels, that I would be taking Finnure out. 'Well, guv'nor,' he said, 'I'd better put a little something in the paddock.'

"When I came in from second lot I found he had erected the most fearsome looking object. I couldn't chicken out, so I took my heart in my mouth, never even let Finnure have a look at it and he flew over the top. Jack Kirby, the hack-man laughed. 'Guv'nor, you won't get left behind in any Cambridge Drag!'

"Alan ('Anger') Lillingston was Master of the Drag at that time and we had a lovely day. It's the only time that I've ever been drag-hunting but I enjoyed every moment of it. It was super. Funnily enough, it's the last day's hunting I ever had.

"The Queen Mother sent Betty and me a Christmas card every year while we were at Freemason Lodge and when Ascot held their special meeting in the Spring of 1983 for the Grand National Appeal, they gave a lunch for all the old-timers who had won the race. The Queen Mother came to the lunch and I was given the honour of sitting on her right. We chatted away for ages and had a wonderful time."

Chapter Eleven

In the autumn of 1953, when Bruce was breaking the Freemason Lodge yearlings for the first time, a magnificent bay filly by Alycidon out of Daily Double, bred by her owner Lady Zia Wernher, combining size, power and quality arrived in the yard.

Bruce says, "The Captain didn't bother much about his two-year-olds, always giving them plenty of time to mature. Originally I hadn't the advantage of a very good team for breaking and, moreover, there were a number of very backward yearlings to deal with. For example the Queen's contingent would arrive from Captain Moore's stud in Ireland with their manes and tails on the floor. They hadn't been touched, scarcely handled at all. We would pick them up off the train and lead them back home and they would stand in the corner of the box, snorting at us. It took an awfully long time, much longer than it takes now to break them. I learnt a lot and from that time I have specialised in breaking yearlings, because for me this is by far the most impressionable time of a horse's life. This is the time when they have to be taught what to do properly, so that they will know it for the rest of their lives. I like to start getting my yearlings in in Doncaster St. Leger week and have them broken by the first week in October, keeping them going until December Sales week. At Freemason Lodge in the paddock we had a boarded sand ring, about thirty feet across, such as I have to this day. The first morning that the yearlings come out they go into that sand ring. They can't get out and you can lunge them and put the roller on them in there. The next day they have a saddle on them and the lads can start driving them. They can drive them round the paddock and into the practice starting-stalls, so that they become used to them before they have even been ridden.

"From the very beginning Meld was obviously going to be a racehorse. However, in April, when she was cantering on Waterhall, she split a pastern and spent the next two months in her box. She was sound by the autumn and first appeared on a racecourse at the end of September, in the five-furlong Newmarket Foal Stakes, ridden by Stan Smith. We had two runners in the race. Harry Carr was on the Queen's Corporal but the filly ran an exceptionally good race to finish second to her stable companion, beaten by only a length.

"When they came back I went to the enclosure for the second rather than the winner. Colonel Bunty Scrope, Lord Derby's former manager and the most knowledgeable of men, said, 'My word, you've picked the right one!' He meant Meld of course."

This was the only defeat of Meld's career. Her next outing was in the six-furlong Quy Maiden Stakes at Newmarket in October and she won as she liked in a field of eighteen, impressing everyone who saw her as the potential Oaks winner of 1955. She wintered well and her trainer reckoned that there was no need to give her a race before the One Thousand Guineas.

Bruce says, "She had such character and a wonderful temperament. If you were kind to her she repaid it a hundredfold. The Captain had her three-year-old career all laid out beforehand. Ridden by Harry Carr, she won the One Thousand Guineas comfortably and then, with no preparatory race over the distance, went straight for the Oaks in which she beat that good filly Ark Royal by six lengths. Then she reverted to a mile for the Coronation Stakes at Ascot, which she won by five lengths from Gloria Nicky.

"Her last race was to be the St Leger, for which she was odds-on favourite. But, by the beginning of September, most of Newmarket had been severely hit by a bad coughing epidemic. We had fifty-two horses in the yard and, on the day that Meld left for Doncaster, fifty-one of them were coughing. I was worried out of my mind. I adored that filly. Somehow, some way I was determined that she should win the fillies Triple Crown and establish for herself the place in history which she deserved. I was up to my arms in disinfectant. Every sort and kind seemed to be everywhere.

"The Captain and Harry Carr had had a terrible month trying to keep Meld isolated, not only from her stable companions but also from horses from other stables, all potential carriers of the cough which, while not serious in itself, necessitated a lay-off of at least a week. If you work a horse with a cough, he is likely to become broken-winded or to incur further symptoms.

"The whole town was in a sorry state. You seldom saw any horses galloping, just long strings walking or trotting, thoroughly depressed. I suppose it was a foretaste of what was to come with the spread of the terrible rhinopneumonitis ('the Virus'). But thirty years ago we were blissfully unaccustomed to such soul-destroying situations.

"During a long dry August, Meld used to go out on her own. We were forever looking for places where we could take her away from the dust. Moreover we had to get sufficient fast work into her before her final great test. Miraculously Meld escaped the cough and I breathed a sigh of relief when I handed her over to George Archibald, the former jump jockey and trainer, who had now become our travelling headman, and watched the box leave for the north.

"After first lot the next morning, the Captain asked me, 'Would you like to go to the Leger, Hobbs?'

"'No, Captain,' I answered, 'not this year, thank you very much.'

"The day wore on with the usual routine, treating the coughers, seeing that disinfectant was spread throughout the yard, making sure that they were all watered, fed and done-up properly before I left for my cottage. I can scarcely remember what I did that morning. It was like a dream. I was in a state of limbo. I could eat no lunch, neither could I bring myself either to watch the race on television or to listen to it on the radio. I got in my little car and went off. I just wanted to be alone.

"At the top of the Waterhall crossroads I stopped. Many years ago a gypsy shepherd boy lost one of his sheep and was so upset that he hanged himself. The Romanies buried him and made a grave for him there, which is now simply known as Boy's Grave. Nobody sees them put there, but from that day to this there are always fresh flowers on the grave.

"This was where I went in my car that September afternoon and sat there with a book until I knew that the race had been run. I drove back to be greeted by the old gardener, waving his arms in the middle of the road, telling me that Meld had won. Lester Piggott, rider of the runner-up, Nucleus, had lodged an objection – unprecedented at that time in a Classic race – which had been considered by the stewards to be frivolous and was overruled with as little delay as possible. Later Harry Carr was to say that, disregarding rumours about her coughing beforehand, he knew in the paddock and on the way to post that Meld was not her true self. He gave her as easy a race as possible and, when she went into a clear lead halfway up the straight, he naturally moved over to the rails. He had neither impeded nor taken the ground of Piggott on Nucleus, who now challenged on the outside but failed by three-quarters of a length to catch our gallant, sickening filly. I learnt that Meld, in fact, coughed in the paddock beforehand and, when she came home I took her temperature. It was 103 degrees. She lay on the floor of her box for forty-eight hours.

"The touts at Newmarket had never liked her because, in her work, she was never spectacular but always did just enough. She was undoubtedly one of the greatest fillies ever to grace the British turf and

I believe that the reason why she did not produce an outstanding animal until Charlottown won the Derby in 1966 was that she had given so much to racing."

When buying horses – and Bruce is one of the most outstanding judges in the world – colour is an important point. He always avoids washy bays and washy chestnuts as much as that rather dirty light-liver chestnut, which frequently characterises a nutty individual. Horses of a washy colour with silver or flaxen manes and tails are apt to be soft. Bruce likes a rich hard bay, brown or grey. Many people hate black ("Isn't it the colour of the funeral horses?" say the Irish) and breeders will always try to describe horses of that colour as brown, if possible. Certainly there have been some pretty vicious blacks of both sexes but, from the time he helped to train Zarathustra, Bruce keeps an open mind.

Zarathustra, who was bred by Sir Harold Gray, was a horse of the highest class. During the four seasons he was in training, he won from five furlongs to two miles five furlongs. A black son of Persian Gulf, he was originally trained in Ireland by Michael Hurley, for whom he won three five-furlong races as a juvenile. The following season he won the Desmond Plate at the Curragh, the Irish Derby and the Irish St Leger. At four he won the Royal Whip at the Curragh and the Chippenham Stakes at Newmarket and, as a five-year-old, after running unplaced in the Irish Lincoln, he came to Freemason Lodge.

He won in succession the Ascot Stakes with 9 stone by five lengths, the July Stayers Stakes at Sandown, the Goodwood Cup and the Shakespeare Stakes at Birmingham. He was second in the Jockey Club Cup. In that race, however, at the end of the season, he cracked a cannon bone and had to have two months in his box.

Bruce says, "The Captain would normally work on Tuesdays, Thursdays and Saturdays. He liked plenty of slow, steady walking and trotting to muscle the horses up. As far as galloping was concerned, a Classic horse would do one bit of work over the distance of his race, but otherwise it would all be work of nine furlongs either on Racecourse Side or, in hard weather, the Limekilns. Before Atlas won the Doncaster Cup he had never run or worked for more than a mile and a quarter.

"From the day that Zarathustra came out of his box sound again as a six-year-old, his campaign was mapped out. He was to win the Gold Cup. The chap who looked after him was particularly fond of the bottle but he never failed to turn up to ride his horse, who had to be exercised both in the morning and again in the late afternoon. As he rode out of the yard, you could always see a quarter bottle in his back pocket! Nevertheless Zarathustra duly won the Ascot Gold Cup, from a strong field which included Cambremer, Tissot, Hornbeam, Atlas,

French Beige and Donald. Eventually his lad signed the pledge and became an excellent travelling headman to Staff Ingham."

As he grew older, winning the Derby became an obsession with the Captain. After Aureole's defeat by Pinza in 1953, he wrote to his famous American owner William Woodward, "We CANNOT win the Derby, second again! No excuse." There had been so many near misses.

I am not anti-bookmakers. After all, I had a very happy association with Bill Hill, who was the biggest of them all. But I would like to see the Australian system adopted here, whereby there are bookmakers on the course and all off-course betting is done through the tote machine.

Bruce has no doubt that the Queen's Mulberry Harbour was doped before the Oaks of 1957, from which she returned "absolutely staggering with eyes glazed". Her Majesty may have been somewhat consoled that her outsider, Carrozza, trained by Noel Murless, won the race. The following year, after Freemason Lodge had won the Two Thousand Guineas with Her Majesty's Pall Mall, Bruce is convinced that one of the greatest animals, Alcide, had suffered the same fate before the Derby. "He was definitely done," says Bruce. "He was a very good horse who would certainly have won the 1958 Derby."

A strongly made medium-sized bay of tremendous quality, Alcide was bred by his owner Sir Humphrey de Trafford, a contemporary of the Captain, who had already been a member of the Jockey Club for nearly forty years and was as keen as his trainer to win the Epsom Classic. Alcide was by Lord Derby's great stayer Alycidon out of the King Salmon mare Chenille, who also bred Lightning, the dam of Parthia.

After Bruce had broken him and got him going, Alcide was given plenty of time, particularly as he was a late foal. In his second and final start as a two-year-old, the prestigious seven-furlong Horris Hill Stakes at Newbury in October, he made up a lot of ground in tremendous style to win by one and a half lengths and was noted by many good judges as the probable winner of the 1958 Derby. That winter there were four Classic colts at Freemason Lodge, Pall Mall, who was obviously, like his sire Palestine, only a miler, and three possible Derby candidates, the Queen's Miner's Lamp, the disappointing Bald Eagle and Alcide.

Although Alcide and Pall Mall were easy to handle, Miner's Lamp was a real problem. Bruce says, "The Captain was away in the United States on leave in the new year and Miner's Lamp was climbing his box and getting worse. Clearly something had to be done, so Captain Moore instructed me to get a goat as a companion for Miner's Lamp to see if that would do any good. We put Miner's Lamp and the goat in adjoining boxes for several days, to get them used to each other, and I then put them in together. A few hours later Tom Pitts, the blacksmith, came rushing up to report that he had heard scuffling in Miner's Lamp's box, had looked in and had been horrified to see that Miner's Lamp was chewing the unfortunate goat and was evidently intending to eat him. So we did not persevere with the experiment! We had to think again and Dr Brook, who had been so successful with Aureole, came down to try to calm Miner's Lamp. He seemed to have some definite effect and we also put a net above him in his box to stop him climbing.

"When racing started, Alcide performed like a true Derby winner, trained by a master. The Captain decided that, although he had plenty of speed, he would miss the Guineas, which Pall Mall duly won, and concentrate on Epsom. His first race of the season, therefore, was the one-and-a-quarter mile Royal Stakes at Sandown on 26th April, when he was beaten a short head by Snow Cat, trained by Noel Murless and ridden by Lester Piggott. Ten days later Alcide won the Chester Vase, which has often been regarded as a Derby trial, but was not particularly impressive.

"Now the Captain knew the strength of his colt and he approached the Derby with real confidence. Alcide's final race before Epsom was the Lingfield Derby trial, in which he displayed his very best form, utterly pulverising his opponents, among whom was Snow Cat, winning by twelve lengths. It was hardly surprising that the money poured on him for the Derby."

Bruce says, "Eight days later, we came to evening stables to find Alcide in his box, standing there in agony. There was a large lump or swelling on his near-side back ribs, reminiscent of what Grey Sovereign had suffered. There is no doubt that he had been 'got at' and had been given a vicious blow which had probably broken a rib. We never established whether he had actually broken anything, but he was in such pain that he could hardly move. He had to be scratched from the Derby, which was won by the Irish outsider Hard Ridden, who had cost Sir Victor Sassoon only 270 guineas as a yearling and was clearly not in the same class as Alcide. Once again the nobblers had succeeded."

After a long rest Alcide reappeared in the Great Voltigeur Stakes at the York August meeting. Starting slowly, as usual, he stormed through his field in the straight to win as he liked by twelve lengths.

Bruce says, "Old Ray Pulford, who had been at the Queen's Hampton Court Stud, had arrived in Newmarket and was watching Alcide's final gallop before the St Leger, over the full mile and three quarters on racecourse side. When they pulled up, Ray said, 'I've never seen anything like that. He'll win the Leger all right. He'll win it with his leg tied up!'

"Betty and I went to Doncaster, where we always stayed with Druie and John Bowett. I watched the race from the little trainers stand above the weighing-in room, with Fulke Walwyn, who had just married Sir Humphrey de Trafford's daughter, Cath. Although he started a hot favourite at 9 to 4 on, Alcide was last round the final bend and, as they turned for home, Fulke said, 'God, Bruce, that horse is no good.' I said, 'Wait a minute.' No sooner were the words out of my mouth than Harry started a long run, came whizzing through on the inside and won by eight lengths, from None Nicer with Nagami third. My word, they cheered him as he entered the unsaddling enclosure. In his reminiscences *Queen's Jockey*, Harry said, 'He was the best colt I have ever ridden but he, and he alone, decided when the time had come in a race to throw off his lethargy and get down to business in earnest.'"

The following year Alcide's target was the Ascot Gold Cup. First time out he was narrowly beaten in the Jockey Club Cup and then, benefiting from that outing, he won the one-and-a-half-mile Victor Wild Stakes at Kempton by twenty lengths, in a time that shattered the course record and was nearly nine seconds below the average for the course. He went on to win the Winston Churchill Stakes at Hurst Park comfortably.

There then occurred another drama at Freemason Lodge. The previous year Sir Humphrey de Trafford had introduced another bay colt, from the same family as Alcide, called Parthia. By Persian Gulf, he was out of Lightning, who was a half-sister to Alcide.

Too big and backward to be raced seriously as a two-year-old, his best performance in his first season was when he finished third in the Dewhurst Stakes at Newmarket. Now, in 1959, he first won the one-and-a-quarter-mile White Rose Stakes at Hurst Park and then the Dee Stakes over the same distance at Chester. He was a lazy colt who did only what was required of him and no more, so that he did not impress the critics but, like Alcide, he duly won the Lingfield Derby Trial and was strongly fancied for the Derby.

Bruce says, "After our experience in 1958, the Captain employed a security man, a nightwatchman, who used to sit in the tack-room, which backed onto our cottage, and periodically patrolled the yard during the night. In the early hours of Sunday morning, there was a violent rattling on the communicating door from the tack-room. I leapt out of bed and ran down to be told by a very shaken security man, 'Alcide has gone! His box door is open and he's gone!'

"'Wait there,' I said and ran upstairs to put on a sweater and a pair of trousers before organising search parties. As I dressed I glanced out of the bedroom window which overlooked the bottom yard and there I saw Alcide having a word with the fillies. I picked up a bridle from the tack-room and, as I went out, I met the secretary, Sue Babbington-Hill, who had heard the commotion, in her dressing-gown. I told her that it was all right, went down, walked quietly up to Alcide, comforted him, talked to him and put on his bridle. Then I brought him back to his box. Clearly someone had let him out. The villains had been in the yard again.

"By now dawn had broken and I knew that all was well. Sue said, 'Somebody must tell the Captain,' obviously hoping that it would not have to be her. 'Leave this to me,' I said, 'I want a vet to see the horse first.' So I telephoned Fred Day, apologised for getting him out so early, told him roughly what had happened and said, 'I don't think there's anything wrong with the horse because he looks perfectly all right from my cursory examination, but I'd like you to see him before I wake the Captain.'

"'Fine,' he said and within minutes had arrived. Fred gave the colt a thorough examination, muttered, 'Someone must have opened the bloody door,' got back in his car and drove off.

"'The old gardener told me as I walked towards the house, 'You'll never wake the Captain. He'll be very cross if you wake him at this hour.'

"'I don't give a damn,' I said. 'I'm going to get him out of bed.' I rattled on the door. 'What's the matter?' said the Captain.

"'I'm sorry to get you out so early, but Alcide has been let out of his box and I found him down with the fillies. He's back in his box, the vet has looked at him and passed him one hundred per cent OK.' The Captain said never another word but went straight back to bed.

"Nobody ever discovered who was responsible but it is a fair assumption that the nobblers made the mistake of going to Alcide instead of Parthia. The two horses were just three boxes apart and there would have been no point in nobbling Alcide at this stage, because there was no ante-post betting on the Gold Cup. On the other hand, if they could have eliminated Parthia as they had done Alcide the previous year, they would once again have reaped a nice harvest in the ante-post market on the Derby.

"Parthia won the Derby all right, achieving their greatest ambitions for Sir Humphrey, the Captain and Harry Carr, who was a very sick man at this time, owing to kidney trouble from too much wasting. There but for the grace of God go I, was my constant thought, remembering how much wasting I had had to do after the war.

"Alcide, who had been held up in his work with a rapped joint, was narrowly beaten in the Gold Cup but scored a tremendous triumph in the King George VI and Queen Elizabeth Stakes at Ascot in July. The next day Harry Carr was in the London Clinic with a temperature of

104, where, under the care of the Queen's doctor, Lord Evans, he spent the next fortnight.

"When Parthia won the Derby, Betty received a silk scarf, with all the Derby winners on it, which she treasures to this day."

The Captain, who had been second on the trainers' list in both 1956 and 1957, was leading trainer for the fifth time in his life in 1958 and now, in 1959, he finished champion once again with prize money of £109,389, running into six figures for the first time ever.

During that winter Bruce and Betty reviewed the situation. Intensely loyal as ever, Bruce had, entirely on his own, reorganised Freemason Lodge and created the wonderful team which had brought it back to its former glory. The Phoenix had risen from the ashes. By the spring of 1960 Captain Bruce Hobbs, MC, had transformed a scruffy shambles into the proudest, smartest string of racehorses in the world. But Bruce himself, with a wife and growing daughter, was getting nowhere at all. He was still "Hobbs" – earning £20 a week and a fiver a winner – rather taken for granted, part of the furniture. He was fond of the Captain and admired the great man immensely. But, at seventy-three, Cecil Boyd-Rochfort showed no sign of retiring. Besides, his tall slim stepson, Henry Cecil, was growing up. Bruce had learnt a lot, given his all, and in his fortieth year could see no future.

Time and again he looked at the letter, in parts curiously worded, which he had received from the Captain back in the winter of 1952.

Freemason Lodge
Newmarket

November 10th

Dear Hobbs,

I have your letter and very pleased you have accepted my offer and will come here, and especially as I have known your family so many years. With regard to salary I really cannot afford more than £10 a week, and I think if you consider it you should earn quite a good income, you have a free house and the coal which we are allowed, light etc. £5 a winner should at least come to another £150 which would be £670 a year. Also my owners are good and give good presents for big winners.

I have the best lot of horses I have had in years so with luck it should be worth a good deal to you.

Trainers today are really making nothing, expenses have gone up so much and I lost a great deal of money last year.

There is no hurry about the house as I will have to give my headman notice and time to get out so the 22nd December should give us both time.

I am sure wise if you can get a good man, and his wife to look after you and I can employ the man in the yard looking after the Hacks and make himself generally useful.

With regard to responsibility I am always here except my holiday once a year and hardly ever go away except racing.

There is another point, if you get on well, and my owners like you there is always the possibility you might take over the stable when I retire and this is a very big asset as I have the finest owners in the country, who only want the best horses.

I have spoken to only two people, Mr John Rogerson who strongly advises you to take it, also Sir Humphrey de Trafford who said he knew you well and hoped you would come to me.

I am sure wise if you could come and see me and look around the place. I am shooting a good deal now racing finished, but give you dates I am sure to be here all day on November 17th, 21st, 24, 25, 26 and whole week December 1st. The other days I am only away for the day as shooting nearby.

By all means bring your hack, I can get rid of one as I have already 6 with ponies for the children and teach the apprentices on.

Yrs faithfully

C. Boyd-Rochfort

Harry Carr says of Bruce that he "is a great horseman, a great disciplinarian and has everything a trainer needs. He has always been very fair with his men. At Freemason Lodge he got all the rights he could for them and they worked hard for him. In those days we were very close. I was living in Murray Lodge until I moved out to my stud in 1959."

But there was no sign of the Captain retiring and now it was clear that he would not be handing over the yard to his assistant. Bruce says, "The whole place had just got on top of me. I'd had eight years flat out and I couldn't see any light at the end of the tunnel. So I thought I must have a change. I had discussed the situation with the Captain and he had told me that he couldn't promise anything. I was just rising forty and I knew that the time had come for me to make a change.

I had an offer from an old family friend, Colonel "Gibby" Gibson of the saddling firm. He asked me to work for him as a salesman with a view to becoming a director of the company. I decided to give it a go and gave six months' notice to the Captain. He was not best pleased and, in fact, it was not for sometime that he became friendly towards me again. I was very fond of him, his beautiful wife and their family. It would have been different perhaps if only he could have given me some help in furthering my own career. No-one was better qualified to do so. But he didn't. I was very sorry that it had to end this way."

During the remaining nine seasons in which he trained, Captain Boyd-Rochfort had to be content with very much less spectacular success. In contrast to his triumphs of that great season, the following year he had only twelve winners of thirteen races worth £18,852.

Chapter Twelve

It gave Bruce no satisfaction to watch the decline of the Captain's fortunes after he left him. "He was a great trainer and I learnt an awful lot from him," he says.

Furthermore, during the time at Freemason Lodge, the rift in their marriage, which had become so serious while they were at Compton, was healed for Bruce and Betty. Bruce explains, "I was only eighteen when war started and, after that completely dedicated horse-orientated upbringing, I was very naive. I loved the Army, working and playing and, make no mistake, I played hard; and when I was demobilised, I was not at all ready for marriage. I was not mature enough to accept the responsibilities and I was still wild. Betty was a saint to stay with me. During my eight years at Freemason Lodge, with all the responsibility thrust upon me as assistant to the Royal Trainer, I began to appreciate the true value of a proper marriage and now accepted my own responsibility towards my wife and child. In other words I grew up. By 1960, when we left Freemason Lodge, I had grown up all right."

At the end of the 1966 season the Queen sent six yearlings into the care of Bruce's friend Major Dick Hern, who was to become the new Royal Trainer. The Royal horses were going back to downland because the village of West Ilsley is close to Bruce's former haunts, Compton and Letcombe.

Harry Carr had retired in the middle of 1964 and in the New Year Honours List of 1968 Captain Boyd-Rochfort was created KCVO. At the end of that season Sir Cecil handed over his string to his stepson Henry Cecil. The last winner that Harry rode was on one of Bruce's horses.

Bruce and Betty moved from Bury Road to tiny Kensington Cottage at Kennett.

Hobblette was now growing into a lovely girl with tremendous charisma who was greatly admired wherever she went. In their quiet way the Hobbs family had made many good friends, as they were soon to discover.

Not only the racing world but also important people outside the industry were worried when Bruce left racing to become a travelling salesman, or "rep" as he would now be known, to a saddler, albeit the master saddler Colonel Gibson. There were even questions asked in the House of Commons about the fact that this talented young man, lacking the necessary financial support, had been forced out of the game. Bruce says proudly, "Yes, I'm even in *Hansard*."

So he travelled the countryside selling saddlery. "I wasn't paid very well but I got by," he says. "They gave me a car and I drove all over the country, visiting old friends, using my name from the jockey world. During the nine months I was there, I sold a lot of tack. When I called on friends, I think the obvious reaction was embarrassment, mostly on their part at finding me in this role.

"What I enjoyed most was seeing the routines of other stables. Some of the things I saw were absolutely horrifying. However, who was I to criticise? I was in the unique position of having been brought up with horses all my life, believing that nothing but the best was good enough for them, and was lucky enough never to have known anything but the best. Now I discovered that there were others less fortunate, less scrupulous, less knowledgeable.

"There were bright moments. One hot June afternoon I went to a rather scruffy little stable, where the trainer had a filly who kept knocking herself behind, with a result that he needed a special boot for her. As we approached this filly in the yard, she had her head over the door with her ears laid back and a wicked look in her eye. The trainer opened the door and told the filly to move back. She turned round with her head in the corner and I thought she was going to kick him but, without turning a hair, he walked straight up between her hind legs to show me what kind of boot he wanted!

"I learnt a great deal about saddlery and it did me a lot of good, giving me time to think without being constantly bound up in racing and routine. Gibby was a past master. He had some wonderful contacts in Walsall who, although some of them were retired, had immense stocks of every kind of saddlery and bit that he might want. I met some fascinating people, including Major Hellyer from Oakham, who introduced me to 'E'-type saddles, the sort without trees, which I have used ever since. I still use rugs and exercise sheets which I bought for £5 and rollers for which I paid the equivalent of 75 pence.

"Gibson's had a good line in pricker boots – leather shin-boots with tin-tacks sticking out to stop horses from chewing their bandages. It is usually only yearlings and two-year-olds who do this. So when a certain famous show-jumping star asked to buy some of these boots, presumably for use on his old stagers, I asked him why. He said, 'I'll turn them inside out with the tin-tacks sticking into their shins. When they hit a pole with those, it'll be better than any form of rapping. Let them feel those nails in their shins and that'll larn 'em. They won't knock one again. They'll jump over the moon rather than have that happen! I'll take several pairs. How much do you want for them?'

"I told him exactly what I thought of him, refused to sell him any, left the yard and have not seen him since."

Bruce was still worried about leaving Freemason Lodge on such bad terms with the Captain. "He was so annoyed when I left that he never even said goodbye. So, after a little while with Gibson's, I was told that there was a job to be done at Freemason Lodge. I said to Gibby, 'Let me do this one.' He remonstrated but I insisted.

"I drove round to Freemason Lodge and asked to see the Captain. He came out and said, 'Hello. How are you?'

"From that day until he died we were very good friends. But I had to make the first move. I asked him what he wanted done, what special saddle he wanted altered or something like that, and luckily Gibson's did the job right. Right up to his death we never stopped writing to each other and, whenever I had a decent winner, the first person to telephone was Sir Cecil."

One of the Hobbs's many friends was old Mrs Cicely Lambton, widow of one of the world's greatest trainers, the Hon. George Lambton, whose autobiography, *Men and Horses I Have Known*, is widely recognised as a classic in racing literature. Cicely Lambton, a raving beauty in her day, was much loved, widely respected and knew everybody in Newmarket.

"One evening Mrs. Lambton asked us to a drinks party," says Bruce. "Suspecting that we were not at all happy, she took Betty on one side and asked her about the situation. Betty told her that I was miserable away from horses and would dearly love to get back into racing. The next thing I knew was a telephone call from Jack Clayton. Norman Bertie's eyesight was going – he was nearly blind – and a new rule said that a trainer must lease his own premises and hold the licence in his own name. Bertie had held the licence for Jack for some years. So now Jack had to take out the licence and asked me to go as his assistant trainer."

Major Jack Clayton, a tall, elegantly dressed man, usually in a grey suit with a white shirt and blue tie, came from an old Northumbrian family, was educated at Eton and Oxford and had become a keen racing enthusiast from the time that his mother and sister moved to Newmarket following his father's death in 1914.

A fearless, but unsuccessful, gambler in his youth, Jack, in 1929, bought the Bedford Cottage yard (now Bedford House where Luca Cumani trains) next door to his mother's home at Newmarket, and formed a private stable. Despite severe injury to a hip in boyhood which prevented him from ever riding a horse, he served with the Welsh Guards during the Second World War while his sister Jane managed the horses at Bedford Cottage.

In 1947 Norman Bertie, who had been travelling headman to the great Fred Darling at Beckhampton, was appointed trainer at Bedford Cottage. That is to say, as with women trainers who were not allowed to hold licences in those days but had to train in the name of a man, Norman held the licence for the stable in the Bury Road on behalf of Jack Clayton. During this time they won the Derby of 1953, as we have seen, with Sir Victor Sassoon's Pinza and the 1951 One Thousand Guineas with Belle of All. Now, in 1961, just as Norman Bertie was going blind, the Jockey Club insisted that Jack should train in his own name. Among Jack's owners was Mrs James A. de Rothschild, for whom Bruce still happily trains today.

Bruce says, "It was roughly the same set-up as at Freemason Lodge except that now, not only did I run the place but I used to work out all the gallops for Jack, discuss things with him the night before and decide what work was to be done. During this period we lived at Green Lodge, a large house looking out over that wide expanse of grass on the Bury side of Newmarket called the Severals.

"I had been told that Jack was a very difficult person, but in two years we never had a cross word. I helped him to train twenty-five winners the first season and eighteen in 1963. I enjoyed it there. Jack was a gentleman in every sense of the word and his sister Jane was a truly lovely person. She was always in the foreground, coming round stables at night with Jack, but she would never interfere in the yard. Right up to her death the other day, she was always Miss Clayton to me and I had the greatest respect for her.

"One of the most popular visitors to Bedford House, as it now was, was Scobie Breasley. The great Australian jockey was always treated like an honoured guest if he deigned to come down to ride for us. One morning we were working on the Limekilns and he kept us waiting for ten minutes. Eventually he arrived in his Rolls and his chauffeur got out, took the rug across his knees and out stepped Scobie to get a proper telling-off from me for being late. He did it again one day when we were working on Racecourse Side and he got the same treatment from me again. Time is time!

"Breasley was one of the few people who could enter 'The Holy of Holies' at Bedford House. He went in through the front door. We went in through the office!

"I advertised in the *Sporting Life* for a headman, and, after several interviews, the one I liked far the best was Brian Lunness. He had served his time with Jack Waugh, who spoke very highly of him as hard-working, honest and intelligent, but at that moment he was out of racing. I took him on. He came to Bedford House and we gave him the bottom yard. Brian and I got on terribly well because he was more of my own age and a very smart chap.

"Miss Clayton was a very sporting lady with a considerable interest in coursing and an incredibly fierce Alsatian, who earned the notice on the gate of Bedford House, 'BEWARE OF THE DOG – THIS IS MEANT!' She was a leading light in the Red Cross, in which she was helped tremendously by Betty and by Sir Jack Jarvis's daughter Vivian, the splendid Commandant of the organisation. We will never forget one particular day when they laid on three cooks to produce a marvellous outing for thirty-five disabled children.

Betty and I loved our time at Green Lodge but, when I saw an advertisement in the Racing Calendar under a box number, seeking a private trainer, I felt that I must apply. I knew that it was David Robinson. There were fifty-four applicants for the job. I told Jack Clayton what I had done and said that I knew that I was under contract to him until the end of the year but that I would like to go for the interview. Typically he said, 'Go with my blessing.' I got the job. I told Jack that I would take only one man with me and that not until the end of the year. I took Brian Lunness as my travelling headman. He was, of course, later to set up training on his own. So I went to David Robinson for the 1963 and '64 seasons."

Many rich men and women have spent fortunes trying to buy success on the Turf. The failures have been plentiful. The tall, square-jawed television-rental tycoon had acquired his love of racing from boyhood when he used to bicycle from Cambridge to Newmarket, fourteen miles away. He bought his first radio shop in 1937 and had twelve shops when the TV-rental boom started in 1954. Thereafter he amassed a fortune and came into racing, determined to make business methods succeed in the sport that was fast becoming an industry.

He never seemed to stay with any one trainer for long, although for a time he appeared to settle down happily with Geoffrey Brooke, who won the 1955 Two Thousand Guineas for him with Our Babu.

Now, having bought twenty-four yearlings at the sales in 1963, he installed Bruce as his private trainer at Carlburg, still in the Bury Road at Newmarket.

"I enjoyed my time with Jack Clayton," Bruce says. "We got on particularly well and, much later, I was very honoured to be asked by Miss Clayton to act as an usher at her brother's funeral. After Jack's death Mrs de Rothschild telephoned to ask if I would have her horses.

A complete circle, because the first winner I ever rode was for her late husband.

"David Robinson had just bought Carlburg from our great friends Fergy and Judy Sutherland. Robinson had paid a lot for the place and was prepared to spend thousands upon it. It was gutted and rebuilt and I was given almost carte blanche to do what I liked, spend what money I wanted and design the yard to suit myself. 'I want it as modern as you can make it,' he said, showing me the plan. I noticed that inside the yard there was to be a pathway with kerb stones and right-angled beds. I said, 'We can't have that.'

"'Why not?'

"'You will have horses walking over those edges, cutting their fetlock joints.'

"This was the trouble all the time with David Robinson. He didn't know horses and, although he had the very best intentions, he had to be guided. I think that even at that early stage I knew that I would never be able to get on the same wavelength as him."

At that time David Robinson was still feeling his way. In ten years' time he would have one hundred and fifty-seven horses, divided between two trainers. In the years between, he was leading owner and, more than once, had over one hundred winners in a season. He was later to form a team of experts, headed by Lord Harrington and Jack Colling as well as a vet and his three private trainers, to advise and buy yearlings, most of which would be early maturing two-year-olds. The team became known as Robinson's Rangers.

Traditionally, successful owners had been horse breeders. But Robinson saw no point in following the Derby, Rosebery, Aga Khan, Boussac and Astor tradition. For one thing it would have taken too long.

"I feel sorry for owners who are landed with unsound horses, some of which never even see a racecourse," Robinson once told me. "We leave any chance as far away as possible and never buy unsoundness. Any horse with an 'if' is struck out right away. We may have some who WON'T race – but virtually none who CAN'T. My team, Robinson's Rangers, work hard and are worth their weight in gold."

The team would buy about fifty yearlings each autumn and a number of foals. But selection was not enough. The Robinson formula for planned improvement and success would then take over. His three stables would be adjacent and inter-linked, each trainer having about forty horses. The animals would be graded into three colours on their ability; red for outstanding, blue for good and green for fair. All the horses would be graded red as two-year-olds and regraded after they had shown their ability on the racecourse. Therefore, they could earn colour promotion or relegation, but only on racecourse performance.

Racecourses would be similarly graded and only red horses ran at the ten red courses in Britain, blue at the twelve blue courses and the remainder at green courses. Even jockeys would be graded. He said, "I change the system only if there is a big race; say at a green meeting, then a red horse might drop in class."

The nerve-centre would be the operations room that linked the stables. Briefing would take place every Sunday morning. Each of the three trainers would study the Racing Calendar, listing the races they considered suitable and making their case at the weekly conference. Robinson and Roy Allen, an old business associate, would then make the decisions. The operations room would have a list of all the meetings for the next two months.

One wall would have a list of all his horses over the age of two. Another would have a list of two-year-olds. Plaques would denote suggested entries, and pegs indicated definite runners. Each horse would have his form figures attached to his name. Robinson and his team would be able to tell at a glance the efficiency and progress of any animal. Apart from the stimulus that he imparted to the bloodstock sales, David Robinson's great value to racing was that he provided several hundred runners during the season, everyone of them a trier. Although his annual outlay on yearlings was enormous, it was reckoned that if one or two turned out top-notchers, they would cover the cost of the remainder when sold as stallions.

Robert Sangster has since admitted to me that this example inspired him to initiate his own operation on a far higher scale, buying the most likely potential stallions in the world as yearlings, racing them, and either standing them at stud or selling those that realised their potential, thereby showing a considerable profit on his multi-million pound outlay and at the same time creating a worldwide Turf empire.

But then Robert Sangster knows about horses. David Robinson did not in the same way, and therein lies the difference.

Unfortunately, because of Robinson's lack of specialist knowledge, even those members of the racing establishment who tried to understand him – and there were some, Bruce included – could never really see eye to eye with him.

But all this was in the future, after Robinson had dispensed with Bruce's services, and the only thing that mattered to Bruce when he started training for Robinson was that he was at last training in his own name on the Flat.

"Keith Freeman had been buying the horses at that time," Bruce says. "I had got to know him well during my days with the Captain and he had become a very good friend. We liked the same type of animal and hit if off straight away. I hoped that I would last three years with David Robinson because I realised that he was paying good money for well-bought horses and, if I couldn't train that sort of animal, then I didn't deserve to have a training licence.

"It took me a long time to have my first winner and I could feel the Robinsons becoming edgy. However, it came in the end on Saturday May 16th 1964 at Newmarket when Harry Carr won the Blue Peter Stakes for maiden two-year-olds with Mr David Robinson's Ward Drill, 'Trained B. Hobbs, Newmarket'. It was a great thrill.

"We had the advantage of living in the big house at Carlburg, while the Robinsons lived some way away in a little village called Westoning, about six miles outside Bedford on the way to Woburn at a house called Flitwick Manor. He had a secretary called Miss Umney who kept a constant finger on the pulse and at the end of every month I used to get a costing. This stated what it had cost to feed each horse and informed me that perhaps I was using too much hay or not enough straw. I think it was all very good for me and I know that it was to help me in the long-run when I set up on my own.

"By the end of the season several horses hadn't run, which niggled Mr Robinson, but we had had nineteen winners and he appeared to be satisfied. Indeed, he took us to Scotland for a week's fishing and David and Mabel Robinson were very kind. You could never talk business to him after seven o'clock at night. As soon as he had had his first drink, that was it. As a very busy man, he liked to relax after work."

The second season, 1965, when Sea Bird II won the Derby, was not much fun for Bruce. "I was too 'Newmarket' for David Robinson," he says. "I just couldn't adapt myself to his business methods. I imagine it would have been different if he had had any feeling for or understanding of horses, but, as it was, I couldn't communicate with him the way he expected me to. I was too much of a horseman and not enough of a businessman. That's really where we clashed."

Nevertheless, there were certain significant advantages in the set-up. Realising after a short while that a new headman was required, Robinson and Bruce had advertised in the *Sporting Life* and received an application from Ted Molyneux, whom Bruce had met as a staff sergeant in the Veterinary Corps, looking after remounts in the Middle East. He was at this time with the Didcot trainer J. C. Waugh, who independently wrote to Bruce recommending him. Ted became almost part of the Hobbs family and stayed with them until he retired through ill-health sixteen years later.

Then there was Suvretta, with whom Bruce won four consecutive races during the season, including the Hare Park Handicap at Newmarket on Thursday, 8th July, a momentous day in the history of British racing because, for the first time, under the guidance of Jockey Club Steward Tom Blackwell, who always had the best interests of racing at heart, starting-stalls were used.

Critics of stalls, including old-timers like Sir Jack Jarvis, were silenced in fifty seconds on Newmarket Heath. This was the time that it took to start the Chesterfield Stakes from the moment that the starter, Alec Marsh, called the twelve runners in until he pressed the button and they flew out of their stalls, galloping straight and true. So great was the interest in the first British starting-stalls event that five hundred people walked the six furlongs from the Newmarket stands down to the start to watch. As anticipated, the secret of the stalls' success was the surprising sense of anti-climax. It was all so quiet, simple and superbly efficient. Seven of the twelve jockeys had no experience of stalls. One was a 7lb.-claiming apprentice. One two-year-old had never run before.

Gone were all the old shouting and the jostling, the kicking and cursing as the starter called the horses in. Gone were the crossing and the bumping as they left the gate.

Lester Piggott, who had considerable experience of stalls outside Britain, got slightly the best of the break and duly won on Track Spare. Great Nephew, now one of the world's most famous stallions, who had behaved badly before the start at Epsom and Ascot when he had shown a marked dislike for the old-fashioned starting-gate, being left on both occasions, now came out splendidly to finish third.

Before the race Great Nephew's trainer, Sir Jack Jarvis, had said, "Regardless of the result I think stalls are awful." Afterwards he commented reluctantly, "Well, I suppose they might be all right for short races."

This was yet another year when British racing was desperately troubled by coughing and Bruce did outstandingly well for David Robinson. But by 20th August when he scored his twenty-third victory of the season with My Swanee at Lingfield, he was already under orders to go, and his successor had been named as Jimmy Thompson, the former jockey who rode well in the north and for a time in France before losing the sight of one eye.

"It got to the stage where David Robinson said that he wouldn't buy me any yearlings. I was called to Bedford and told that our association was not working out and that I ought to resign. I had been advised not to resign and so, in the end, David Robinson gave me three months' notice. I don't in any way want to knock the Robinsons. They were very upright, honourable people and everything at all times was absolutely above board with the staff."

Although David Robinson had never shown any wish to take part in the administration of racing, he bought Kempton Park in 1969, hoping to give the racing world the benefit of his ideas of how a modern racecourse ought to be run. This might have been a tremendous shot in the arm for British racing, providing a blueprint for the future and an example for other courses to live up to. However, lacking support from the areas that mattered, planning permission was not forthcoming and Kempton went on much the same as before until Mr Robinson resold it to the Levy Board.

"So I served out my three months' notice," says Bruce, "and left. I insisted that one of the directors should come and see the house before I handed over the keys. We had the house scrubbed from top to bottom; there wasn't a thing out of place and the yard was immaculate. David Robinson came over, shook hands and said goodbye. There was no bitterness, no rancour. We both respected each other but there was no way in which we could ever see eye to eye. He took my daughter cruising in Italy and took us fishing in Scotland. I owe him a lot. He was very good to me. He is still alive, living in the area, and on the rare occasions when we see each other on the road, we wave, although I haven't spoken three words to him since. He had one hundred and fifty horses and now he has none. He never used to come and see them saddled or visit them in the box. He was paying me a fair salary, with a company car and all expenses, including light and fuel in the house. I had trained forty-five winners and many placed horses in my own name during the two seasons. That was what really mattered. Furthermore, although we had to surrender the company car and had nowhere to live, we were at last in the black with the bank.

"Moreover, on the home front things had taken a happy turn. Our darling daughter Hobblette had fallen terribly in love with the best young man whom Betty and I could ever have chosen for her. Charles Dimsdale, born and bred at the family home in Hertfordshire, is the direct descendant of the first Baron Dimsdale, who was honoured for vaccinating Catherine the Great of Russia. He is also the grandson of Kitty Barclay, whose father Edward founded the Puckeridge Foxhounds. They married in February."

Chapter Thirteen

Three hundred years after King Charles II inaugurated the Newmarket Town Plate, Bruce Hobbs moved into Palace House Stables where the Merry Monarch kept his horses. By the end of May 1965 the Hobbses knew that they would be leaving David Robinson. In fact, Bruce stayed on at Carlburg until the end of the season in November. But, naturally worried about the forthcoming loss of Bruce's job and the fact that once again they would have nowhere to live, Betty telephoned Joan Gray, who, with her husband Colonel Douglas Gray, shortly to become Director of the National Stud, had become such good friends.

"Joan immediately came down to see me," says Betty, "and, after considerable thought, I told her that what we would like most would be to find some people to form a syndicate to back Bruce as a trainer. Within a few days she came back to me and asked if Bruce could meet Tom Blackwell at Epsom on Derby Day."

That was a good Derby Meeting for Bruce. On the first day at Epsom, he won the Ashtead Stakes with Suvretta and, in the prestigious St James's Stakes immediately after the Derby, David Robinson's Enrico, trained by Bruce and ridden by Jimmy Lindley, beat Alan Adare, the mount of Lester Piggott, by half a length. So the omens were particularly auspicious when, primed by a double at one of the world's greatest fixtures, Bruce in his top hat and morning coat kept his rendezvous with Tom Blackwell, who was at the time a very active and popular Steward of the Jockey Club.

Tom Blackwell lived at Langham Hall, Bury St Edmunds, where he had built a stud in 1960. After Harrow, he had gone to Cambridge and was a contemporary there of Henry Cecil's father and Simon Lycett-Green, Major Frank Beale, later of the British Bloodstock Agency, and John Dimsdale, the well-known amateur rider, who would have been

Hobblette's father-in-law if he had not been killed in a steeplechase at Huntingdon. Developing a lively interest in racing at an early age, Tom had many winners trained for him by Geoffrey Barling before the war and, on the outbreak of hostilities joined the Coldstream Guards.

His considerable business experience, combined with much energy and determination, subsequently made him a most effective Turf administrator. He was Steward of the Jockey Club from 1964 to 1966 and, as Senior Steward in 1966 was largely responsible for the introduction of starting-stalls. In 1974 he headed the Jockey Club committee which surveyed the entire question of manpower in the racing industry.

Tom, whose recent death has been such a blow to us all, was the most hospitable of men, loving to share the good things of life with his friends. Unlike most racing men, moreover, he was particularly well-known in the golfing world. He won the Jubilee Vase at St Andrews at an early age and for several years played for the old Harrovians in the Halford Hewitt Cup. He was Captain of the Royal and Ancient Golf Club. Apart from other business interests, he was Chairman of Turf Newspapers Limited and formerly a Director of Tote Investors Limited.

Colonel Douglas Gray says, "When I suggested Bruce to Tom Blackwell, I told him that here was a man who was not only an outstanding trainer but possessed quite exceptional integrity."

As a result Tom Blackwell formed a company consisting of himself, Jocelyn Hambro, Jim Philipps, and David Wills. After much discussion they took a lease on Palace House Stables. Bruce has since joined the Board as a director.

Major Jocelyn Hambro, MC, a banker of international repute, was educated at Eton and, like Tom, served during the war in the Coldstream Guards, being severely wounded in Normandy in 1944. His intelligence, business experience and enthusiasm have made him an invaluable asset to the Jockey Club. At this time his mares were kept with Tom Blackwell at Langham Hall Stud. His trainer was Geoffrey Brooke.

The Honourable Jim Philipps, third son of the late Lord Milford, whose racing interests he inherited, including the Dalham Hall Stud at Newmarket, was also educated at Eton and had a great deal of experience in the administration of racing and of the Tote. Originally, like his father, Jim Philipps was a patron of Sir Jack Jarvis's stable but there was a rift over the career of Great Nephew, who was soon to leave Newmarket for the Chantilly stables of Etienne Pollet.

David Wills, another old Etonian who had served in World War Two with the Cameron Highlanders, owned Hadrian Stud at

Newmarket, where he bred Tomy Lee, winner of the Kentucky Derby. Another Jarvis owner, the best racehorse to carry his colours was Happy Laughter who won the One Thousand Guineas in 1953.

"At last Betty and I knew where we were going," says Bruce, "With any ordinary luck this would be our last move."

Go down that narrow little lane parallel to Newmarket High Street, round the back of the famous Rutland Arms Hotel and past Nell Gwyn's Cottage, and there, on the left, are the gates of Palace House opposite the steps of the old palace. A secret underground passage is reputed to connect Palace House with Nell Gwyn's Cottage but nowadays Charles would not have to go there to collect his oranges, because, just at the top of the lane, so close to Palace House that Betty calls it her deep freeze, is Waitrose, where all Newmarket society now seems to meet.

During the war Palace House stable-yard had been commandeered by the Army, with Jewish refugees billeted in the house. It was then leased by Harry Jelliss junior, who trained there for Dorothy Paget. When his horses left and the stables were empty, Jack Jarvis took it on as his second yard, employing Jelliss, who was living in Palace House, as his assistant.Jack Jarvis, whose main training establishment was Park Lodge, gave up Palace House in 1964 and soon Harry Jelliss moved out.

During their moves first from Tyler's Cottage, then to the large house, Green Lodge, and even larger Carlburg, Bruce and Betty had collected plenty of furniture including, with the help of their parents, some very attractive antiques. So, that winter, when Palace House was being done up ready for them to move in, they had the wherewithal to furnish it.

Betty says, "Knowing that we were leaving Carlburg with nowhere to go for the winter, General Poole's widow Margaret, who lived next door to Freemason Lodge and had become a very good friend of ours, offered us her house for the whole of that winter, during which she was going to the United States to stay with her daughter. Not only her house, but her cook as well! Sadly that nice house has now been pulled down and the site belongs to Freemason Lodge. Margaret Poole is now dead. Other friends who rallied round during this period were Geoff and Joan Hull. He had been a regular Gunner and was now managing Someries Stud, while she was the daughter of the famous vet, Brayley Reynolds. Geoff died a while ago, but his wife and children are still good friends of ours.

"Then there were Hugh and Ann Rosselli. He is a cousin of Sir Thomas Pilkington and that is how Tommy came into our lives."

Bruce says, "Tommy has had horses with me for ten years now. He and his beautiful wife Sue live near Hitchin, where they have a fabulous estate. His mother, Liz Burke, of Stackallan Stud, County Meath, knew me as a small boy in Leicestershire.

"Ever since our association with the Rogersons – remember that Eileen Rogerson was a Joel – we had been very friendly with and fond of Paddy and Dana Brudenell-Bruce. Dana, also a Joel, was the niece of Eileen Rogerson. One evening when I was out, Paddy came down to Carlburg and asked Betty where I was. He said he had just come round to say that if we needed a couple of horses to get us going, he would love to send us them. So, at the sales, I bought for him Wandering Eyes, one of the first animals I had trained for David Robinson. I paid only 2,000 guineas for him and also bought them a yearling as well by King's Bench. Both horses won.

"At the end of his four-year-old season, although Wandering Eyes was still winning, Paddy told me, 'From now on, that's your horse. Anything you win is yours.' He gave this good, genuine horse to me. As time went on, there were increasing enquiries to buy him, particularly for New Zealand because he was by one of their favourite stallions, Palestine. Clarence Hailey was trying to do the deal and every time he approached me, I put the price up. In the end I couldn't say no. He went out to New Zealand and was champion sire with his first crop. He was what I call a fun horse. In the winter I used to ride him myself. He couldn't bear rain or snow on his face and so we had to put him at the back of the string. He would twist his head away as soon as anything came down from the sky. Paddy and Dana are a wonderful couple, who have helped many people over difficult times, quietly and discreetly.

"It's incredible to think that when I started at Palace House, I was charging 17 guineas a week in training fees. Now my fees are £120 basic. Apart from the company who set me up – Jim Philipps, David Wills and Tom Blackwell were already sending me horses and Jocelyn Hambro was to do so when Geoffrey Brooke retired the following year – a number of very good owners came to me. Mrs Jules (Patsy) Bricken, an American who had had horses in Ireland with Stuart Murless but never before in England, came to me.

"I was a bit doubtful when William Hill, the bookmaker, asked me to train for him and I asked Tom Blackwell, who was, remember, at that time a Steward of the Jockey Club, but he said that he didn't mind. William and I got on terribly well. As I was starting, I got the yearlings that he had bred which did not fetch their reserve in the sale ring. I learnt a great deal from him, particularly when he told me, 'First win an egg-and-spoon race and then we can start upgrading the horse.'

"One of the first two horses I had from him came from Bill Elsey's stable. This was a filly by Ballymoss called Ice Ballet, who had been placed as a two-year-old but had arthritis of her knee. She was a nice grey mare, and I had her covered by Romulus while she was still in training. Carrying her foal, she won at Alexandra Park on the Monday and at Beverley on the Friday of the same week. Then she produced a grey filly foal.

'When she went up to the sales William told me, 'Bid this filly up to 2,000 guineas but if you get on the wrong leg, it doesn't matter.' I got on the wrong leg and the filly was knocked down to me. So there I was stuck with her, when one of my owners, Mrs Tony (Clare) Villar, came up and said, 'Who is that for?' I said, 'I don't know, do you want it?'

"'Yes,' she said. The filly turned out to be Tanara, who won four races and was the dam of Count Pahlen, the handsome grey colt who most appropriately won the William Hill Futurity at Doncaster in 1981.

"When we moved into Palace House on 7th February, 1966, two days after Hobblette's wedding, we had thirty-five horses. My first two-year-old runner from the yard was Eric The Red, owned by the famous actor Peter O'Toole. It was a great start because he won the Blue Mantle Stakes at Ascot on 2nd April by a short head.

"Another of my first owners at Palace House was our old friend Julian Wilson, the excellent BBC racing correspondent.

"Ted Molyneux had come with me and was a tower of strength as my headman. The apprentices whom I had signed on at Carlburg were indentured to me and not to David Robinson, and so I was acting within the Rules of Racing when I took them with me. Geoffrey Brooke very kindly looked after them during that winter."

By the start of the 1967 season Bruce had sixty horses stabled in two separate yards. To judge his immense popularity and the goodwill which he had engendered during the time when he and Betty had been struggling, here is a list of his owners at the start of his second season:

Mrs W.M. Impey; Miss O. Bridges; Mr Frank S. Burton; Mrs J. Bricken; Mrs C. Brudenell-Bruce; Mr T.F. Blackwell; Lady Carton de Wiart; Mr E.R. Charles; Mr Ralph Colman; Mr A. Dormer; Lt. Col. N.E. Frieze; Captain G. Fane, DSC; Mrs C.H. Gosling; Mrs Vernon Harriss; Mr William Hill; Mr R.E. Hibbert; Lt. Col. G.H. Illingworth; Captain G. Booth-Jones; Mr J. Kenny; Mr Peter Larkin; Sir Martin Lindsay, Bart., CBE, DSO; Mr J.M.E. Lowinsky; Mr Stanhope Joel; Mr R.B. Moller; Major and Mrs J.P. Philipps; Lady Susan Pilkington; Mr and Mrs John Rogerson; Mr O.H. Rosselli; the Marquess of Tavistock; Mr H.D.H. Wills; Mr J.H. Weller-Poley; Mr Alan Walker; Mr Frank Yardley; Mr A.W.N. Lake; Captain M.T.H. Wills; Mr Peter O'Toole; Mr Julian Wilson.

Bruce had twenty-three winners in 1966 and twenty-six the following year.

After her honeymoon in France, the Hobblette had left for Kenya, where Charles was a land agent. "Her departure left a great hole in our lives," says Bruce.

Bruce is lucky to have had a steady supply of potentially high-class horses, not only from his fellow directors, of whom Jocelyn Hambro has now established a splendid Waverton on the site of William Hill's Sezincote and stands his successful stallions Vaigly Great and Monsanto there, but also from the studs of other owner-breeders.

In addition, Bruce goes to all the yearling sales in England and sometimes in Ireland. Over the years his buying has impressed me so much that I now rate him as the best judge of a yearling in the country.

One of the most important factors affecting buying at the yearling sales is to get your eye in. The real experts will have been looking at yearlings round the studs for some weeks, if they can spare the time away from their training stables. But even they must keep looking at lots of yearlings to tune their eye after seeing older horses every day.

The true-born horseman, Bruce does not allow himself to pre-judge an animal on the strength of the catalogue. "In my opinion conformation is ninety-nine per cent of the business," he says. "The Stud Book doesn't matter as much as people think. If the yearling looks right to my eye, then if the pedigree fits, I'll bid for him. In fact, I take a chance with a horse with a moderate pedigree if I like his looks.

"Although I have had a great deal of success in two-year-old races, I do not by any means regard myself as a two-year-old trainer like, say, Atty Persse or Paddy Prendergast. I cannot force horses. In fact I don't usually have a two-year-old winner until the second Newmarket Meeting – the Guineas fixture. And I'm not really fussy about distance. When buying horses, once I've found the individual and the pedigree fits, I don't mind whether it's a sprinter or a stayer so long as I've got the right sort of customer for that animal.

"Very often I buy horses on my own, but if I have a specific order to fill, then it may not be quite so easy. I may have found something else which I like, then I ring up the man who has given me the commission and say, 'I'm sorry, I haven't got quite what you wanted but in my opinion this is a particularly nice horse and I should think he will be a winner.' Nine times out of ten he'll say, 'All right, let's have a go.'"

In order to get his eye in, Bruce, unlike many of his rivals, likes to go to the Doncaster St Leger Sales, which always start the round of public auctions in this country and Ireland. "I like to go there, not only to get my eye in but because there are also nice horses to be bought there if you take your time.

"In general I hate spending big money on yearlings. I've done that only once and I don't regret it. The horse was Eva, Lady Rosebery's Crested Grebe, by Blakeney, who won as a two-year-old over a mile at Sandown, beating twenty-three rivals. He cost 40,000 guineas.

"I suppose that Hotfoot, the first horse I bought for Tony Villar and his mother, Betty Fyfe-Jameson, for only 3,000 guineas, has given me particular pleasure."

Racing from two to four years old, Hotfoot won nine good races and £32,298 in England alone. When he retired in 1970, Hotfoot was syndicated at £3,500 a share, giving him a stallion value of £140,000.

By the start of the 1984 stud season Hotfoot, who stands nearby at Pat McCalmont's Gazeley Stud, Newmarket, had sired the winners of 527 races and £1,439,962, including Hot Grove who was so narrowly defeated in the Derby by The Minstrel, Tachypous who, trained by Bruce, won the Middle Park Stakes and was runner-up in the Two Thousand Guineas, Free State and Count Pahlen.

It is quite remarkable how, throughout his training career, Bruce has managed to achieve Classic status for horses which he has bought for so little. Hotfoot, after all, finished second in the Irish Two Thousand Guineas. Speaking of the owners, Bruce says: "We met them through Colonel Denzil Holder, owner of the Upend Stud. They had never had a horse on the Flat and Tony wanted to share a horse with his mother, thinking that it would cheer her up after the death of her husband. So he came to us in our second season and I bought him Hotfoot. Other good horses I've had for the Villars have been Touch Paper, whom I bought for very little money at Doncaster and trained to win the Stewards Cup at Goodwood, and Take A Reef, whom I also bought cheaply with Tony. He was top of the three-year-old Free Handicap.

"Another one which gave me great pleasure to train was a little filly for whom I paid 1,250 guineas called Catherine Wheel. She was the first horse that I bought for Tom Blackwell. Catherine Wheel finished third in the One Thousand Guineas won by Sir Noel Murless's top-class filly Altesse Royale, and won the Musidora Stakes at York and the New Ham Stakes and Nassau Stakes at Goodwood. Since I started, I have been placed in the first three in no fewer than eleven English Classic races.

"My first stable jockey was Stan Clayton, the best judge of a gallop that I have ever known. He could tell me more in two seconds than the majority of them could in twenty minutes. He then became my assistant trainer for two or three years before Edward Hide's brother, Tony, came to join me.

"John Gorton, the South African jockey, came next but initially was not particularly good with the staff. Once he overcame the problem, however, he got on very well. Geoff Lewis, who succeeded him, was always great value and we got on very well together."

All the time Ted Molyneux was still with Bruce as headman. "I brought him on from David Robinson's. He was a brilliant feeder and a very good organiser. We referred to him affectionately as 'Nanny' because he was so good at nursing horses. He was a complete master of his craft and utterly reliable. Unhappily he had a serious heart attack and had to retire, although he kept on working for as long as he could. Ted will always be a great friend of ours.

"Jocelyn Hambro came to me as soon as Geoffrey Brooke retired. In 1968 Jack Jarvis died. When Betty saw him a week beforehand, he told her that he had not much longer to live. Betty said, 'Don't be so stupid,' but he said, 'I can't wait to go and join little Ethel.' Ethel, his wife, had died several years earlier and had sadly not lived to see Jack receive his richly deserved knighthood.

"He died on the 18th December, just as he was preparing for his annual holiday in South Africa. He had trained for the Roseberys for nearly fifty years. First for the only man ever to win a Derby while Prime Minister of England and then for the fifth Earl, Harry Rosebery, for whom he won the Derby with Blue Peter and Ocean Swell."

When Bruce took over Park Lodge and the Rosebery horses, he got on particularly well with the grand old man, who had been such a conspicuously successful captain of Surrey. "Lord and Lady Rosebery were so delightful to us," says Bruce. "Whenever we went to dinner with them, I would first bring up old cricket history to help the conversation. At the very mention of the names of C. B. Fry and Archie Trumper, his Lordship's eyes would light up. He had a wonderful brain and it was fascinating to talk to him. The one thing he always wanted with his horses was for them to run often. He was especially keen for them to appear at his favourite Scottish courses, Ayr and Musselburgh (Edinburgh), and luckily I was able to provide him with a fair number of winners in Scotland."

While training for Lord Rosebery, Bruce had more than a hundred horses to supervise in three separate yards, Park Lodge, Palace House and Albert House. "I like to get round all my horses at least once a day," he says.

At the Rosebery dispersal sale Bruce bought Chil the Kite for Lady Rosebery and did very well with the horse. "He won for us at Ascot, Goodwood, York and Ayr," he says, "before he was shipped to America. Lady Rosebery has had horses with me ever since. I can't tell you what an incredible enthusiast Lord Rosebery was. In August 1973, the year before his death at the age of ninety-two, I won the Gordon Stakes for him at Goodwood with Duke of Ragusa. I thought

I was pretty quick getting down to the winners enclosure but Lord Rosebery, in his wheel-chair, was there first!"

Bruce maintains that, during that period, he was the first English-based trainer to have more than a hundred horses in his charge. "When I took over Park Lodge and was spring-cleaning the entire place, I discovered all the old white coats which the lads used to wear at evening stables in the old days. One of the best horses I trained for Lord Rosebery was Tom Cribb, who was quite a challenge because he was savage. But, I mastered him all right and we won some decent races with him, including the Northumberland Plate."

Chapter Fourteen

"'The Way to the Stars' – that's what Stilvi means in Greek and that's how Betty and I feel about that wonderful mare and the family who own her. They, Tom Blackwell and Jocelyn Hambro became part of our lives."

Back in 1945 it had been the Rogersons who had come to the resue of the disillusioned young officer, frustrated by weight from returning to the only life that he had known outside the Army. John and Eileen had set him up as a trainer. Throughout all the vicissitudes of Bruce's life since those days at Letcombe, they had remained steadfastly loyal. Now, in 1970, a quarter of a century later, the vital shot in the arm which every trainer needs came from their daughter, Valda, and her husband Nick Embiricos, better known now as the owners of Bob Champion's fabulous Grand National winner Aldaniti.

Nick was a business associate and close friend of George Cambanis, a tall, dark, quietly-spoken Greek shipowner with twinkling brown eyes and a wonderful sense of humour, a gift which he shared with his delightful tall wife Lenior, whose father had been aide to the King of Greece and who herself was Lady-in-Waiting to Queen Frederika. Bearing one of the proudest and most respected names in their native country, the Cambanises had suffered badly during the German occupation. Their family home and stud is at Pikermi, a small village about twenty kilometres from Athens. George, a senior member of the Greek Jockey Club, who had previously trained in England with the late Joe Lawson, asked Nick Embiricos to recommend another Englishman who would buy and train horses to carry the famous "black, white spots" – the Cambanis colours. With complete confidence Nick nominated Bruce.

George Cambanis went to Kempton Park one Saturday to inspect Nick's choice. Later he was to admit, "I saw a man whom I thought to be Hobbs and didn't like the look of him at all. Luckily, when I opened the *Sporting Life* on Monday morning, it carried a picture of Bruce and I knew that I had seen the wrong chap. Just as well, because I couldn't possibly have sent horses to that other man!"

When the letter arrived from Greece asking him to buy two yearlings, Bruce's secretary Eric Rhodes, who had been with Joe Lawson, told Bruce what wonderful owners the Cambanises were.

"How right he was!" Bruce agrees. "Without exaggeration I can say that they have always been pure heaven for us. I don't think we have ever met any more sincere, genuine people than George, Lenior and the members of their family.

"In those days the larger October Open Yearling Sales were held at Newmarket in the first week of October and Tattersalls' more select Houghton Sales a fortnight later. At the first sale I bought Palestis, who went on to win three races and was successful at stud in Greece. George Cambanis was coming over for the Houghton Sales and was anxious to see what I was going to buy for him. I got more and more worried when he failed to turn up and my nap selection, a really athletic bay filly by Derring-Do out of Djerella, with big ears on a lovely head and powerful quarters, was already parading and would shortly be going into the ring. George arrived just in time, inspected the filly, approved my selection and instructed me to go to 6,000 guineas, which was a fair price at the time. He stood with me as I bid for this wonderful walker with her long sweeping stride. At 5,800 guineas I was 'on the wrong leg' and my bid was capped at 6,000 guineas. He nudged me and I went to 6,200, at which figure she was knocked down to me. Ryan Price and Mick Easterby were the underbidders. I don't believe that Mick has got over it to this day!

"We broke her, and the very first time I watched her coming up the yearling canter on Warren Hill, bringing her hind legs right underneath her, I knew that here without a doubt was a true racehorse. I ran Stilvi for the first time in the five-furlong Wills Embassy Stakes on the Rous course at Newmarket on May 29th, 1971. Ridden by John Gorton, she made all the running. Five lengths in front of her field at halfway, she won as she liked. Stilvi went on to win the Star Stakes and the prestigious National Stakes at Sandown, where she lost ground by jumping the road on both occasions.

"Although she went wrong for a while towards the end of that season, she made a splendid comeback in her first race of 1972, the six-furlong Duke of York Stakes at York in May, winning by a short head and a neck from Shiny Tenth and Royal Captive, shooting out of the stalls and leading for five furlongs, but tiring in the final furlong and only just holding on.

"In the King George Stakes at Goodwood two months later, she put up a magnificent performance, rallying in great style under pressure throughout the final furlong and getting up on the post to beat David Robinson's top-class sprinter Deep Diver by a short head. In doing so she broke the five-furlong course record on the famous Sussex track. Stilvi was runner-up in both her other races, including the Nunthorpe Stakes at York in August. Described by *Timeform* as, 'very genuine', she earned a high rating in that publication of 130. Betty became particularly fond of Stilvi and they still get on well together."

Betty says, "We have the most wonderful affinity, which started in a very simple way. I often go round the yard after lunch – before the horses start their daily nap – just talking to them through the bars. After a time Stilvi would always neigh when she heard me coming. She used to love to see me. As she was going to live at Pat McCalmont's Gazeley Stud near here, where another of my favourites, Hotfoot, stands as a stallion, I suggested to Bruce that if Stilvi's owner, George Cambanis, agreed and the blood-lines were right, it would be a great opportunity for a 'marriage of convenience'. George, such a sweet man, and Bruce, the expert, agreed with my idea. My love affair with Stilvi resulted in her producing a top-class first foal called Tachypous, who lived up to his Greek name of 'Swift Foot'."

Bruce says, "Tachypous was a cracking good horse and we have not seen the best of him yet as a stallion. This fine, rangy, most attractive first foal of Stilvi's stands 16 hands 1 inch."

Here was obviously a true racehorse like his dam. The winter months pass slowly for a Flat-race trainer until the steady cantering begins. This is the first stage of building preparation before, as they say in Ireland, "steeling them into their fast work." Now begins the most exciting stage of a trainer's life, when he will learn whether any of his geese are likely to be swans. For a few weeks, until he has the chance of testing them against other people's horses, he can dream, and dreams are the stuff of which racing is made – "They all go fast past posts and bushes" is the cynical old phrase, but while they are doing so, it can be immensely exciting. Some three-year-olds will have improved out of all recognition since their two-year-old days. The backward horse, whom you did not hurry last season, will reward your patience by revelling in work over a longer distance. The cheapest yearling that you suspected might go a bit now confirms your hope.

Knowing and loving Stilvi, Bruce could barely restrain his impatience to see whether her first foal, her beautiful son, had inherited her brilliance. A true horseman like Bruce, riding out on his hack with the string, can see so much more than the trainer who goes to the gallops in a motor-car. He can talk to the lads, see the horses in their slow paces and appreciate how they feel. Bruce has always insisted on wearing a hard hat as an example to the lads. "I know that it may not look as good as a tweed cap," he says, "but what does that matter? It's much more important that the trainer should show that he too needs protection for his head, in case, as has happened many times, he should fall from his hack. If the lads are compelled to wear head protection – quite rightly, in my opinion – then the trainer should do so as well."

Bruce has been very lucky with his hacks. Having been used to Finnure, when he arrived at Palace House Bruce telephoned his old friend Frenchy Nicholson. "I said, 'Frenchy, I haven't got a hack. Can you help?' He said, 'I've just the thing for you, a horse called Buffer belonging to Lady Sefton, who was unbeaten in five steeplechases at Sandown, and winner in all of sixteen races'. When he arrived with me he was eleven years old and he was twenty-five when I had to have him put down. Then, knowing that he had to go, I telephoned Frenchy again and this time it was David Nicholson, his son, who is training jumpers so splendidly at Condicote near Stow-on-the-Wold, who sent me my new hack. This was a grand horse called Bob, standing 15 hands 2 inches, and I was even better off than before.

"All my hacks learn quickly to stand still and, with the exception of Finnure, will remain on their own peacefully waiting when I get off and put the reins through the stirrup-leather. Although they have been racehorses themselves, they quietly crop grass and never think of running away. This is essential for a trainer.

"Bob is still going strong but I have another little hack as well, called Jam, a good horse with whom I won seven races for Mrs de Rothschild but who broke down. When he broke down for the third time, his owner asked me if I could make a hack of him. I told her, 'I'm afraid I can't do with him at the moment, Mrs de Rothschild.' Three years went by and she told me, 'I've got to do something with Jam.' So I told her that I would have him back as a hack and would see what I could do. Within three weeks that horse had settled back into stable routine and, as it was obvious that he was enjoying himself, Mrs de Rothschild agreed that we could have another go with him.

"Zara Pratt was riding out for me in the summer of 1983 and I asked her whether she would like a ride in the Newmarket Town Plate, the oldest race in England, with a continuous history since its inauguration by King Charles II in 1665. She was delighted with the idea and, during a somewhat depressing season, the one real thrill I had was watching this little horse and his girl jockey – running over three miles six furlongs against thirty-one others. I went down to the start. Harry Carr was the starter and off they went, right across the flat. As I walked back, I could see that Jam was leading by a long way and I thought that the little horse must have run away with Zara. Not a bit of it. I came up with Harry Carr again. 'Bruce, this horse of yours is five hundred yards in front!' he said. Believe me, Jam won by two hundred yards. So, once again, more than three hundred years on, the Newmarket Town Plate had been won by a horse from Palace House Stables.

"As I sat on my hack, watching the two-year-olds work in the spring of 1976, I realised that Tachypous was every bit as good as I had hoped – as I had dreamt all through the winter. He had his mother's glorious stride and, as he came up hard held, he was revelling in his work. My spirits lifted just as the larks rose from the Heath into the sky on that lovely morning.

"Tachypous took to racing like a duck to water. For his second racecourse outing we went to Newbury where he won the five-furlong Berkshire Stakes most impressively. Indeed he did it so well that I looked forward to great things in the autumn, and even began to dream of next year's Classics."

One of the most prestigious and important tests for a two-year-old is the six-furlong Middle Park Stakes at Newmarket. It is now generously sponsored, like a number of other important races, by the William Hill Organisation. In the days of the old deeply-entrenched traditional Jockey Club, when sponsorship was first mooted, it met with considerable opposition. Completely ignoring the impoverished state of the racing industry, one old nobleman spoke for nearly all the members at the meeting of the Club, when he exclaimed, "Disgusting! The very idea of sponsoring races at Newmarket is quite intolerable. The next thing we shall hear is that somebody wants to rename the Dewhurst or the Middle Park Stakes!"

Lord Rosebery had been sitting quietly. Now, at last, he entered the argument – but not on the side of the majority. "Gentlemen," he said, "Does anyone know which was the first sponsored race in Britain?" There was no answer. "Well, I'll tell you," said Rosebery. "The first sponsored race in this country was the Middle Park Stakes, sponsored by the Middle Park Stud!" He sat down amid understandable consternation.

So it was for the William Hill Middle Park Stakes, always regarded as one of the main pointers for the following year's Classics, that Bruce aimed Tachypous.

Every now and again the hard graft of a trainer's life is brightened as he watches his horses on the gallops. He will hope one morning to receive that sudden inspired thrill when his horse seems to shout out, "I will win!" These moments come all too seldom to the average trainer. "As he gallops up to you and passes you," Bruce explains, "you can scarcely recognise him as the same animal you have watched working. His entire action and his outrageous confidence and well-being give him a sort of star quality, so that he seems to flash. If you have a betting owner and the horse gives you this sign when you clear him out on the day before his race, you cannot wait to get back to breakfast and telephone so that the owner can have a good bet. Of course, many horses will win for you without it, but it is only this flashing action that inspires that real confidence beforehand."

Such was the case with Tachypous the day before the Middle Park Stakes. As he rode back to Palace House, Bruce could scarcely believe that the following day he had a good chance of winning this famous Group One race, even though he had already twice won the fillies counterpart, the William Hill Cheveley Park Stakes, with Jacinth and Cry of Truth. Over breakfast he said quietly to Betty, "I think we should nearly win tomorrow."

Indeed he did. Although the Irish challenger Nebbiolo, a hard tough bay colt trained by Kevin Prendergast, was strongly fancied, Tachypous beat him comfortably by a length. The colt wintered well and Bruce sent him down to Newbury for his first outing of 1977, in the seven-furlong Greenham Stakes, now known as the Clerical Medical Greenham Stakes, which has not the best of reputations as a trial for the Guineas. It seems that the courses are too dissimilar and, moreover, that individual horses can make such different amounts of improvement in the time between the trial and the Classic. The going was very soft, which Tachypous resented, and he could finish only second, beaten one and a half lengths by He Loves Me, to whom he was giving 5 lbs. Returning to Newmarket for the Two Thousand Guineas, itself, George Cambanis's colt ran a cracking good race, defeating the subsequent dual Derby winner, Robert Sangster's The Minstrel, but failing by just a length to overhaul Nebbiolo. Thereafter, although worried by leg trouble, which was to enforce his retirement before the end of the season, he was third in the St James's Palace Stakes at Royal Ascot and second, beaten three-quarters of a length by North Stoke, in the Land of Burns Stakes at Ayr in July. Gunner B was no less than six lengths further back in third place. That was Tachypous's last race and he retired to stud, where he has already sired Group winners like Travel On.

By now Bruce was looking at Stilvi's next foal, a strong, rangy, good-looking chestnut by Brigadier Gerard, called Taxiarchos. Third in the Acomb Stakes at York in August behind the Queen's Tartan Pimpernel from two starts in his first season, Taxiarchos won three nice races as a three-year-old and was exported to South Africa, where he is a successful sire. "He was a pretty decent horse," says Bruce, "but not top-class. He beat Homing at Sandown and is getting plenty of winners in South Africa."

Stilvi's next foal was by Busted, the big bay son of Crepello, who, trained by Sir Noel Murless for his breeder, the late Stanhope Joel, was unbeaten "Horse of the Year" and European champion of 1967.

The mating with Stilvi produced a chestnut colt with four white legs and a white face. "He was a very, very plain foal and yearling," says Bruce. "What you would call, in a human being, a gangling youth. By mid-summer of his yearling season he was so weak that it was touch and go whether we would send him to the sales or not. However, we decided not to sell and it soon became clear that, although he would take a long time to mature, he was always going to be a good horse. By the beginning of September he was fit to run but was still backward and in need of a race. So I sent him to Doncaster for the Ribero Stakes, which has since been renamed, to my delight, the Yorkshire Dragoon Stakes. He ran understandably green and finished third. That race was just what he needed. In the Clarence House Stakes at Ascot he left the gate like a cork out of a bottle, strode right away over the last two furlongs and beat the Queen's Classic hope Milford by a long-looking ten lengths. The following month I ran him in the seven-furlong William Hill Dewhurst Stakes at Newmarket which is regarded as even more of a Classic trial than the Middle Park. The Dewhurst is also a Group One contest and has been won in the past by some top-class horses. So when, always on the bridle and never looking in the slightest danger, he beat More Light, a previous good winner from the stable of my old friend Dick Hern, with incredible ease, he was immediately installed at a very short price as winter favourite for the Two Thousand Guineas. His name of course was Tromos.

"Tromos wintered all right but, from the end of February, he never showed the sparkle that he had the year before. I received a lot of stick from the Press but there was nothing I could do about it and the criticism was totally unjustified. I told George Cambanis that I was not happy and that, although I would run him in the Craven Stakes at the first Newmarket Meeting, I knew that he would not win, even though *Timeform* at the end of the 1978 season had stated, "Clearly a two-year-old of the highest class and will take the world of beating next year.'

"Even so, he might still have won, wrong as he was in himself, if 'Kipper' Lynch, riding to orders, had not steadied Tromos in the early stages instead of letting him make the running as he had always done in the past. Stilvi and her children hate to be disappointed. Tromos was disappointed on this occasion and he was well beaten by Henry Cecil's Lyphard's Wish.

"I was worried out of my mind. Here was a colt who was capable on breeding and performance of winning both the Guineas and the Derby, but he was completely wrong. I had in my care the champion two-year-old of Europe, probably of the whole world, with the Classics at his mercy, but a colt who was clearly in such poor shape that there was no way in which he could run in them. The worst feature was that I had no idea of the reason and could not, therefore, cure him or alleviate his suffering. He missed the Guineas and had still not recovered by the time of the Derby.

"George Cambanis did not want to sell him but I received such a big offer from the United States that I suggested that George should come over. He met the Americans and a magnificent half-share deal was set up with the Pillar Stud, Kentucky, subject to examination by their own veterinary surgeon. One of the first things that the American vet did was to put an instrument down Tromos's gullet, enabling him to examine that area. He discovered ulcers all the way down inside and diagnosed a streptococcus infection of the throat and chest. This form of inspection is now general practice.

"The deal went through and Tromos was exported to the United States. After two seasons as a stallion, he died with colic from a twisted gut. I have high hopes of Jaggery (USA), a likely-looking bay colt from the first crop of that unfortunate champion.

"There was nothing wrong with Stilvi's next foal, Tyrnavos, a magnificent, strong, good-bodied, most attractive colt by the all-quality Derby winner Blakeney, one of the two half-brother winners of the Epsom Classic, bred, owned and trained by Arthur Budgett and now standing at the National Stud in Newmarket. From three starts as a two-year-old, Tyrnavos comfortably won the valuable Roberre Trophy Stakes over seven furlongs at Ascot in September and then finished second to Robert Sangster's Vincent O'Brien-trained unbeaten two-year-old champion, Monteverdi, in the Dewhurst. When Tyrnavos retired for the winter, I had high hopes for the Classics."

During the winter, from two to three, Tyrnavos developed into a superb, powerful specimen of a thoroughbred racehorse. It was obvious to Bruce from the beginning that he needed a lot of work. He won the Craven Stakes, sponsored now by Ladbrokes, over the Two Thousand Guineas course on the Rowley Mile. But a week before the Guineas, he went lame in his shoulder and missed two vital bits of work. In the circumstances he did well to finish fourth, two lengths behind Hello Gorgeous, in the Mecca-Dante Stakes at York and, when he went to Epsom for the Derby, Bruce was extremely hopeful.

Bruce says, "The horse had a very rough race. In the old days, I suppose, that would have been it. But now compensation was at hand in the form of the valuable Irish Sweeps Derby at the Curragh. My colt was supremely well and, as Edward Hide was retained to ride in England on that day, I was lucky enough to secure the services of Tony Murray, who was based in Ireland. Tony is the son of my old friend, Paddy Murray, from the Letcombe jumping days, who wisely sent his boy to be trained as a jockey by that master of his craft, Frenchy Nicholson. Tyrnavos travelled over and two days before the race

Tony, who had worked the colt on the Curragh, telephoned to say that he was delighted with him. 'He gave me a wonderful feel' he said, 'and I'm sure he has a great chance.'

"I flew over with George and Lenior Cambanis. We were met at Dublin Airport by John Walsh of the Curragh Bloodstock Agency, who had arranged everything for us. We stayed at the Royal Hibernian, were taken out to the Curragh by the CBA (Curragh Bloodstock Agency), shown round the Irish National Stud and given a splendid lunch. Despite the big crowd on the course, we were shown into an ideal place from which to watch the Classic. I had told Tony, 'This family don't like being disapppointed. If he wants to make the running, let him.'"

And Classic indeed it was, that Irish Sweeps Derby of 1980 with its vast first prize of £142,195, making it the most valuable race ever run in Ireland. The English Derby was worth only a little more and Henbit, sidelined for the rest of the season through cracking a cannon-bone in his off-fore leg, was the only notable absentee from that race. No fewer than seven of those who had finished behind him at the beginning of the month at Epsom lined up in the field of thirteen at the Curragh.

Among these were the Epsom Derby runner-up, Master Willie, the third, Rankin, the fourth, Pelerin, and the fifth, Garrido, as well as the Irish Two Thousand Guineas winner Nikoli, the last Classic winner to be trained by the great Irish trainer Paddy Prendergast, who had died ten days before the Sweeps Derby. But none of these could finish in the first three at the Irish Sweeps Derby as Bruce Hobbs's 25 to 1 outsider, Tyrnavos, now led all the way to turn the form-book upside down and vindicate his trainer's faith.

None of the Derby colts had been out again in the meanwhile and not surprisingly Master Willie, who had come so close to catching Henbit in the final furlong at Epsom, was now made the 7 to 4 favourite. Nikoli, the Epsom favourite, was at 4 to 1, but he sweated up badly on the way to the start and was difficult to persuade into the stalls, Christy Roche having dismounted in an attempt to calm him down. With Lester Piggott booked for Pelerin, the Epsom fourth was made a 13 to 2 chance while the only raider from France, the Italian Derby winner Garrido, was at 10s.

As a result of Nikoli's antics at the start, both Rankin and Tyrnavos backed out of their stalls and Greville Starkey seemed quite anxious about Rankin, trotting him around to see whether the knock the colt had sustained had lamed him at all. By the time that Rankin was back in his starting-stall, the race was nine minutes late.

None of the jockeys seemed particularly anxious to make the running and Tony Murray sent Tyrnavos to the front, followed by

Henbit's stable companion, Prince Bee, and the Nijinsky Stakes winner, Ramian. At the mile post, Tyrnavos was still bowling along in front but Cobbler's Cove had now moved up to dispute second place with Prince Bee, with Master Willie also closing up to the leaders. As they turned into the straight Master Willie strode up to within a length of Tyrnavos, with Cobbler's Cove, Ramian and Prince Bee all well there still and Philippe Paquet making a forward move on Garrido. With three furlongs to run, Master Willie got within half a length of Tyrnavos, but the favourite's effort fizzled out soon after that and Prince Bee burst through a gap to emerge as the principal danger.

Tyrnavos, meanwhile, trained to the minute by Bruce, was still galloping along in fine style with not the remotest suggestion that his stamina might run out and, as he came into the final furlong with a two-length advantage over Prince Bee, it was already clear that he had the race in safe keeping.

At the post Tyrnavos was a length and a half clear of Dick Hern's Prince Bee, with Ramian keeping third place for Ireland, another two and a half lengths away. A length and a half behind him, Garrido just snatched fourth prize from Master Willie on the line and then came Pelerin and Rankin, but Nikoli, who was never prominent at any stage, was a disappointing tenth.

Epsom, with its sharp turns and gradients, has been known to tell a lie and the Derby had occasionally been won by a non-stayer. But the Curragh, one of the stiffest, fairest galloping courses in the world, tells the truth and the form book says that, in the circumstances, Tyrnavos should have won at Epsom on 4th June. So his first Classic victory was a major triumph for Bruce and, of course, for his delightful owners who had bred the winner from their own lovely mare, Stilvi.

Bruce says, "George, Lenior and I were escorted to a celebration party in the Turf Club rooms before flying back to London that night, complete with the magnificent trophy, which is now in Greece. As a result of their impeccable organisation and wonderful unsolicited hospitality on this occasion, the Curragh Bloodstock Agency have done all our business ever since." He adds, "It was quite a day because, on the same afternoon, we won two races at Newmarket."

Tyrnavos ran once more, ridden by Edward Hide in the King George VI and Queen Elizabeth Diamond Stakes at Ascot, but having been taken on by the pacemaker in the early stages, he was all but knocked over the rail early in the straight and, through no fault of Hide's, lost all chance. On his return to Newmarket, he was retired to the Gazeley Stud, where he is already siring some excellent produce.

Henrietta Micklem, the horse artist, says, "Tyrnavos's bright, bold intelligent head was a joy to paint. If he passes that intelligence, strength and quality on to his stock, they are sure to be winners."

Meanwhile Stilvi's fifth foal, Tolmi, a most attractive well-made, strong compact bay filly by Great Nephew, the sire of Derby winner Grundy, was already showing her paces at Newmarket. First time out, at the July Meeting in 1980, she drew right away from her field in the final one and a half furlongs, to win contemptuously from twenty rivals and then, at the big Ascot Meeting at the end of the month, although starting slowly, she won the six-furlong Princess Margaret Stakes in impressive style, earning the *Timeform* comment, "Has the pedigree and conformation to match her very smart form and will take all the beating in the top fillies' races."

Incidentally, Bruce won the first three races on that day at Newmarket, the other two being with Scintillating Air, and Stumped in the Group Three Child Stakes.

As her half-brother had done the year before, Tolmi wintered splendidly, but, like him, she suffered a setback in that absolutely vital period just before the Guineas.

Bruce says, "Tolmi had been working like a dream but ten days before the One Thousand, she came in from exercise lame behind, and I called out to Betty, 'Come and look at our Classic hope!' I had been so full of confidence. My vet, Allan Heath, treated her twice a day and within seventy-two hours she was sound again but, determined not to run her in the Classic at half-cock, I worked her on Side Hill. In spite of a thunderstorm, she moved beautifully, ridden by Ray Cochrane, and pulled up sound. But I knew that she would go into that race short of work.

"At this time George Cambanis was far from well. Since the previous year he had been suffering from heart trouble and had recently had pneumonia. Against everybody's advice he came over to watch the One Thousand Guineas. Edward Hide rode a super race but in the last hundred yards that lack of work told its tale and Tolmi was beaten a neck by Mr Jim Joel's Fairy Footsteps. That was the last race that George Cambanis saw. He was unable to come to Royal Ascot to see his lovely filly win the Coronation Stakes, and he died in July. On the morning of his death he spoke to me from the island of Andros. About ten o'clock that evening I received a telephone call from Nick Embiricos, telling me that George had collapsed and died. We were shattered."

As I write, Tolmi, at Gazeley Stud, has a yearling by Posse, a foal by Bustino and has been covered by Ile de Bourbon.

Stilvi's next foal, Tenea, a dark bay daughter of the champion miler Reform, chipped a bone in her knee after one start and never ran again. But, when Bruce sent her to the December Sales of 1982, she was to create history in another way as Europe's first million-guineas horse. The most thrilling bloodstock sale, admirably conducted by Richard

Mildmay-White, soon resolved into a duel between Sir Philip Payne-Gallwey and New York publisher Joe Albritton, who, in a hushed ring, finally gave best at 1,020,000 guineas. The previous record was 730,000 guineas.

"I never expected we would have to go so far and the powder was running dry," declared Sir Philip, who had bought the filly for a syndicate headed by Stavros Niarchos and Robert Sangster to mate with the Derby winner Golden Fleece.

Amid all the excitement Bruce was typically concerned about Tenea's stable-lad. This was Yorkshireman Roy Collins, who served his time with Geoffrey Brooke, and is married with two children and had at the time been with Bruce for eighteen years. In addition to being well-looked after by Lenior Cambanis, he received £1,020 plus a £50 bonus from Tattersalls. "A splendid fellow", says Bruce, "and a first-class stableman who hadn't had a winner that year and really deserved this windfall."

Stilvi's next foal was Telios, a small, beautifully-turned rich chestnut colt by champion sire Mill Reef. Lightly raced but a Newmarket winner as a two-year-old in 1983, he is, as I write, looking sensational in his box at Palace House, poised for his three-year-old season. He stands only 15 hands 2½ inches but Mill Reef was a small horse, and he is bigger than Hyperion! Bruce says, "He's big enough if he's good enough!"

The next foal, a full-sister to Tyrnavos, will not race. Bruce says, "A fortnight before birth, probably due to the way that Stilvi rolled over, or something like that, the filly received a pre-natal injury, and she was born wrong. But, thanks to the expert nursing and attention that she received at Gazeley Stud, they managed to keep her alive and she will definitely be able to breed. I think that's a triumph in itself for Pat McCalmont and his staff."

More recently Stilvi had a big chestnut yearling colt by Grundy on whom Bruce is particularly keen and who may well keep him training for a bit longer. By the time this book is published, she should have foaled to Final Straw, whose first crop of yearlings averaged over 100,000 guineas and will have been covered by the sire of the moment, Shirley Heights, who has a sensational international book of mares at the Royal Studs, Sandringham.

In the 1984 stud season, three heroines of five Classics are among the eighteen Group and Listed winners of twenty-nine races visiting Shirley Heights at Sandringham. The dual Derby winner's remarkable list includes the Queen's Highclere (One Thousand Guineas and French Oaks); Juliette Marny (Oaks and Irish Oaks) and One in a Million, who won the One Thousand Guineas for her breeder Jocelyn Hambro. Among other well-known mares to be covered by the handsome nine-year-old stallion are of course Stilvi and the late Tom Blackwell's Vielle, whom Bruce trained to be second in the Oaks of 1980.

"Tom Blackwell's death was a terrible blow for us," Bruce says. "He was a great loss to racing and to us personally because he was a very great friend and confidant. Always in and out of the house, he was well liked by all the staff because of his cheerful kindness, generosity and enthusiastic interest in everything to do with Palace House. His place on the Board has been taken by another old friend, Lord Fairhaven. We had fair success for Tom, I'm happy to say, and his stud was being constantly upgraded. One of my buys which gave me the greatest pleasure to train was the first horse I bought for Tom, the little filly called Catherine Wheel for whom I paid only 1,250 guineas. She was third in the One Thousand Guineas, won the Musidora Stakes at York, the New Ham Stakes and the Nassau Stakes at Goodwood and other races. Vielle also won the Nassau Stakes. Then there was his Goodwood Cup winner Richmond Fair. Mrs Tiggy-winkle who won the New Ham Stakes at Goodwood, and Princess Eboli with whom we won the Cheshire and Lancashire Oaks. There are only about half a dozen mares on his lovely stud at his home, Langham Hall near Bury St. Edmunds, but they are all superbly bred and have nominations to all the best stallions. Tom's daughter, Caroline Holland-Martin, a delightful person, is very keen and knowledgeable about bloodstock.

"I think that one of the proudest moments of Tom's life was on King George VI and Queen Elizabeth Diamond day at Ascot, when his daughter Caroline rode the winner of the ladies race on his own mare Hurdy Gurdy, described by Tom – because Caroline had been with us for some time here at Palace House – as, 'Horse and jockey both trained by Bruce Hobbs'; and to crown a beautiful day his son, Charles, had his first winner when Le Patron won the last race. We celebrated so well that Tom asked me to drive him back and, I'm happy to say, we made it! It was one of my proudest moments of my life when I was asked by the family to be an usher at Tom's memorial service."

It was, of course, Tom who had brought in Jocelyn Hambro at the beginning, because Jocelyn kept his brood mares at Langham Hall then. John Wilkinson, a tough Yorkshire horsemaster of the old school, who was Tom's stud-groom, is now the manager of Jocelyn's superb model Waverton Stud in Gloucestershire, which used to be William Hill's Sezincote. There he stands those successful young stallions, Monsanto and Vaigly Great, and it was there that he bred the 1983 Oaks runner-up Acclimatise.

"If Tyrnavos's Irish Sweeps Derby was one of the happiest days in our lives," says Bruce, "then the 1983 Oaks was undoubtedly one of the saddest. Jocelyn, a wonderfully brave man, steadfast and loyal not only to us, his friends, but to himself and his standards, has suffered a double tragedy in the last ten years, losing first one wife and then another from cancer. Elizabeth Hambro, who had longed to watch Acclimatise run in the Oaks, died two nights before the race. Honouring her wish, although of course, he did not attend the meeting himself, Jocelyn insisted that the filly ran. She is top-class on her day but she has two ways of running. She is like the little girl with the curl. When she's good, she's very very good . . . Although she gets one and a half miles, she is really more effective at ten furlongs and has a brilliant turn of speed. Acclimatise was beaten at Epsom by an exceptional filly in Sun Princess, who really stays, as she showed when winning the St Leger and finishing second in the Arc de Triomphe. We had decided to send Acclimatise to stud, but when Cormorant Wood had such a successful autumn, culminating in the Champion Stakes at Newmarket, we decided that, because we had decisively beaten Barry Hills's filly, it would be a good idea to keep our filly in training as a four-year-old too. When I suggested the idea to Jocelyn, he was only too ready. He is a great supporter. And, you know, even at my age, you do need a confidant from time to time. During the last year, when I was so unwell until my operation at the end of 1983, Jocelyn was a marvellous support to both Betty and me."

Bruce often talks about the other directors who have contributed so much to the success of the Palace House venture. "Jim Philipps was a tremendous supporter in the beginning," he says, "and David Wills is so charming, considerate and tremendously loyal. I have unfortunately had only two half-decent animals for him. Hecla so nearly beat Mill Reef in the International Stakes at Kempton and Sleat won the Sun Chariot Stakes for him. He deserves a great deal more. We are very fond of him and his charming wife Eva.

"We have been lucky in all our wonderful owners, who have been so good to us. Happily, despite George Cambanis's death, his family are carrying on with racing on the same scale as before. They have been so kind to us and Betty and I have loved staying with them in Greece. We have a happy arrangement whereby horses that are suitable to race and breed in Greece go out there whenever I see fit and fillies may come back here to breed.

"Bill Hill was very good to us. I trained his horses right up until the time that he died. I was winning races and we were both happy. He was a good owner. It was he who bred the brilliant filly Jacinth, who, like Cry of Truth, bred by her owner, Pearl Lawson Johnston, won the Cheveley Park Stakes for me. Jacinth was by Red God out of Jaffa, who had been bred at the Brook Stud and sold as a yearling to Bill Hill for 3,000 guineas, and whom I also trained. Sir Kenneth Butt, acting on behalf of the Brook Stud, paid 16,500 guineas for Jacinth as a yearling from the William Hill Stud's draft at the Houghton Sales, thus returning the blood to the stud.

"Jacinth's defeat by Sir Noel Murless's Mysterious in the One Thousand Guineas was one of the disappointments of my training career. She was not quite right and I was so worried beforehand because I had not been able to give her a race before the Guineas. What's more, having bumped her head on the gate the previous season, she hated starting-stalls. It was she who made me have wooden practice-stalls erected, a design that has been copied by others. That was one race that I did not watch. Brian Lunness went down to the start with her and, as I say, she was just unlucky enough to find one too good for her in Mysterious on the day. She was a tremendously good three-year-old over a mile, and I won not only the Coronation Stakes but the Falmouth Stakes and the Goodwood Mile with her.

"Another who was difficult to start, because of his size, was Scallywag, an enormous grey horse. It hurt him to stand in the stalls as he had to arch his back. So I had a special trace made, three foot long with two clips to go round the back of the gate, to give him greater space. The Stewards approved and I used it to such effect that he ran third in the St Leger."

Bruce has nothing but praise for the key members of his staff, including a magnificent breaking-in team. "Frank Crozier is not only a first-class travelling headman," he says, "but also a great breaker-in of yearlings and terribly loyal. My headman, Pip Payne, who has been with me now in that capacity for four years, is the only son of my dear friend Bill Payne, who now happily lives only a stone's throw away from Palace House in Newmarket. Pip is a great support to me and a very good organiser. We mentioned Roy Collins as the lad who did Tenea. He has been with me twenty years and used to be second travelling man. It was he who won the 8 stone 7 lb stable-lads' boxing title at the Hilton Hotel and was virtually unbeaten in the ring. But, when he was taken ill with back pains, cancer was diagnosed and he did not work for twelve months. Talk about Bob Champion. Roy is a miracle too. He is a keep-fit fanatic and plays a great part in the stable-lads' marathon walks. He's an old fashioned sort, who is always singing as he goes about his work.

My late secretary, Eric Rhodes, who had been a prisoner-of-war with the Japs, was with me for eighteen years. A marvellous secretary, who knew every department of Weatherbys inside out. For the last eleven years he was assisted by a wonderful girl, Vicki Hibble, who is now number one, helped by Michael Fenton.

On the subject of jockeys Bruce has no doubt. "In my time two jockeys have stood out head and shoulders above anybody else: Sir Gordon Richards and Lester Piggott. There have been many other top-class jockeys, Charlie Eliott, Scobie Breasley, Harry Carr, Freddie Fox and, still, Joe Mercer who is the stylist that the youngsters should model themselves on.

"I well recall my first spring in Newmarket. I was standing on Warren Hill, waiting for the Captain's horses to come up, and next to me was George Colling, to whom Joe's brother, the late Manny Mercer, was apprenticed. Something of his was playing up at the bottom of the canter and he said, 'It's come to a thing, Bruce. This is 1953. You can only train your horses today the way your labour will allow.' Things have not improved. Every yard now has three lots, which really cannot be a good thing, so that horses by and large are not getting enough exercise, and in consequence they are much less sound today. They don't stand the work. Like all the old trainers, I still insist that a horse should be out of its box limbering up for at least three-quarters of an hour before it does its first canter.

"The pattern of racing has changed, inasmuch as horses are treated as a commodity. The emphasis now is on a quick return because of the economic climate. Unfortunately, it would seem to me that winning the Triple Crown doesn't mean as much. You have a horse to win the Guineas; you have another horse to win the Derby; and, unfortunately, the St Leger doesn't count anymore, which is a tragedy. It's all been done by money. The Arc de Triomphe has taken over from the St Leger.

"Economics are such that now, the moment horses have won a decent race, they are rushed off to stud because they are worth so much money as long as they have won. If they are beaten, then they are devalued.

"Racing now is so commercial that when a mare has a foal, as long as the little animal is still breathing when it comes out, it has to be kept alive, no matter what its shape or size, so that it can be got to the sales. In the old days, the worst stock would be knocked on the head.

"Newmarket has reached saturation point now, unless they build more and more of these artificial gallops. We have an enormous amount of grass, but no matter what you do, there are certain places where people will go and work and there are certain places where they won't. I'm not terribly fond of the artificial surfaces, these all-weather gallops. I would certainly never really allow a horse to gallop flat out on them. Half speed; yes – but full speed, definitely no. I find that the horses never seem to let themselves go properly. They're not sure of their footing. Mind, I think that the artificial gallops are improving, but even an artificial will not stand two hundred horses going up it in one morning."

Bruce and Betty are so fond of their grandchildren and inordinately proud of them. Sixteen-year-old Rupert Dimsdale, who is at Harrow, is an excellent shot but it is Tana who loves the horses and is so happy riding out with her grandfather. Georgina is still not old enough to have decided in which way she will turn her talents. Their grandparents are so happy to be able to dedicate this story to them.

Much of Bruce and Betty's comfort at home is due to Mrs 'Milly' Millington, who has been with them for twenty-five years, longer than anyone else, as Betty's righthand man in the house much loved by Hobblette and the grandchildren.

There have been many dogs but now the trio consists of the pekes, Lamb Chop and the beautiful young Mrs Ding, and Pepper, the wire-haired dachsund. The family is completed by Nettles, a twelve-year-old black cat who has mothered many puppies.

Bruce says, "I have only one way of doing things and, as long as I continue to train, I am not going to compromise. I believe that horses in training should be looked after in the best possible way and that this entails not only the best forage and the exercise which our grandfathers, who were much nearer to the animal than we are today, believed essential but also the care of top-class disciplined staff. I know that I may go on about discipline because I have always appreciated it. But, just as I have always been brought up with horses, so, in any department of the horse world, discipline is a must.

"I intend to retire within the next two years but, if I find that I have a really promising young horse like, perhaps, Stilvi's foal by Grundy, I could be tempted to stay on, if only on a limited scale for a short while. Otherwise I shall be seeking some administrative job in racing. I want to retire while I'm still active and while I've got some mileage, so that Betty and I can enjoy some of the things that we couldn't do when we were young – particularly travelling."

I think back to those wartime days when Nurse Betty Winder, the future Mrs Bruce Hobbs, was looking after handicapped patients in the old workhouse at Wantage, serving as a hospital, and one afternoon an orderly rushed up. "Nurse," he said excitedly, "one of your patients, one of the men, has gone off down the drive and is going out onto the road, the main road!"

Betty answered, "Well, that's all right. They're allowed to."

"He's got his tin hat and his gas-mask," said the orderly.

"Well, that's all right. He should have them."

"Of course he should. But that's all he's wearing. He's got nothing else on at all!"

Apart from his horse-knowledge and his integrity, Bruce too was naked when he went out into the adult world. The struggle has been tough but these two qualities, helped by his Christian faith and that greatest of all human virtues, unswerving loyalty, have moulded him into a real man, the finest of all British sporting gentlemen.

Index

Above Board 115
Acclimatise 167-8
Acre 83-4, 87
Aga Khan 141
Agility 87
Aintree 11-12, 29-31, 42, 47, 49-51, 87, 123
  see also Grand National
Airborne 109
Airgead Sios 54, 58-9
Al Malakaiya 88
Alamein 93-4, 99
Alan Adare 146
Albert House 153
Albritton, Joe 166
Alcide 129-32
Aldaniti, 108, 155
Alexandra Park 150
Alexandria 91-2, 95
Algeria 99-100, 102
Allen, Roy 142
Ally Sloper 11
Altcar 48
Altesse Royale 152
Alycidon 125, 129
Angelola 115
Angers, Avril 63
Annaly, Lord 8
Anthony, Ivor 10-11, 24, 45, 47, 53, 112
  Jack 11, 29, 31, 47, 54, 57, 105-8
  Owen 45, 47
Anzio 100-1
Archibald, George 127
Argur 117
Ariona 102
Ark Royal 126
Arkle 30
Armida 36
Ascetic's Silver 11
Ascot 58, 113, 117, 119, 121, 124, 126, 128, 131-2, 144, 150, 153, 160-2, 164-5, 167
Astor family 105, 141
Atlas 128
Auchinleck, General 90-1, 93
Aunt May 11
Aureole 115-20, 129-30
Ayr 153, 160
Azzib 90

Babbington-Hill, Sue 132
Badminton 87
Bagatelle 56
Baggrave Hall 22
Bailey, Willie 107
Bald Eagle 129
Baldoyle 10, 114
Ballymacad 12
Ballymoss 149
Barbour, Frank 30
Barclay, Colonel 93
Barker, George 27
Barling, Geoffrey 147
Barnet, James 116
Barton, Billy 31
Bath 68-9
Battleship ix, 49-64, 69
Baxter, Jack 39
Beale, Major Frank 146
Beaufort, Duke of 22
Beckhampton 29, 93, 139
Bedford House 139-40
Beeby, Eileen 113
  George 26, 33, 56, 107, 111-15

Beeby—*Contd.*
Harry 7, 33, 111
Bell, Ossie 32
Belle of All 139
Belmont Park 10, 66
Belper, Lord 25
Belvoir Hunt 14, 16, 22, 25, 27, 124
Benny, Jack 67
Bertie, Norman 117, 138-9
Beverley 150
Bicester, Lord 107, 112-14, 123
Big Game 115
Bird RSM 69
Birmingham 39, 113, 128
Black Tulip 36
Blackwell, Charles 167
Tom 143, 146-7, 149-50, 152, 155, 167
Blakeney 152, 162
Blandford, Marquess of 18
Blow, Simon 16
Blue Peter 153
Bob 158
Bogskar 47
Bombo 18
Booth-Jones, Captain G. 150
Bostwick, Brother 10
Pete 10, 23, 27
Boussac, M. 141
Bowett, Druie 131
John 131
Boyd-Rochfort, Arthur 117, 120
Sir Cecil ix, 110, 113-23, 125-36, 138, 142, 170
Mrs. Hamilton 114
Rohays 120
Breasley, Scobie 139, 170
Bricken, Mrs. Jules (Patsy) 149-50
Bridges, Miss O. 150
Brigadier Gerard 160
Brindisi 100
British Bloodstock Agency 146
Brixworth 5
Brook, Dr. Charles 117-18, 130
Brook Stud 168-9
Brooke, Geoffrey 140, 147, 149-50, 153, 166
Brown, Eric 36
Brown, Tony 29
Brudenell-Bruce, Mrs. C. 150
Dana 149
Paddy 149
Buckfastleigh 37, 47
Budge, Donald 54
Budgett, Arthur 36, 162
Buffer 158
Bungay 37
Burghley, Lord 107
Burghley Horse Trials 107
Burke, Liz 149
Burnaby, Major Algie 22
Burrows, Royce 121
Burton, Frank S. 150
Busted 160
Bustino 165
Butt, Sir Kenneth 169

C-in-C 109
California 8
Cairo 90-2
Cambanis, George 155-7, 160-5, 168
Lenior 155-6, 163-4, 166
Cambremer 128
Cambridge Drag Hounds 124
Cardiff 37
Carey, Tommy 42-3
Carlburg 140-1, 143, 146, 148-50
Carlos-Clarke, Charlie 18
Diana *see* Walwyn, Diana
Sandy 18
Carr, Harry 111, 113-14, 116-19, 121-2, 126-7, 131-2, 134, 136, 143, 158, 170
Joan 113
Carrozza 129
Catherine Wheel 152, 167
Cecil, David 117, 120
Henry 117, 120, 133, 136, 146, 161
Cesarewitch 115
Chaddsford 27
Chamberlain, Neville 69, 112
Chamier 119
Champion, Bob 108, 155, 169
Chantilly, 147
Chaplin, Henry 8
Charles II, King 115, 146, 158
Charles, E.R. 150
Charlottown 128
Cheltenham 2-3, 29, 51-5, 62, 92, 101, 105
Gold Cup 24, 29-31, 42, 48, 62, 92, 109, 112, 123
Chenille 129
Chepstow 39-40
Chester 131
Vase 130
Chil the Kite 153
Cicero 8
Clark, Ambrose 9-12, 14, 16-17, 22-4, 28, 33, 49, 65
Mrs. Ambrose (Florence) 24, 34, 44, 52, 56, 61, 65
Robert Sterling 9
Stephen 9

Clark — *Contd.*
Major-General 91
Clayton, Major Jack 117, 138-40
Jane 139-40
Stan 152
Cobbler's Cove 164
Cochrane, Ray 165
Colling, Bob 105
George 170
Jack 105-6, 141
Roy 166-169
Colman, Ralph 150
Compton 111-14, 136
Condicote 158
Cooleen 48, 53
Cormorant Wood 168
Corporal 126
Cottage Rake 109, 123
Cottesmore Hunt 14, 41
Cottrell, Harry 28
Cottrill, Harry 32
Count Pahlen 150
Courage, Edward 2
Coventry, Harry 36
Cowbridge 37
Craven Lodge *see* Melton Mowbray
Crepello 160
Crested Grebe 152
Cropwell Court 7
Croxton Park 23, 26
Crozier, Frank 169
Crump, Neville 73-4, 76, 80-1, 84, 109, 114
Cry of Truth 160, 168
Cumani, Luca 139
Cundell, Frank 74, 76, 80-1, 109
Ken 112
Curragh, the 128, 162-4
Curragh Bloodstock Agency 112, 163-4

Daily Double 125
Dalham Hall Stud 147
Dalziel, Lord Hamilton of 16
Dante 108
Darling, Fred 36, 93, 139
Davy Jones 53
Day, Fred 119-20, 132
de Burgh, John 112
de Pret, Jack 17
de Rothschild, Jimmy 36
Mrs. James A. 139-40, 158
de Trafford, Cath 131
Sir Humphrey 129, 131-2, 134
de Wiart, Lady Carton 150
Deep Diver 157
Delachance 56, 59
Delaware Park 66
Derby 37
Derby, the 8-9, 36, 42, 48, 106, 108-9, 112, 115, 117, 128-33, 139, 143, 146, 152-3, 160-6, 170
Irish 119, 121, 128, 162-3, 167
Kentucky 148
Derby, Lord 42, 126, 129, 141
Derring-Do 156
Devon Loch 12
Dewster, Dusty 76
dieting 104
Digby, Lord 63
Dimsdale, Charles 145, 151
Mrs. Charles (Hobblette) 111, 114-15, 120, 137, 145, 147, 150-1, 171
Georgina 171
John 146
Rupert 171
Tana 171
Diolite 32
Djerella 156
Donald 129
Doncaster 118-19, 125-6, 128, 131, 150-2, 161
see also St. Leger
doping 44, 129
Dormer, A. 150
Douglas-Pennant, Major F. 8
Doutelle 121
Dover 74-5
Dowdeswell, Jack 36
Tom 36
Dowson, Dickie 2-3
Druid's Lodge 49
du Pont, William 49
Dufosee, Tony 81
Duke of Ragusa 153
Dunbar 103
Dunchurch Lodge Stud 122
Dunkirk 75

Early Mist 48
East Ilsley 112
Easterby, Mick 156
Walter 37
Easter Hero 29-31, 53, 59, 105
Edouard 39
El Hamma 97
Eliott, Charlie 170
Elizabeth II, Queen 115, 117-18, 121, 123, 125-6, 129-30, 133, 136, 160-1, 166
Elizabeth, Queen Mother 12, 53, 123-4
Elsey, Bill 149
Embiricos, Nick 108, 155, 165

Embiricos — *Contd.*
  Valda (née Rogerson) 108, 155
Enrico 146
Epsom 38, 119, 129-30, 144, 146, 162-4, 168
  see also Derby, the
Eric the Red 150
Eva 152
Evans, Lord 133
Exeter, Marquess of *see* Burghley, Lord

Fairy Footsteps 165
Fane, Captain G. 150
  Lady Augusta 22
Fanshawe, Dick 6
Feakes, Matt 105
Fenton, Michael 169
Feola 115
Field, The 10
Field of Gold 106
Fields Elysian 16
Final Straw 166
Finnure 113-14, 123-4, 158
Fisherman 27
Flitwick Manor 143
Florence 101
Flying Minutes 52-3, 56
Foinavon 30
Foley, Eric 43, 47
Fontwell 109
Fortescue, Earl 15
  Lady Daisy 15
  Lady Margaret 16
Fountain, Sergeant Major 81
Fox, Freddie 170
Francis, Dick ix, 47, 113-14, 123
Free Fare 54
Freeman, Frank 8
  Keith 142
Freemason Lodge 114-17, 120-2, 124-5, 128-9, 131, 133-4, 136, 138-9, 148
French Beige 129
Frieze, Lt. Col. N.E. 150
Furlong, Major Frank 42, 53
Fyfe-Jameson, Betty 152

Garadice 24
Garrido 163-4
Gatwick 11-12
Gazeley Stud 152, 157, 164-6
George VI, King 53, 115
George, Prince 17
Gezira 91
Gibson, Colonel 'Gibby' x, 134, 137
Gillingham 103
Girdlestone, Professor 3, 67
Glenmore Lad 45
Gloria Nicky 126
Gogglegoose 24
Golden Fleece 166
Golden Miller 24, 30, 42, 48, 52-3
Goldsmith, John 37
Goodwood 68, 128, 152-3, 156, 167, 169
Gordon, Hector 68, 80-1
Gorton, John 152, 156
Gosling, Mrs. C.H. 150
Grand National ix, 7-9, 11-12, 24, 27-30, 42, 47-50, 52-3, 55-65, 67-9, 73, 81, 87, 96, 105, 108-9, 114, 123-4, 155
  American 50, 64
  Palestine 87
  Scottish 48, 52
Grant-Lawson, Sir Peter 69, 72
Grately Stable 114
Gray, Colonel Douglas 146-7
  Sir Harold 128
  Joan 146
Great Bowden 6-7, 12
Great Nephew 144, 147, 165
Great Span 31, 81
Greek Jockey Club 155
Gregory, Leonard 18, 21, 24, 33, 36, 48, 56, 73
Grey Sovereign 111-13, 115, 130
Griffin, Joe 48
Griggs, Billy 23
  Walter 23
Grundy 165-6, 171
Gunner B 160
Gurney, Fred 43, 62
Gwilt, Ted 33-4

Hadrian Stud 147
Haifa 76, 78
Hailey, Clarence 149
Halifax, Lord 88
Hambro, Elizabeth 168
  Jocelyn 147, 149, 151, 153, 155, 166-8
Hamey, Tim 36, 51
Hammond, Percy 111
Hampton Court Stud 130
Hanbury, Tom 48
Happy Laughter 148
Hard Ridden 130
Harrington, Lord 141
Harrison, Major Jack 27
Harriss, Mrs. Vernon 150
Hastings, Aubrey 10-12
  Mrs. Aubrey 27
  Peter 27

Haydock 37, 44, 109
He Loves Me 160
Heath, Allan 165
Hearth, Doreen 19
Hecla 168
Hello Gorgeous 162
Hellyer, Major 137
Henbit 163-4
Henry, Prince 17
Herbert, Peter 81
Hern, Dick 105, 136, 161, 164
Hethersett 37
Hibbert, R.E. 150
Hibble, Vicki 169
Hide, Edward 152, 162, 164-5
  Tony 152
Higginson, Mr. 9
Highclere 166
Hill, Barry 168
  William 129, 149-51, 159-61, 167-9
Hitler Youth 101
Hobbs, Betty (née Winder) 74, 99, 107, 112-15, 120-1, 124, 131, 133, 136, 138, 140, 145, 148-50, 155, 157, 160, 165, 168, 171
  Cecil 7
  Hobblette *see* Dimsdale, Mrs. Charles
  Margery (née Robertson) 1, 12-14, 23, 27-8, 31-2, 39-41
  Michael 41
  Nellie (née Pratt) 36, 40-1
  Reg ix-x, 3, 6-14, 20-29, 31-5, 38-41, 44, 47-58, 60-1, 64-7, 69, 73, 92, 105-8, 110
  Susan *see* Leader, Susan
  Captain Tom 5-9, 25
  Tom 7
Hobhouse, Hugh 69, 71, 73
  John 69
Holder, Colonel Denzil 152
Holland-Martin, Caroline 167
Holman, Colonel 42
  Di *see* Nicholson, Di
Holmes, Frank 116-19
Homing 160
Hornbeam 128
Hot Grove 152
Hotfoot 152, 157
Hull, Geoff 148
  Joan 148
Huntingdon 37, 43
Hurdy Gurdy 167
Hurley, Michael 128
Hurst Park 53, 121, 131
Hypericum 115
Hyperion 42, 115, 166

Ice Ballet 149
Ile de Bourbon 165
Illingworth, Col. G.H. 150
Ilston 11
Impey, Mrs. W.M. 150
Ingham, Staff 36, 129
Inglesent 44
Irish National Stud 163

Jacinth 160, 168-9
Jackdaw 24
Jaffa 168
Jaggery 162
Jam 158-9
Jarvis, Ethel 153
  Sir Jack 140, 144, 147-8, 153
  Vivian 140
  Willie 115
Jellis, jnr, Harry 148
Jenin 78, 80
Jerusalem 83, 90
Jockey Club 121, 128-9, 131, 139, 143, 146-7, 149, 159
Joel, Eileen *see* Rogerson, Eileen
  Jim 165
  Stanhope 108, 150, 160
John, Geoffrey 100, 102
Joker's Resort 48
Jones, Bob 116
  Hywell 47
  Mervyn 47
Juliette Marny 166

Karkur 81-2
Kellsboro' Jack 24, 53
Kempton 30, 38, 119, 123, 131, 144, 155, 168
Kennett 136
Kenny, J. 150
King's Bench 149
Kingscote, Maurice 108
Kirby, Jack 124
Koko 30

Ladbrokes 162
Lady Marvel ('Kiss Me') 7, 19, 24-7
Lady Nelson 11
Lake, A.W.N. 150
Lambourn 3, 6, 21, 25, 28-9, 32-42, 49, 54, 56, 62, 64, 70, 106-7, 109-10
Lambton, Mrs. Cicely 138
  Hon. George 52, 138
Langham Hall 146-7, 167

Larkin, Peter 150
Lawson, Joe 155-6
Lawson Johnston, Pearl 168
Le Patron 167
Leader, Susan (née Hobbs) 41
Lehane, Johnny 46
Leicester 6-7, 19, 21, 51
Letcombe Regis 29, 31, 105-8, 111, 136, 162
Levy Board 145
Lewis, Geoff 153
Lightning 129, 131
Lillingston, Alan ('Anger') 124
Limerock 12
Lindley, Jimmy 146
Lindsay, Sir Martin 150
Lingfield 117, 130-1, 144
Lockinge 107
Long Island 8-9, 11-13, 20, 65-6
Lonsdale, Earl of 16
Lord Harrington's Hunt 7
Louis, Joe 66-7
Lowenstein, Captain 30-1
Lowesby 18
Lowinsky, J.M.E. 150
Ludlow 53
Lunness, Brian 140, 169
Lycett-Green, Gladys 87
  Simon 87-8, 90-3, 95-6, 100, 146
Lynch, 'Kipper' 161
Lyphard's Wish 161

Mackinney, Reagan 66
Madison, James 65
Maguire, Johnny 55
Maher, Danny 7-8
Man o'War 50
Mandarin 30
Manifesto 7
Mareth 95-6
Margaret, Princess 123
Marlborough 111
Marseilles 75-6
Marsh, Alec 144
  Marcus 36-7, 42, 122
  Michael 23
Marshall, Bryan 109
  William 15
Martyr, Major 'Tubby' 81
Maryland 9
Master Willie 163-4
Masters, Sister 3
Maxwell, Freddie 36-7
McCalmont, Pat 152, 157, 166
McAlpine, Di 41
  Malcolm 41
McNeil, Tommy 54-5
Mecca organisation 162
Medinine 95
Medoc II 92
Meld ix, 125-7
Mellon, Paul 45
Melton Mowbray 1, 7, 11, 14-17, 23-4, 26-7, 29, 41, 106, 111
  Craven Lodge 16-17, 26-7
  Warwick Lodge 11, 16-18, 20-3, 28
Melville, Whyte 7, 16
Men and Horses I Have Known 138
Mena 91
Mercer, Joe 170
  Manny 170
Mereworth Stud, Lexington 50
Meynell Foxhounds 22, 108
Micklem, Henrietta 164
Middle Park Stud 159
Milburn, Rupert 82
Mildmay, Anthony 53
Mildmay-White, Richard 165-6
Milford 161
Milford, Lord 147
Military Cross 97-8
Mill Reef 166, 168
Millington, Mrs. 'Milly' 171
Miner's Lamp 129-30
Minton, David 'Minty' 112
Minuf 93
Moller, R.B. 150
Molony, Martin 110, 112-13
  Tim 109-110
Molyneux, Ted 91, 143, 150, 153
Monsanto 151, 167
Monteverdi 162
Montgomery, Field Marshall 93-6
Moore, Captain Charles 118-19, 122, 124-5, 129
  Dan 58-60
More Light 161
Morgan, Danny 39, 53
Morse Code 48
Moseley, Colonel 'Babe' 87
Mrs. Tiggywinkle 167
Mulberry Harbour 129
Murless, Sir Noel 29, 129-30, 152, 160, 169
  Stuart 149
Murray, Paddy 108, 162
  Tony 108, 162-3
Musselburgh 153
My Prince 30
My Swanee 144

Mysterious 169

Nagami 131
Naples 100, 102
Nasrullah 112
Nathaniya 91
National Hunt racing ix, 2, 37, 42, 51, 53-4, 69, 105, 107-8
National Stud 115, 146, 162
Nearula 115, 117
Nebbiolo 160
Never Say Die 9
Neville Holt prep. school 23, 28-9
New England 9
New York 65
  Jockey Club 9
Newbury 37-8, 40, 44-5, 51, 53-4, 68, 129, 159-60
Newcombe, Kay 21
  Wilson 21
Newmarket x, 8, 16, 23, 38, 48, 106, 108, 114-17, 120, 122-4, 126-8, 130-1, 133, 138-40, 143-4, 146-8, 151-2, 156, 158-62, 164-6, 168-70
  see also Albert House; Palace House; Park Lodge
Newton Abbot 42, 109
Niarchos, Stavros 166
Nicholson, David 158
  Di (née Holman) 42
  Frenchy 39-40, 42-3, 47, 62, 68, 92, 105, 108-9, 158, 162
Nikoli 163-4
Nimbus 112
Nimrod 15
Nitsdale 6
Niven, David 18
None Nicer 131
No Reckoning 39
Norfolk, Lavinia Duchess of 25
North, Geoffrey Ford 98
North Stoke 160
Nottingham 39, 50-1
Nucleus 127

Oakham 137
O'Brien, Vincent 109, 123, 162
Ocean Swell 153
Ogbourne 109
Old Berks Foxhounds 107
Oldtown Stud 112
Ollerton 73-4
Olympia International Horse Show 7, 19, 24
One in a Million 166
Osborne 121
Oswestry 37
O'Toole, Peter 150
Our Babu 140
Over the Open 11
Oxford 1, 3

Page, H.S. 11
Paget, Dorothy 24, 42, 53, 148
Palace House ix, 146-50, 158-60, 166-9
Palestine 78-91
Palestine (horse) 129, 149
Palestis 156
Pall Mall 129-30
Palmer, Noel 81
Paquet, Philippe 164
Paris 31
Park Lodge 153-4
Parkinson, Kenneth 92
Parthia 129, 131-3
Parvin, Billy 2
Payne, Bill 30-1, 81, 83-4, 87, 101-2, 169
  Pip 169
Payne-Gallwey, Sir Philip 166
Peacock, Matt 108
Pearl 14
Peel, Major Hugh 12
Pelerin 163-4
Pepper, Peggy 14
Perry, Frank 116, 122
Perryman, Dick 108-9
Perrywinkle 55
Persian Gulf 128, 131
Pershore 43, 51
Persse, Atty 8, 10-11, 35-6, 107, 109-10, 114, 151
Pettifer, Tom 81, 83-4, 87, 97, 102
Philipps, Jim 147, 149, 168
  Major and Mrs. J.P. 150
Piggott, Ernie 12
  Keith 109
  Lester ix, 12, 47, 109, 127, 130, 144, 146, 163, 170
Pilkington, Lady Susan 148, 150
  Sir Thomas 27, 148
Pikermi 155
Pillar Stud 162
Pinza 117, 129, 139
Pitts, Tom 130
Plattes, Gabriel 15
Poethlyn 12
Pollet, Etienne 147
polo 10, 21, 23, 26, 65, 91, 107
Pony Club 22, 107
Poole, Margaret 148

Poor Lad 32
Popham 21
Popham Down 30
Portal, Lord 115
Portobello 105-6
Posse 165
Pratt, Fred 36, 40-1, 54
  Nellie *see* Hobbs, Nellie
  Zara 158
Premonition 117, 119, 121-2
Prendergast, Kevin 160
  Paddy 151, 163
Price, Ryan 156
Prince Bee 164
Prince Regent 48
Princess Eboli 167
Pucka Belle 53
Pulford, Ray 130
Pytchley Foxhounds 5-6, 8, 12
Pytchley Statesman 6
Python Scheme 102

Quarentine 50, 64
Queen's Jockey 131
Quorn Hunt 6-7, 14, 16, 22, 25-7, 95

Rajpipla, Majarajah of 42
Ramlan 164
Ramleh Vale Foxhounds 82
Rank, J.V. 48-9, 53
Rankin 163-4
Red Gold 168
Red Rum 63
Rees, Bill 68
  Dick 31
  Peggy 68
Reform 165
Rehovoth 82
Reynolds, Brayley 148
Reynoldstown 42, 48, 53
Rhodes, Eric 156, 169
Richards, Sir Gordon 29, 117, 170
Richmond Fair 167
Rimell, Fred ix, 2, 21, 35, 47, 55, 59-60, 109
Robertson, Florence 13, 18
  Margery *see* Hobbs, Margery
Robinson, David 140-6, 149-50, 153, 157
  Mabel 143-4
  Noel 93
Roche, Christy 163
Rock Sand 8
Rodbourne, Harry 38
  John 38
Rogerson, Eileen (née Joel) 106, 108-9, 111, 114, 149-50, 155
  John 106, 108-9, 111, 114, 134, 149-50, 155
  Valda *see* Embiricos, Valda
Roimond 113
Rollo, Prim 18-19
Rome 101
Rommel 91-2, 94
Romulus 150
Rosebery, Lady 152-3
  Lord 141, 153-4
Rosh Pinna 87
Rosselli, Ann 148
  O.H. 148, 150
Rosslyn Park 65
Royal Captive 156
Royal Danieli ix, 58-60
Royal Mail 53, 55
Royal Serenade 113
Rubio 8-9
Rucker, Sir Arthur and Lady 112
Ryan, Jim 49, 58

St. Bartholomew's School 34
St. George, Ferris 81-2
St. John, Edward 92
St. Lawrence, 'Touche' Gaisford 90
St. Leger ix, 115, 117-19, 121, 125-7, 130, 151, 168-70
  Irish 128
Salisbury 109
Salmon, Walker J. 50
Sandown 51, 54, 119, 128, 130, 152, 156, 158, 160
Sandringham 117, 166
Sangster, Robert 142, 160, 162
Sarafand 84
Sassoon, Sir Victor 117, 130, 139
Scallywag 169
Sceptre 8
Schmeling, Max 66-7
Scott, Mrs. Marion du Pont 49-53, 55, 57-9, 61, 64-6
  Randolph 49, 65
Scottish Union 48
Scratchley, Sandy 37-8, 40
Scrope, Colonel Bunty 126
Sea Bird II 143
Seasick 50
Sefton, Lady 158
  Lord 92, 107
Seven Barrows 28, 32, 34
Sezincote 151, 167
Shedden, John 88, 91

Sheila's Cottage 109
Sheriffe, Monica 17, 22, 25
Shiny Tenth 156
Shirley Heights 166
Silver Fame 112-13
Skegness 23
Sleat 168
Smith, Eph 119
  Stan 126
Smyth, Ron 105
Snow Cat 130
Someries Stud 148
Somerset Yeomanry, North 68-80, 82, 84, 90
Sorley Boy 24
Soueida 89-90
Southern Hero 48
Spares, Charlie 43
Spearmint 8
Spence, Major Jimmy 72, 81
  Judy 72
Sport of Queens, The 123
Sporting Life 140, 143, 156
Stackallan Stud 149
Stalbridge, Lord 47
Stalker, Charlie 47
Stamford 107
Stanton, Major Doodle 81-2
Starkey, Greville 163
Stephenson, Colonel Francis 84, 87, 90-1
  Willie 43
Stilvi 155-7, 160-1, 164-7, 171
Stoddard, Louis 10, 66
Stratford-on-Avon 34-6, 53
Strutt, Lavinia *see* Norfolk, Lavinia Duchess of
Sun Castle 115
Sun Chariot 115
Sun Princess 168
Surtees, R.S. 1
Sutherland, Fergy 124, 141
  Judy 124, 141
Suvretta 143, 146
Swindon 2
Syria 88-90

Tachypous 152, 157, 159-60
Take A Reef 152
Takvor Pacha 56, 59
Tanara 150
Tannihill, Captain 100
Tarporley 28
Tartan Pimpernel 160
Taunton 39, 44
Tavistock, Marquess of 150
Taxiarchos 160
Teal 114
Telios 166
Teme Willow 55
Templeman, Fred 32
Tenea 165-6, 169
The Chase 109
The Minstrel 152, 160
The Tetrarch (the 'Spotted Wonder') 8, 10-11, 110
Thomas, Hugh Lloyd 55
Thomond II 42
Thompson, Jimmy 144
  Percy 57
Thornton, William 65
Thorpe Satchville 30
Thoughtless II 34
Timber Wolf 48
Time Step 105-6
Timeform 157, 161, 165
Tipperary Tim 31, 53
Tmimi 95
Tissot 128
Tolmi 165
Tom Cribb 154
Tom Thumb 4, 18, 22
Tomy Lee 148
Tongue, George 27
Topness 37
Torquay 37, 47, 68
Touch Paper 152
Toulson, Vin 23
Towcester 8, 39
Track Spare 144
Travel On 160
Tripoli 95
Tromos 161-2
Trouble Maker 49
Tudor Era 122
Tunis 97, 99
Turnell, Andy 109
  Bob 108-9, 111
Tuxford 74
Typhoon 104
Tyrnavos 162-4, 166-7

Umney, Miss 143
Underdown, Teddy 40
Upend Stud 152
Uppingham 23, 28
Ursulus 105
Utoxeter 51

Vaigly Great 151, 167
Vaughan, Major General 16

Vielle 167
Villar, Tony 152
Villar, Mrs. Tony (Clare) 150
Virginia 9, 49, 58, 65

Wadsworth, Major Austin 9-10
Wales, Prince of (later Edward VIII) 16-17, 55
Walker, Alan 150
Walsall, 137
Walsh, John 163
Walwyn, Diana (née Carlos-Clark) 18-19, 25, 106
  Fulke 18, 42, 53, 56, 69, 105-6, 131
Wandering Eyes 149
War Risk 108
War Vessel 49-50, 52, 57
Ward Drill 143
Warner, Ben 42, 47
Warrender, John 23
  Sir Victor 23
Warwick, Countess of 16
Warwick Lodge *see* Melton Mowbray
Waugh, J.C. 143
  Jack 140
Waverton 151, 167
Weatherbys 169
Weedon 81
Weller-Poley, J.H. 150
Wernher, Lady Zia 125
West Ilsley 105, 112, 136
Weston-super-Mare 70-2
Whally, Sergeant 81
What Have You 56
Whitney, Jock 31, 105
Whitton family 23
Wilkinson, John 167
Williams, Evan 53
Williamson, George 7-8
Wills, David 147, 149, 168
  Eva 168
  H.D.H. 150
  Captain M.T.H. 150
Wilson, Gerry 39-40, 42-3, 46-7, 53, 62, 110
  Julian 150
Wincanton 38-9
Winder, Colonel Aston 107
  Betty *see* Hobbs, Betty
Windsor 105, 113
Windsor Lad 36, 42
Wingfield, Tony 96, 98, 122-3
Winter, Major 'Pop' 107
Withington, Fred 8
Wolverhampton 36, 38, 44, 51
Wood, Captain Peter 88, 93
Woodward, William 129
Woore Hunt 37
Workman 59-60
Wragg, Harry 113
Wyatt, Brigadier Willie 117, 121-2

Yardley, Frank 150
Yattenden 112
York 115, 130, 152-3, 156-7, 160, 162, 167
Yorkshire Dragoons 83-103, 107

Zarathustra 128